My Way Or No Way

By

Brenda M. Hampton

ISBN: 1-4140-4618-9 (e-book)
ISBN: 1-4140-4617-0 (Paperback)
ISBN: 1-4140-5398-3 (Dust Jacket)

This book is printed on acid free paper.

1stBooks - rev. 01/21/04

Acknowledgments

Special thanks to the women of St. Louis Sisters United who believe in everything that I stand for, who support me, and who share my vision of maintaining a successful organization for women.

An extended thanks to:

Teresa Clay and Carlos Turner from the Platinum Hood Award Winning Flipside Newszine Newspaper for recognizing my hard work and acknowledging it. Your comments and the opportunity for allowing me to SHINE was greatly appreciated. Thanks for keeping it real in the Flipside and for constantly exploring St. Louis' talented individuals to the fullest.

Brad Sanders, a.k.a. Ti-Rone, for taking time out of your busy schedule to read *Two's Enough Three's A Crowd*. The opportunity to be on "live" radio with you was a dream come true and I thank God for placing you in my life at the right time.

Anthony L. Cowins, for making *My Way Or No Way* the phenomenal piece of work that it is. Words can not express how thankful I am to you for giving this fun-filled novel a new life. You are an awesome man and I'm sure that "Jaylin" thanks you for your creativeness and your ability to keep it real as he does. I truly hope that after all is said and done that you'll have the opportunity to shine as well. Good luck with your modeling career and there's no doubt in my mind that success is well within your reach.

Carl Johnson (First World) and Sheryl Perry & Elaine Cammack (Knowing Books & Café) for sharing my novels with your customers. It's people like you all who make the difference in this world and I truly appreciate you going over and beyond to make things happen for me.

Joyce M. Hampton, my sister, for constantly believing in EVERYTHING that I do, and supporting my ideas. As my sister, I can never remember a time that you doubted my career decisions in life, good or bad, and you always had faith in me no matter what. This time, we're going all the way. God never said it was going to be easy for us, because it never has, but he has most certainly opened the door

iv

and allowed us to come through. Remember that I'm counting on you, Judge Joyce M. Hampton, to do your thang as well and I'll be there smiling next to you, as you have never let me down and always stood by me.

Regina M. Walton, my sister, for sending your encouraging e-mails and cards when I most certainly needed them the most. Being so caught up in my work, and to open up a card sent by you meant more to me than you will ever know. Thanks for being a part of my life and keep on being the beautiful, encouraging, and spiritual woman that you are.

Phyllis M. Payne, my mother, for teaching me to be independent and giving me the courage to make it on my own. Without your guidance over the years, there's no way any of this would be possible. You installed the necessary values for three beautiful daughters to survive in this world and God could not have given me a better mother than you.

Monique, Monica, and Aaron, my children, for showing your love, support, and understanding, as I continue to make a way for all of us. Thanks for embracing my passion for writing and for allowing me to stay focused on the important things in life.

Aaron Littlejohn, the awesome man in my life, thank you for putting up with me. I know this change in our life has been a fast-paced and interesting one and being the man that you are has made all of the difference. Thanks for your patience, your support, and for understanding how important my writing is to me.

Finally, a more extended thanks to the Lord Jesus Christ who shows me every day that with him leading my life ALL things are most certainly possible.

Because It's My Fans Reviews That Really Count!!

Alice Douglas...*Two's Enough Three's A Crowd* is one of the best books I've read in a long time. Jaylin, "kept it real." I admired him for telling the truth and the women had a choice to either roll with him or roll on. I recommend this book to every true book reader there is.

Teresa Clay...You owe it to yourself to pick up a novel published by Brenda M. Hampton. Not could I put *Two's Enough Three's A Crowd* down, but when I did, I found myself wrestling with my roommate to get it back. Definitely a "Modern Masterpiece."

Gina Bell...Only books written by Brenda M. Hampton will I read. Jaylin, my baby daddy, got it going on. I was hooked on him and everything about him. I love how he tells it like it is and I'm dying to read the sequel.

Valerie Craig...Phenomenal. I didn't sleep until I was finished. I loved Jaylin's character and understood his challenges. Brenda, I didn't know you had it in you but you've made a true book reader out of me.

Geneta Jacobs...truly a delightful treat. *Two's Enough Three's A Crowd* was a genuine, and realistic story. Hampton is a gifted author and has truly inspired me to continue with my writing.

Terrie Weaver...By far, the best book I ever read. *Two's Enough Three's A Crowd* will make women aware of the many Jaylins of the world and he was a realistic example of what it could be like dealing with a man like him.

Monica Brown-Weaver...*Two's Enough Three's A Crowd* was the best book ever because it became a reality for me and slapped me right in the face. It encouraged me to take a look at my own situation and encouraged me to move forward and never look back.

Because It's My Fans Reviews That Really Count!!

Nicholus Hughes... *Two's Enough Three's A Crowd* is a straight page-turner. When the fellas wanted to go out, I declined until I was completely finished. I enjoyed reading the male characters and could relate to them. Ms. Hampton inspired me to start reading all over again.

Michael McCullom... Hampton did an excellent job speaking from a man's point of view. I thought a brotha wrote *Two's Enough Three's A Crowd* and I was quite surprised to find out that it was written by a female. The elements of the book and its well put together story line kept me from beginning to end.

Lawrence Lewis... *Two's Enough Three's A Crowd* was an excellent read. It kept me tuned in, as I couldn't believe how into it I was as a first time reader.

Thanks to all of the above who went out of their way to share with me how much *Two's Enough Three's A Crowd* impacted their lives. I appreciate the wonderful comments more than you know and for the many individuals that I missed, please know that I am grateful for your support because without you, there is no way for my success.

Brenda M. Hampton

TWO'S ENOUGH THREE'S A CROWD

Later that night, I smiled as I stood on my balcony drinking a glass of wine. I looked up at the stars as a south wind was blowing, and lifted my glass up to Mama. Nokea's decision had made me realize how important it was for me to have someone in my life to love. I tilted my wineglass upside down, poured the wine out over the balcony, and thought about where I'd go from here. Going forward, it was going to be "MY WAY OR NO WAY."

MY WAY OR NO WAY

JAYLIN

I crashed out in a lawn chair on the balcony, and was awakened by Scorpio's kiss on my lips. She rubbed her fingers through my naturally curly hair, and straightened my thick eyebrows. I slowly opened my eyes and just stared because I was in no mood for fucking. All I wanted to know is why? Why didn't Nokea give me what I wanted? She said that she loved me and for damn sure knew how much I loved her, so why? Why did she just walk away from the altar? I was humiliated. Fucking downright pissed off and was seriously ready to kick somebody's ass. After she left me standing there looking like a fool, I didn't know what to do but walk away my damn self.

I continued in deep thought, and Scorpio kissed me on the lips again. She stared deeply into my gray eyes, and I turned my head so she wouldn't kiss me again. I sat calmly thinking about how the Atomic Dog in me was getting ready to come out, and whoever crossed me this time was going to pay.

Trying to get my attention, Scorpio put her hands on my face. "Say, I know you're hurting, but I'm just trying to get a smile out of you. If you didn't want to be bothered, then why did you call me to come over?"

Ignoring her, I got up and went into my room. I loosened my tie and unbuttoned my shirt. When I went into the closet, Scorpio followed. "You haven't said anything to me since I walked through that door. Whenever you want to talk, just let me know. I'm not going to pressure you," she said.

Feeling sorry for me, she helped me out of my shirt, and laid it across her arm. Then she removed my belt, and unzipped my pants. When she squatted down to help me out of them, a pleasant thought came to mind.

"Give me some head," I asked softly.

"What?" she said looking up.

5

"You heard me."

"Jaylin, you know better coming to me like that. You haven't said anything all night, but you have the nerve to ask for some head."

I looked down at her still squatted in front of me. "Listen!" I yelled. "Are you going to do it or not? If not, then get the hell out of my closet! I'm not in the mood for any bullshit!"

Scorpio stood up, laid my shirt on my shoulder, and left the closet without saying a word. I quickly grabbed her arm. "And where do you think you're going?" I asked.

"I'm going home." She snatched away and snapped. "You are one crazy high-yellow Negro. I don't have the time or energy to curse you the hell out because I'm trying to be patient and understand what you're going through. Mackenzie told me about what happened, and I didn't want you being alone. That's why I came, but I'm not going to let you dump on me because some other bitch fucked your day up."

"She's not a bitch, so watch your damn mouth, okay?"

"Defend the BITCH if you want—that's your choice. But I call it as I see fit. In the meantime, I'm getting the hell out of here. Call me when you calm your ass down."

Scorpio grabbed her purse off the chaise and headed towards the bedroom door. I dashed out of the closet and stood in front of the door so she wouldn't leave. "Hey, I'm sorry. Don't go. It's been a messed up day, and I really need you to stay." I gave her a quick peck on the lips, and when she didn't kiss me back, I knew she was pissed.

"Jaylin, your kissing me bullshit ain't going to work this time. I'm sorry too, but I'm going home tonight. So, please move out of my way."

She tried to move my arm that was blocking her from leaving the room.

"I said stay," I begged.

"And I said I'm leaving. Now, move your arm so I can go."

I raised my arm and let her pass by. When she reached the stairs, I ran up behind her and begged again. "Don't go, Scorpio. Make love to me, on the stairs, like you did when we first met. Please...I need you to relax my mind and put me at ease for the night."

She ignored me and continued down the steps. I hurried down after her and stood in front of her. Then I picked her up, and carried her back up the steps. She pounded my back, kicked her legs and yelled for me to put her down.

When we reached the top, I dropped her to the floor and lay on top of her. I held her arms together, so she wouldn't hit me, and pulled my boxers down.

"Jaylin, I said no!" she yelled. "Not tonight, baby, please! I don't feel comfortable letting you do this to me, especially after how you've treated me."

"I'm sorry! Damn! How many times do I have to say it?"

We continued struggling. And after I removed my boxers, she got away and crawled her way to my bedroom door. As she neared the bedroom, I grabbed her legs, lifted up her skirt, and crawled my body on top of hers.

Not being able to move, she lay on her stomach and tears began to roll down her face. "Jaylin, I told you I didn't want this. Why are you forcing yourself on me?"

I moved her hair to the side, and kissed the back of her neck. "Because, I need you, baby. Can't you tell how much I'm hurting?" I said, rubbing her ass, then moving her panties slightly over to the side.

I fondled her insides and the juices started to flow. "Can I have you now?" I whispered in her ear. "I'm dying to be inside of you."

Her tears slowed, as her resisting stopped. She then nodded and I went for it. I eased myself inside of her and started to stroke. Relieved, I closed my eyes, as her insides felt wet, juicy, and warm.

After a few minutes of having my way with her, she slowed down and forced me up with her body. "Let's go to the bed Jaylin. You're hurting me on the floor, and I really need to get comfortable."

I raised up and walked over to the bed. I rested one leg on the floor, so she knew I was ready for a ride. She stood at the door and looked at me with a smile.

"I told you not tonight, but you insisted on having your way."

"Always, baby. Always." I winked.

"Goodnight, Jaylin. I love you." She blew me a kiss and flew down the stairs so I couldn't catch her. By the time I got out of bed and made it to the stairs, she was closing the front door behind her. I was left there holding a hard dick in my hand. Furious, I went back into my room, grabbed a *Brown Sugar* magazine, and worked it down myself. Couldn't believe Scorpio played me, but I'd be damn sure to make her pay for it later.

After lying across my bed for hours soaking about Nokea, I finally got my ass up to take a shower. The water gushed out on me, as I pressed my hands against the wall and thought about my dramatic day. Scorpio, claiming to love me so much, had the nerve to walk out on me at a time like this and leave me hanging. Nokea, she never would have left me if I asked her to stay. That was one of my many reasoning for loving her so much. Even that bitch Felicia gave me what I wanted, but I just couldn't deal with her whorish-ass ways. She was, without a doubt, what I called a straight-up scantless freak. And then to turn around and sleep with Stephon after all that good-ass loving I kicked down? I laughed to myself and realized that I must have taught her well.

Saturday night was working on Sunday night by the time I moseyed out of bed. The phone woke me up several times throughout the night, but I ignored it and took my butt right back to sleep.

Hungry, I went into the kitchen to look for something to eat. It was pathetic—couldn't find shit. There was a small container of strawberry ice cream in the freezer, so I reached for it. I hopped up on a stool and started to eat it in the dark. I licked the ice cream, and wished it were Nokea. The last time we made love was so right. All I could think about was her bright smile, her scent, and her silky sexy little body that I held in my arms that day. And not only was she heavy on my mind, but my son. What was I going to do about him? Simone had already taken my daughter away, and I'd be damn if I let another one go. Thing is, though, I'm not ready to talk to Nokea or Stephon after how they played me. As soon as I can get myself together I'll be the first to let both of them know how I really feel about them stabbing me in my goddamn back.

I finished up my ice cream and reached for the phone to check my messages. There were seven messages and I listened to them one by one. Scorpio called explaining why she left me hanging last night, and then she called again and reminded me about picking up Mackenzie today. I had so much shit on my mind that I forgot. Angela called, telling me she wasn't going to make it for work tomorrow because she was ill. Brashaney called, telling me how bad she wanted me to fuck her, and Stephon called insisting that we needed to talk. Calls seven and eight were Nokea. She felt like she owed me an explanation and wanted to come by. I deleted each message. The only person I wanted to talk to was Mackenzie, so I called Scorpio's place and asked for her.

"I was wondering when you were going to call," Scorpio said, angrily. "Mackenzie has been asking for you all day long."

"Well, put her on the phone."

"I will. Before I do, though, I want to talk to you about last night."

"Not right now…put Mackenzie on the phone."

"Jaylin, you know you were wrong for—"

"Woman! Didn't you hear what I said? I don't want to hear it. Put Mackenzie on the phone, so I can apologize for not picking her up today."

Scorpio hung up and I called right back. "Helloooo," she said, as if something was funny. I didn't find any humor in her games.

"Don't make me disrespect you. Now, I'm asking you nicely to give the phone to Mackenzie."

"She's asleep right now. I hope you didn't expect her to stay up all night waiting for you." I hung up on Scorpio, and she called back as I was getting ready to go over to her place. I didn't answer because I already knew Mackenzie was upset with me.

Scorpio hesitated to open the door, but when I reminded her I had a key to let myself in, then she opened it. I walked by her and went into Mackenzie's room. I climbed into bed with her, and rubbed my nose against hers to wake her. She moved and I reached for the lamp and turned it on so she could see me. She sat up in bed and smiled. I knew she had been crying because I could see the dried up tears on her face.

"Why were you crying?" I asked, tickling her to make her smile. She gave me a hard time like Scorpio and wouldn't even crack a smile. "Okay, then I won't tell you what I have planned for us next weekend." She looked at me and pouted. "I guess I'll just have to take Barbie to the circus with me, since you don't want to go."

She smiled. "Are we really going to the circus, Daddy?"

"Yes, and after the circus we're going to stop at McDonald's for hamburgers." She pouted again. "Jack-in-the-Box?" I said. She

9

rolled her eyes. "How about Burger King?" Her eyes looked like they rolled to the back of her head. "Okay, what about one of my favorites? Outback Steakhouse." She smiled and gave me a hug. No doubt about it, I was teaching her to have the best. At five-years-old, I was lucky to get a hamburger from White Castle.

Mackenzie took her arms from around me. "Daddy, why didn't you pick me up today? Did you spend the day with your wife that ran out of the church yesterday?"

Damn, I thought. Now why did she have to go there? "No, Mackenzie, and she's not my wife. Daddy was just tired today. I kind of...got my feelings hurt and wanted to be alone. I know I should have called, but I slept most of the day."

"Did you cry when you got your feelings hurt?"

"A little bit, but, uh...let's talk about something else, Mackenzie, okay?"

"Okay, but your *wife* looked really pretty yesterday. Will you buy me a dress like hers?"

"Mackenzie, I told you that she's not my wife. And yes, she did look pretty. I promise you I'll buy you a dress prettier than hers when you get married."

She hugged me again and pulled the covers back over her so she could get back to sleep. She kind of kicked me out after I told her I would buy her a dress, but I didn't care; she was definitely one person that could get anything she wanted from me.

I quietly closed Mackenzie's door and went into Scorpio's room. She was sitting in bed reading. "Hey, I'll let myself out. I just wanted to say thanks for not making a big deal about me coming over to see Mackenzie."

"You're welcome. I'm glad you came because she was really upset when she didn't hear from you today."

"Well, we worked it out," I said, getting ready to leave.

Scorpio put the book down and opened her legs. "Are you possibly in the mood to work something else out before you go?"

"Maybe. What kind of workout do you have in mind?"

"Did you have to ask?" she said, removing her panties. "I was hoping to get one of those all nighters that I haven't had in a long time."

"Um...I see." I gazed at her pussy. "But, uh...I don't have all night. I gotta get up early for work because my secretary ain't going to be there. So, I'll take a rain-check."

"You know you're just saying that because you got played last night. Aren't you?"

"You're damn right I am. And you know what else?"

"What?"

"I'm going home to call this sweet young tender who's been begging me to fuck her. So, that all nighter you just asked me for, I'm going to have the pleasure of giving it to her."

"Tuh, yeah right. I know you ain't that bold."

"Watch me."

I left Scorpio's house, took my ass home, and called Brashaney. She was there in a flash. I couldn't give her that all nighter I promised Scorpio I'd give, but I damn sure made Brashaney's visit worth it.

Scorpio rang the phone several times throughout the night while we were fucking and sleeping, but when I decided to answer, it was damn near six o'clock in the morning. Taking my time getting to it, Brashaney reached over to answer. "Hello?" she said, sharply. Her eyes bucked, as she grinned and gave the phone to me.

"What?" I yelled.

"You are one low-down, dirty, ignorant, stank-ass Negro, Jaylin. I can't believe how trifling you are. If you want to play games, then hey let the games begin. I guarantee you—"

"Some other time, Scorpio," I said, casually. "I ain't trying to disrespect my company by being on this phone. Now, I told you once not to fuck with me."

I handed the phone to Brashaney and asked her to hang up. When she did, Scorpio called right back. I snatched it up and told Scorpio if she wanted to listen to what was about to go down, feel free. I laid the phone on the nightstand and rolled on top of Brashaney.

"Jaylin, you know I wouldn't enjoy her listening to us having sex," she smiled. "Why don't you just hang up the phone?"

"In a minute." I said, placing her legs high up on my shoulders, then inserting my thang. "Now, do you care about who's listening on the phone?"

11

She closed her eyes and moaned. "Sort of, but I'll feel so much better if you just hang up. "

After stroking Brashaney for a few minutes, and figuring that Scorpio had heard enough, I reached over and slammed the receiver down. I quickly finished my business with Brashaney and tried to get some rest before going to work.

NOKEA

I had mega explaining to do. Daddy was so furious with me for not marrying Stephon that he wasn't even speaking to me. Mama, on the other hand, understood what I was going through. She told me to use the days I had set aside for my honeymoon, and told me to think about what I wanted to do. She knew how messed up I was and told me she'd keep LJ until I got myself together.

I was so screwed up. The only person who was really happy about the whole thing was my best friend, Pat. She didn't want me to be with Jaylin or Stephon, so right after I left the church, she came after me and thanked me for not making the biggest mistake of my life.

Still, I felt terrible leaving Stephon at the altar. And Jaylin, the look on his face I'll never forget. After hours of trying to make sense of the whole thing to Mama and Daddy, I got a room at the Ritz Carlton in Clayton. I've been here since Saturday night trying to figure out what to do. I've called Jaylin trying to work this out with him first, but he refuses to return any of my calls. If I talk to Stephon first, I'm afraid I'll say something to him I really don't mean. My true love, Jaylin, is the one who deserves an explanation as to why I couldn't marry him. Knowing him, though, he'll probably never want to speak to me again.

After a long bubbly bath at the Ritz, I went downstairs to have breakfast. When I finished, I went back to my room and held the phone in my hands. I called Jaylin at work and expected Angela to pick up, but when he answered I was shocked.

"Jaylin," he said again.

"Hi...it's me, Nokea." There was silence. "Jaylin, are you there?"

"Yes, but I can't talk right now."

"Okay, then can we talk later? I'm at the Ritz in Clayton. Will you stop by after work?"

"Yeah."

"Listen, if you're not going to come just tell me. Please don't have me waiting for you. We really need to talk."

"Damn, I said I'll be there," he snapped. "Gotta go."

He hung up.

I hated this side of him, but I knew his attitude was because of me.

I called my parents' house to check on LJ, and when Daddy heard my voice, he gave the phone to Mama. I couldn't believe how he was treating me—like it was his life or something. But I also knew he always wanted the best for me. Mama said LJ was doing fine. She told me to take all the time I needed and to call her if she could help. There was a knock at the door, so I told Mama to kiss LJ for me, then told her I'd see them soon.

When I opened the door, I was so glad to see Pat. After she came in we just held each other with a tight embrace, and then I started to cry on her shoulder. "I know, sweetie, I know exactly how you feel," she said, comforting me.

We walked over to the couch and sat down. "Why don't this bad dream just go away Pat? Why is it just one thing after another?"

"Because, that's just how life is. God never said it was going to be easy."

"Well, I guess I'm failing him too. I can't seem to get anything right. Tell me, what am I doing wrong?"

"Nokea, I didn't come here to give you one of my lectures. I'm here as your best friend and not your psychiatrist. You didn't sound well when we talked yesterday, but I at least wanted to give you time to think about what you need to do. Have you eaten anything yet?"

"Yeah. I just had some breakfast food not too long ago."

"Good. Cause if you hadn't, I was hoping we could order one of those pizzas we ate when you were pregnant."

We laughed.

"Girl, wasn't that a mess," I said. "We should have been ashamed of ourselves."

"We my ass. You should have been ashamed of yourself. I wasn't the one who was pregnant. I worked mine off very well," Pat said, gloating, and holding her waistline.

"And so have I."

"Oh, be quiet. You've always had an awesome petite body. I knew that pizza wasn't going to do a damn thing to your figure. Me, I

14

had to work hard to get those pounds off. Chad and I were at it day end and day out trying to work off those pounds."

"Well, I'm sure the two of you had fun," I said, laughing. I dazed off and thought about the last time Jaylin and I made love.

Pat snapped her fingers in front of my face to get my attention. "Now, what's got your attention that fast?" she asked. I looked at her and smiled. "Forget it. I don't even want to know. When are you going to forget about him and move on Nokea?"

I stood up, walked over by the window, and folded my arms. "I can't, Pat. I've tried so many times to move on, but I can't. I love him so much that it scares me."

"Well, why didn't you just marry his sorry ass? When he stood there making a damn spectacle of himself, you should have just married him."

"Because, the timing wasn't right. That's why."

"And the timing ain't never going to be right if you ask me. I wish like hell you'd just find someone else."

"I know you do, Pat, but that's not going to happen. I wish everyone would just realize that the love we have for each other will never go away."

"Your love or his love? Honestly, I can't see Jaylin wasting anymore of his time on this. You'd better wake up and smell the coffee, because I'm sure he's making up for lost time right now."

"No, he's not. Actually, he's coming over to see me after work today."

"For what? Nokea, I know you ain't going to sleep with him."

"No, no. We're just going to talk. Talk about why I did what I did, about our future, and about LJ."

"Girl, I don't know what to say. I'm staying out of it. Listen, don't even mention his name to me anymore. I don't want to hear it, okay."

"Okay, I won't. But if things don't work out, will you still be there for me?" Pat came over by me and smiled. "Of course I will."

We chatted for a few more hours, and then I walked with her downstairs to the lobby. As we stood there giving our good-byes, Jaylin walked through the door on his cell phone. I rushed Pat off and made her promise not to say anything to him. She didn't, but when she walked by him, she rolled her eyes.

15

"Hello to you too, Pat. Nice to see you," he said, trying to piss her off. She kept her promise and kept on walking.

I walked up to Jaylin and nervously held my hands behind my back. "Thanks for coming. I know you didn't want to, but I guess you figured we needed to talk."

"Yeah, yeah, but keep it short," he said, ending his call. "I have somewhere I need to be within the hour."

What an attitude, I thought, as we walked up the steps. He walked in front of me like he knew where he was headed. I didn't mind because I was checking him out from behind. Looking and smelling good, as usual. Leather shoes were shining, haircut was fresh, Gucci suit was well fitted, but his smile wasn't there. By the time we reached the third floor Jaylin stopped and turned around. "What's your room number?"

"I thought you knew. The elevator would have been quicker, but you seem to know everything, so I'm just following you."

He stepped down and looked at me with a raised eyebrow. "Nokea, I don't have time for games. I just told you my time is minimal so—"

"So, go up one more flight of stairs and turn to your right." He moved over to the side and motioned his hand for me to go in front of him.

"Thank you," I said, smiling and leading us to my room.

After we walked in, Jaylin didn't waste any time. He didn't even sit and just stood by the doorway with his arms folded in front of him. I sat down on the couch hoping that he would sit next to me, but when I asked, he declined.

"You're so upset that you can't even sit next to me? Now, Jaylin, that's taking things a bit too far. Wouldn't you say so?"

"Nokea, cut the act," he said, fuming. "What do you want from me?"

"I'd like for you to relax and come sit next to me so we can talk."

He unfolded his arms, removed his jacket, and put it on the coat hanger by the door. Then he loosened his tie, and headed towards me on the couch.

"Now what?" he asked, sitting down. "What else do you want me to do...Miss, 'I'm calling all the shots around here?'

16

"Please, stop. It's not about what I want. It's about what's in our best interest, and about what the future holds for us."

"Can I answer that question? You know—the one about our future."

"Sure. I'd like to know what you think we should do," I said, feeling that he was about to tell me what I really didn't want to hear.

He rested back on the couch and propped his feet up on the table in front of him. "Nokea, we don't have a future. It's time we go our separate ways for good. I know you love me and I for damn sure still love you, but we are a prime example of two people who love each other and just can't be together. I'm hurting...and bad. I've never felt like this in my entire life, even when I was in that jacked-up orphanage. But right about now, you definitely don't need a man like me in your life. It's only going to get worse for us if we try to be together. So, baby-girl, I'm just being honest."

"Wait a minute, you...you lost me. What do you mean by its only going to get worse? We have a child together and that's going to keep us together forever."

"Right, right, oh, you're so damn right. It's going to keep us together as being loving parents for our son, but that's it. From this moment on, Nokea," he said, pointing his finger at me. "You, your Mama, your Daddy, Stephon, Pat, NOBODY is going to keep me from being with my son. Now, I mean that shit. If you want to make plans, start making plans for me to see him. If you don't, I'll just do what I have to do to make sure this shit works out for me."

"Are you threatening me?"

"Maybe, but more so, I'm just telling you like it is. I don't want this situation to get ugly, but I've been without my son long enough."

"I agree, and I have no intentions of keeping him from you any longer. I just wanted to know about us. Can you really just end it like this?"

"Baby, don't you see? You ended it when you left me standing at the altar. Nobody ever humiliated me like you did. All you had to do was say yes. Simple as that and right now we could be on our honeymoon. You had a choice and I gave you nothing but time. So, now, fuck it. What we could have had is a thing of the past."

17

Jaylin quickly stood up and removed his tie. He rolled it together in his hands, and shook his head. "You really hurt me, Nokea. I know I did a lot of shit to you in the past, but none of it compares to what you did to me."

I stood up next to him. "Jaylin, please know that I wanted more than anything to marry you, but my previously planned wedding with Stephon was not the time or place to do it. There was no way to continue the ceremony with you and you know it. Stephon would have been crushed; my parents would have damn near died, and lets not talk about Pat. It would have been a complete disaster. So please, lets take this one day at a time before we go making any critical decisions."

"Nope, can't do that right now. I had plans to marry you Saturday. You shattered my goddamn dreams, made a fool out of me, and I have to live with that hurt for the rest of my life. I begged you to marry me, Nokea. I stooped to an all-time low and embarrassed the fuck out of myself. To hell with that, this shit is over!" His voice got louder, as he headed towards the door.

I followed behind him. "Please don't leave under these conditions. I understand how you feel, but now is the time for us to heal together. Haven't we hurt each other enough?"

He swung the door open. "I want to see my son on Sunday, Nokea. Make plans for me to do so, or my attorney will be at your place by noon."

He slammed the door.

I wanted to go after him, but I knew he probably needed time to cool off. I just wished he wasn't so damn stubborn and realized we were meant for each other. The more time we waste trying to convince ourselves any differently, then the more bullshit is going to come between us.

Disgusted with the way our conversation went down, I changed clothes so I could go downstairs to mingle for the rest of the evening. I got down to my black lace bra and panties, and there was a knock at the door. I looked out the peephole and saw Jaylin. I quickly opened the door and didn't cover up. "Yes," I said. He looked me up and down before he walked into the room.

"I forgot my jacket."

I reached for his jacket and gave it to him "Here you go."

"Thanks."

"You're welcome. And if there's anything else you forgot, just let me know."

He grinned, walked up to me, and gave me a simple wet peck on the lips. "My son, Nokea. All I forgot was my son."

He left out again.

Later, I went downstairs to get a drink at the bar. I listened to the pianist play soothing music, and I realized it wasn't in my best interest to keep LJ from being with Jaylin any longer. I also thought about what I was going to say to Stephon when I made arrangements to see him on Friday.

I called Stephon late Thursday night and confirmed our arrangement to meet up tomorrow. I insisted that we meet at his place, because I didn't want him visiting me at the hotel.

When I arrived, he was eagerly waiting. "What's up, Shorty?" he said, holding the door open. He was looking so workable with his shirt off and some crisp faded blue jeans on. I still had a thing for his chocolate nicely cut body, but my feelings for Jaylin meant more to me.

"Hi, Stephon," I said, stepping into his house. "Sorry it took so long for me to call, but I really needed time to sort through some things."

He closed the door and asked me to have a seat in the living room. I was nervous because he didn't seem upset, and had a look like he really didn't care.

"Thanks for stopping by. Can I get you anything?" he asked, sitting down next to me.

"No. I'm fine. But how about you?" I asked, patting him on his leg. "I expected you to be livid with me like Jaylin was when I spoke to him."

"So, you already talked to Jaylin, huh?"

"Yes. I spoke to him on Monday. He's really upset, but deep down I know I did the right thing."

"Maybe you did, but what about how you played me, Shorty? You left me hanging too. And then, not to call me until almost a week later? Now, that was foul."

"I know it was, Stephon. And I'm sorry, but I just didn't know what to say to you. After having the baby I thought things would get

19

better between us, but you know I never stopped loving Jaylin. I was wrong to accept your proposal, and by the time I wanted to tell you I couldn't go through with it, it was too late. Mama and Daddy were making plans and so was everybody else. Basically, I just went with the flow. Please forgive me."

Stephon put his hand on top of mine. "Shorty, it was a good thing that you didn't call me after you left the church because I probably would have done something I would have regretted. These past few days I've had time to think about the whole fucked-up situation. I finally realized why you had to walk away. Honestly, neither one of us deserved you, and I'm kind of pleased that things turned out the way they did." Stephon picked my hand up and kissed the back of it. "I do love you, Shorty, but I know there's a man out there who can love you more. Maybe Jaylin. I don't know, but I want to thank you for having the courage to do the right thing."

I put my hand on his cheek and rubbed it. "You don't know how much it means for me to hear you say that. I regret taking our friendship to another level, because I really feel like I'll never be able to get it back."

"Yes you will. I'll always be there for you, Nokea. Just like I was before. This time, though, I promise you that I won't interfere with you and Jaylin's relationship. I'm going to work hard at getting my relationship back with him because he's all I got. I regret like hell playing him, but when you love someone it sometimes makes you do stupid things."

"I wouldn't exactly call loving me stupid. Your love means a lot and it always will. I blame myself for not being honest with you from the beginning."

Stephon pulled me in close to his bare chest then kissed my forehead. I rested my head on his shoulder. "Stay the night with me, Shorty." I pulled myself away, and then he looked at me. "I'm not asking for us to make love. All I want to do is hold you in my arms one last time."

There was no way I was going to tell Stephon no. After what I did to him, the least I could do was allow him to hold me for one more night. He leaned back on the couch, and I laid my body on top of his. Then he wrapped his arms around me, and held me tightly, as if he never wanted to let go.

20

SCORPIO

I was so upset with Jay-Baby trying to play me like he did. He really was out of his mind if he thought, for one minute, I was going to tolerate anymore of his mess. I had much love for the brotha, but what he did the other night was low. First, to try and take something that wasn't even his, then to make me listen to him screw another woman was even lower. Lower than I ever thought he would go. But then again, I should have expected this from him. Especially since he got his male ego crushed. I wasn't mad at Nokea for playing him like she did, because if anybody had it coming, he did.

I just somehow wish I had the nerve to break this off with him. One day I find myself loving him dearly, and the next day I can't stand to be around him. I know that he's probably going to be eating out of Nokea's hands. If not, he's going to be eating everything else in sight.

So, for now, I'm chilling. I got myself somewhat of a new friend, Shane Alexander, and I'm dying to know how Jaylin's going to react when he finds this out. Especially, since Shane is just as educated, fine, sexy and qualified as Jaylin is. He's hooked-up in all the right places: body tight, about six-foot two, Carmel as a Caramello bar can get, and give twisty's a whole new name. The only thing I don't like is the diamond earring in his left ear, but his light-brown eyes allow me to over look it.

I met Shane at Career Days that I went to on Friday. Upset, of course, because Jaylin told me he was going to Nokea's wedding. Something inside of me knew he was planning on stopping her wedding, but I didn't want to tell him he would be wrong for doing so. I'm the last person he would have listened to, but now, I'm sure he wishes somebody had stopped him. No doubt about it, I still love Jaylin, but he needs to be taught many lessons before he will ever think about getting his act together.

I called Jaylin late Friday night to remind him about taking Mackenzie to the circus. She'd been bugging me all week, and since he seemed to be suffering from amnesia lately, I didn't want him forgetting about her.

21

"What time would you like for me to have her ready?" I asked.

"I'll pick her up around ten o'clock in the morning. I'll have to bring her home afterwards, because I have an invitation to a charity ball that I'm supposed to attend tomorrow night. I'll pick her back up early Sunday morning, so that way she can spend the whole day with me."

"Charity Ball, huh? So, who's going to accompany you? I'm sure you have a date."

"None of your business. All you need to know is that I'm not going alone."

"Now, that doesn't surprise me. Is it anyone I know?"

"Naw, you don't know her, but I'm sure you heard her the other night."

"Well, if it's that chick who answered your phone, you really should be searching for a new sex partner. Those moans I listened to sounded pretty damn fake to me. Didn't seem like you were giving it your all like you do when we're together."

"Aw...I gave it my all. You just happen to listen in when I was wrapping things up..."

"Jaylin that bitch was asleep when I called, so whateverrrr...just be on time picking up Mackenzie."

"Sure will. She's one woman who will never have to wait for Jaylin Rogers, baby."

He hung up and even though he was working my nerves, I wasn't about to let him know it.

I put Mackenzie to bed, and sat on my bedroom floor trying to get the homework done I'd been neglecting. I knew I couldn't count on Jaylin to pay my bills forever, so I had to definitely get my priorities together.

Shane was a Math Professor, and since I seemed to struggle with Algebra, I called him to see if he wouldn't mind coming over to help. When we talked at Career Days he offered, but I didn't anticipate on taking him up on his offer so soon. I had a little over one year of school under my belt, and I realized returning to school was the best thing I'd ever done. It sure in the heck beat taking my clothes off for men any day of the week.

I'd decided to get a degree in business. It could probably open many doors and when I talked to Jaylin about it, he thought it was a good choice too. Other than him paying the bills, and being a good father to Mackenzie, a big part of me wanted a committed relationship with him. Crazy, I guess, but when it comes down to it, there is nothing he wouldn't do for me, and nothing I wouldn't do for him.

I was so indulged with my work that when Shane rang the doorbell I hadn't even took a moment to get myself together. My hair was in a ponytail lying on my right shoulder, and I still had on a dirty white T-shirt from cleaning earlier today. My hipster Levi's had dried-up mud on them from working in the garden today and my face was quite pale without any make-up. As I looked in the mirror, I figured this would just have to do. Jaylin said I looked beautiful without make-up, so maybe, just maybe, Shane would feel the same.

"Hello there," I said, smiling, and opening the door for him.

"Hello, Miss Lady, and how have you been?" He searched the room with his eyes.

I closed the door and got a good look at him from behind. Meaty-ass, clean-cut and nice, I thought.

"I've been fine, Shane. Just fine, but I'm getting a slight bit tired of my Algebra class already."

He laughed and followed me into the kitchen. "I think I've heard that statement a million times before. So, that's what I'm here for. I'd love to help."

Realizing that my books were in my bedroom, I asked him to have a seat. He placed his motorcycle helmet on the table, turned the kitchen chair around and straddled it. Lord help me, is all I could say to myself. I looked at him and smiled. "Can I get you anything?" I asked.

"No, no, I'm fine. But thanks."

I left the kitchen and hurried to get my books. Mr. Alexander wasn't looking too bad. He actually looked a lot better than when I saw him at Career Days in his dark brown suit. And boy did I have a thing for a man who could ride a motorcycle. Pants were gripping his ass in all the right places, and scent was nothing to play with. Whew, I thought—but that earring. The earring had to go.

I gathered my things and went back into the kitchen. "Here, let me help you with your things," he said, standing up taking my books.

"Thank you." I sat down across the table from him, so I could gaze into his pretty eyes. Besides, I knew the further away I stayed the better.

After two hours of him explaining Algebra, and now, I was even more confused. I gave up about an hour ago, and decided to enjoy this thickness of a man that was now sitting beside me. Half way through our session, I pretended not to hear and moved closer. I even got up a few times to see if he'd notice me, but Shane was all about teaching.

I took a deep breath. "Shane," I said, moving my ponytail to the other side, then massaging my neck. "I've taken in enough for one night. I'll never be able to understand all this stuff."

"Yes you will. It's not as hard as you think it is. You'll master it in no time. I promise, but you can't go giving up on it."

"That's easy for you to say. You've probably done this most of your life. This is really something new to me. I mean, I remember Algebra in high school, but that was so long ago."

"Well, again, that's what I'm here for. Give it some more time, and with me being your tutor, you'll know this stuff in no time at all."

"If you say so," I said, yawning.

He stood up and stretched his arms. Again, I couldn't help but notice a nice size hump in his pants.

"Don't let me keep you up any longer, Scorpio." He smiled and took his helmet off the table. "When would you like to get together again?"

"I have a test on Wednesday. Would you be able to pencil me in on Tuesday night?"

"It'll have to be late. I have a class until eight o'clock, but after that I'm free."

"That's fine. I'll call you on Tuesday morning to confirm."

I walked Shane to the door and really hated to see him go. He sped off on his motorcycle and waved goodbye. Really nice, I thought, and maybe he was just what I needed to get Jay-Baby to straighten up and fly right.

JAYLIN

I got up early Saturday morning because I had a busy ass day ahead of me. I was already late picking Mackenzie up, and still had to stop by the plaza to pick up my tuxedo by five.

I'd decided to take Brashaney with me. I felt bad about fucking her all the time, and wanted to give her a taste of what it felt like being on the outside of Jaylin's world. She was thrilled when I asked her to go, and since I was already running late, I asked her to meet me at my place by seven o'clock tonight. She agreed.

When I pulled up Mackenzie was looking out of the window. She had her hands on her face and was already pouting. I knew I was late, but damn. Seems as if I couldn't please anybody these days.

I, at least, thought she would smile after she saw me, but she didn't. And when I break the news about bringing her home after dinner, I know she's really going to throw a fit.

Scorpio opened the door and rolled her eyes. I gave her a slight push in her back.

"Shut up, and I'm not in the mood to hear your mouth," I said.

"I haven't said a word. You're going to hear it from Mackenzie, so what the hell?"

Mackenzie walked to the door and took my hand. "Are you ready now?" she asked, looking up at me.

"Yeah, baby, lets go." I licked my tongue out at Scorpio and she smiled.

"You know, you could have asked me to go. I like the circus too," she said, standing in the doorway.

"Damn, I could have, couldn't I? But I think they got enough clowns there already, so maybe next time." She slammed the door, as Mackenzie and I laughed.

We enjoyed the Universoul Circus. I had never been to a circus before, and really felt like I missed out as a kid. Mackenzie for damn sure didn't miss out on anything. She had to have everything she could get her hands on.

When we left, I was down three hundred bucks, and she was all smiles. Knowing that I had to break the news about taking her back home, I thought all the shit I bought would make it easier. It wasn't and she cried and cried. Damn near made me wanna cry. So, after we left Outback Steakhouse, I called Nanny B to see if she would come watch Mackenzie while I went to the charity ball. She said it was fine, and told me she would be there by the time we got home.

We stopped at Plaza Frontenac and picked up my tuxedo, then drove back to my place. When we got there, as promised, Nanny B was parked in the driveway. I was running tremendously late because it started raining, and I took my time driving with Mackenzie in the car. So, as soon as I got into the house, I jetted upstairs, took a shower, and changed into my black Tuxedo. After I trimmed my beard down and gazed at the mirror, I turned to the left first, then to the right. I rubbed my goatee straight with the tip of my fingers and smiled. The mirror didn't lie—I was one fine-ass brotha who knew he had it going on. Mr. Schmidt was definitely going to be proud of me tonight and since I was the one who he had chosen to represent his company, and hand out the check, I had to make sure I had no flaws in my attire.

Just when I started wondering what the hell was taking Brashaney so long, I heard the doorbell ring. Nanny B and Mackenzie were coming out of the kitchen, as I jogged downstairs to open the door. I looked Brashaney up and down because I shockingly had a problem with this hot-pink silk long dress she was wearing. It was pretty, but I thought it was much too loud for the black-tie occasion. Her accessories were silver, and when I looked down and saw mud caked on the heel of her shoe I damn near fell out. If that wasn't enough, she didn't even have the decency to have her nails and toes done. Polish was chipped and looked a mess. This was, without a doubt, a no-no for a man like me.

"Hey, baby, wha…what's up with the way you're looking? Didn't I explain to you how important tonight was for me?"

She put her hands on her hips. "Excuse me! What do you mean by the way I'm looking?" She looked down at herself. "For your information, I went over and beyond for you tonight. Don't be so damn critical."

Nanny B and Mackenzie looked at me, said hello to Brashaney, and went back into the kitchen.

I stood there for a minute trying to figure out if I was going to work with her tonight or not. "Okay, your hair looks nice, the dress is pretty, but couldn't you have at least had your nails and toes done? I could have given you the money to get them done if you didn't have it." She rolled her eyes, and headed towards the living room. When I looked down, the mud on her shoes tracked up my damn floor. "Whoa…wait a minute! Don't go any further. I do not want that shit you got on your shoes all over my carpet. Just stay there for one minute."

Brashaney stood there with her arms folded and was mad as hell. She rolled her eyes, and turned her head and waited, as I quickly ran back upstairs. I sat down on my bed, grabbed the phone, and started to dial. Scorpio answered the phone sounding like she was asleep.

"Wake up," I said. "It's too early for you to be sleeping on a Saturday night."

"Well, you know, this clown needs all the sleep she can get," she mumbled.

"Yeah, you do…but, uh, I need a favor."

"What?"

"Do you remember that black dress I bought you when we went to the Bahamas?"

"Yes."

"Put it on, comb your hair, and put on those shoes I bought you too. I'll be there in less than an hour to pick you up."

"Jaylin, are you crazy? I'm tired. Besides, I thought you had a date for this damn charity ball tonight."

"I do. Well…I did. Anyway, I'll explain it to you later. Just do what I asked, okay?"

"No, it's not okay, but I'll do it because you seem desperate. Next time, get your shit together ahead of—"

I cleared my throat. "Desperate? Never. In need… yes. So, get dressed, and I owe you one."

"Oh, you owe me more than one."

"Okay, then two, damn! Hurry up and don't wear your hair down. Pin it up at the top and let the back dangle on your shoulders how I like it."

"Now, that's asking too much. That shit takes time. If you give me two hours then maybe I can get it together like that Your Heinous."

"One hour, that's all you got. I'll be there in one hour."

I hung up and ran back downstairs to break the news to Brashaney. She just didn't make the cut. Sorry, but she wasn't fit to be in Jaylin Rogers' circle.

"Don't give me any excuses, Jaylin." She said, pointing her finger at me, fuming. "I know exactly what you're up to. I swear...this is the last time you're going to play my ass. You don't ever have to worry about me calling your house again. You are a cold cruel motherfucker and you don't even deserve to have a woman like me."

I shook my head. "You're right, I don't," I said, escorting her to the door. "But can we talk about this some other time? I really need to be going." Brashaney reached up and tried to smack me. I let her get away with that shit one time before, but she wasn't going to fuck up my handsome face tonight. I grabbed her wrist and squeezed it as tight as I could.

"DO NOT!" I yelled. "Touch my damn face, Brashaney. You're taking shit a bit too far, so please...get in your car and take your ass home."

She snatched her wrist away from me. "Ooo...I swear this is it! You better not ever call my house for as long as you live."

She followed behind me running her mouth, as I walked to my car. I opened the door and looked at her. "I promise you, I will never call you again."

I grinned, got in my car, and slammed the door. I heard a clunk when she walked past my Cedes, so I hopped out to see if she'd fucked it up. "Don't play, silly-ass," I said, looking down at my car to make sure everything was cool. She gave me the finger, and walked abruptly to her car.

After backing out of the driveway, I reached for my cell phone to call my baby Mackenzie. I forgot to tell her goodbye, after messing around with Brashaney, and when Nanny B answered, I asked her to put Mackenzie on the phone. She blew me a kiss, and told me how handsome I looked. I smiled because that was all the approval I needed.

29

It was ten minutes after eight when I honked the horn outside of Scorpio's condo. Normally, out of respect, I would go to the door. But since I had already called to let her know I was around the corner, I expected her to be outside waiting. I got out, leaned against the Cedes and waited.

Almost five minutes later, she strolled her ass out taking her time. But when I saw how amazing she was looking, I couldn't do nothing but smile. She wore the black satin dress I bought her, her hair was just like I had asked and was pinned up as a few strands dangled on her shoulders. Her make-up was flawless, and her thick perfectly arched eyebrows could have put her on the front of *Essence Magazine*. Her scent gave me a rise and smelled just like a bed of roses. To make her complete, her fingernails and toenails were polished to perfection. It made me feel good to have a woman like her by my side. Smiling, I quickly opened the door for her and winked.

"Don't go being all nice to me now," she said, grinning, and getting into the car.

"Just be quiet. Did anybody ever tell you that you talk too much?"

"No, but did anybody tell you that you're a control freak?"

"All the time, baby." I gave her a peck on the cheek and closed the door. I ran over to the driver's side and got in.

"So, what happened to your date?" I knew she couldn't wait to ask.

"She didn't make the cut."

"Negro, please. So, now, women got to audition in order to be with you, huh?"

"No, nothing like that, but there are certain things I'm particular about."

"Certain things like what, Jaylin?"

"Like a woman's hair, her skin, her smell, her clothes, her nails, her make-up, her ass, her pus…" I rubbed my hand on Scorpio's leg near the good stuff.

"Okay, I got your point. But who in the hell are you critiquing us like you do?"

"I'm J-A-Y-L-I-N, if you wanna be with me, you got to fit in."

30

"So, you're a rapper now, huh? You are so damn full of yourself it's ridiculous. And by the way, please don't quit your day job because *that* was pathetic."

We both laughed.

"Anyway, uh…" I cleared my throat. "Are you gonna shake a brotha down tonight or what? You know it's been a while since I tapped into that pussy…right?"

"So, you're asking now? And if my memory serves me correctly, it's been less than a week since I tapped into that dick…right? Besides, I thought you were the kind of man who just takes what he wants. "

"Yep, that would be me. But you know I wanna take it right now since you're looking all pretty and everythang. However, since we got plans, I don't want to mess you up."

"Was that a compliment?"

"Yes, it was. Gotta hand it to you, baby, you really out did yourself tonight. You know a brotha appreciate it, don't you?"

"Well, he'd better. Cause if he don't, he won't be getting no loving tonight."

"Um…so, does that mean I'm getting some juice tonight?"

"Juice? That depends on how well you arouse me," she said, moving closer, and placing her hand on my goodness.

"Don't play now, Scorpio. I'm already running late. I'll pull this motherfucker over and fuck the shit out of ya."

Scorpio laughed and eased back over to the passenger side.

I flew down highway 40 trying to get to the Adams Mark downtown. By the time Scorpio and I arrived, we were damn near two hours late. The presentations had already started, but there wasn't anything I could do. We quietly walked through the crowd and found our table. Schmidt was so glad to see me; he didn't even seem to care how late I was. He stood up and grinned, as he shook my hand and introduced me to his ugly ass wife—like I'd never met her before. I, in return, introduced the entire table to Scorpio. The men at the table, which was Angela's husband Doug, Roy, and Clay, another one of my co-workers, mouths were wide open. I pulled the chair back for Scorpio, and flattered by all the attention, she crossed her legs in front of her. Considering my past history with Angela, she looked at me and tooted her lips. Avoiding her, I reached over and shook hands with Roy and Clay wives.

The ceremony was too damn long. I found myself getting tired even though the conversation at the table was flowing. They were all up in Scorpio's and my business. Asking questions and shit about how long we've been dating, and where did we meet? But when Roy asked what she did for a living, I quickly intervened.

"She's an entrepreneur. I'm assisting her with her Fashion Merchandising career. She's very creative when it comes to designing clothes, and can model any piece remarkably well."

"Really?" she replied. "That doesn't sound like a bad idea Jaylin. We should talk more about that later." She picked up her wineglass, took a sip, and gave me a crazy stare.

I was glad when they introduced Schmidt's Brokerage and called me to the podium. I stepped up, cracked a few simple-minded jokes, and presented *St. Louis Sisters United* a check for five-thousand dollars. As the audience applauded, I looked around the room and thought, where in the hell were all the black people? Aside from the sistas of STLSU, there must have been just a hand full of us in the entire room. We were missing out on so much that it was ridiculous.

I scanned the room for a while, when I noticed Felicia at a table with her employer. She was staring so hard; I couldn't do anything but nod my head and smile. And after I joked around with the crowd a little while longer, I went back to our table. Schmidt proudly stood up, gave me another handshake, and patted me on the back. When I sat down, Scorpio leaned over, and gave me a quick kiss on the lips.

Shortly after my presentation, it was Felicia's turn. She stepped up to the podium wearing a long white silk strapless fitted dress with slits on both sides. Her braids were wrapped in a French roll and two curls dangled on the sides of her face. She wore a four-tier diamond necklace that sparkled, long shimmering diamond earrings, and a bracelet that matched the necklace. Her shoes looked like a Cinderella glass slipper and for damn sure didn't have any mud caked on them. Classy, I thought. Sure looked classy for a woman who was truly what I call an "under cover ho."

After dinner was served, I was ready to go. Scorpio was making conversations with everybody, even Angela. Fucked me up, because when she finds out Angela and me used to be banging buddies, I was sure her tune would change.

As the night dragged on, the band started playing some old-time boogie-down-ass funky music that had all the white people on their feet looking like complete idiots. I really wasn't up for this shit. I was ready to go and get my fuck on, but Scorpio kept running her mouth and prolonging the night.

"Come on, Jaylin, let's dance." She stood up and reached for my hand.

"Woman, you have got to be out of your mind. I ain't dancing to no bullshit like that," I said, silently.

"Please," she begged. "Trust me, it'll be fun." She tried to pull me out of my seat, but I just sat there with my arms folded. Seeing that I wasn't going to cooperate, she walked off and went over to the musician. He immediately slowed it down and kicked up some jazz by Miles Davis.

"Okay, get up now," she said, coming back over to the table. When I still didn't budge, she leaned down and whispered in my ear, "You know that sex we talked about…"

I stood up. "Come on, damn. I just knew you were going to go there."

Scorpio escorted me to the dance floor. I put my arms around her waist, pulled her in close, and left no breathing room between us.

"Damn, why don't you just pull me to the floor and fuck me?" she said, trying to scoot back.

"Why don't we just get the hell out of here so I can get you out of this tight-ass dress and then fuck you?"

The couple who was dancing next to us heard our conversation and moved away. We looked at each other and cracked up.

"You know I can feel your hard thang pressing against me, don't you?" Scorpio said, moving side to side.

"Baby, please. You of all people should know how big my thang is. It ain't no where near hard. It just can't help itself." Scorpio slid her hand down my back and squeezed my ass. I grinned and slightly moved back, "Quit playing. You don't want to get hurt when we get home do you?"

"Hurt me. By—"

"Excuse me," Felicia interrupted, then looked at Scorpio. "Do you think I can steal your man for a moment?"

"Sure, why not?" Scorpio said, backing away from me. "Take more than a moment if you need it." She looked at me. "Baby, I'm going to go mingle for a while. Don't be too long, okay."

"Hey, you really don't have to," I said, really not wanting to let her go.

"No, no...by all means, dance. A dance never hurt anybody." She looked at Felicia. "Right Felicia?"

"Right, Scorpio. Thanks, sweetie, you're such a charm," Felicia said, with a fake smile.

"Jaylin seems to think so too." Scorpio touched my face and gave me a juicy wet kiss before she walked away.

I held Felicia in my arms and left just a little room in between us. "You know that was kind of bold, don't you?" I asked

"Yes, but, oh well, you know me. Anyway...how have you been doing, Jaylin?"

"Good, good. And you?"

"Couldn't be better. Missing what we had, but Stephon's definitely doing a great job taking your place."

"Ah...so glad to hear that," I said, trying to keep my peace because I knew the bitch was trying to piss me off. "You look nice, though, Felicia, I mean really nice."

"So do you, but would you ever expect anything less from me?"

"No...really can't say I would. Just only if you had the personality to go with the look."

"Ouch! Now, that hurt. I could really say the same about you, but I won't. Besides, you were such a good teacher for me. I only learn from the best. And oh, before I forget, how's the wife and kid. I heard about all your drama with Nokea, but I see you still got the playboy bunny, I mean, stripper or hooker...or whatever you want to call her, with you."

I laughed. "You know, Felicia, you still haven't changed one bit. I thought that maybe after Scorpio took this good-ass fat dick away from you, you'd get some sense. It's really a shame that playboy bunny, stripper, hooker, or whatever you want to call her these days, got more goddamn sense and respect for herself than you ever will have. So, I don't care how spectacular you look tonight, you still the same ole stank-ass, tramp-ass slut that you were when I was with you." I unwrapped my arms from around her waist and walked off the floor. Damn shame she made me go off like that in front of these white people, but I couldn't help myself. I know some of them heard me, so it was definitely time to get the hell out of here. I found Scorpio coming out of the ladies room with Angela laughing like they were the best of friends. I grabbed her and told her I was ready to go. She waved goodbye to Angela and told her she'd call her tomorrow.

"Call her for what?" I asked, as we waited for one of the valets to bring my car.

"Call her because she seems like a nice person. We talked about getting together sometime."

"Well, that ain't going to happen."

"Why? Who are you trying to pick my friends for me?"

"Scorpio, she's my secretary. She knows more about me than anybody does. I don't want her sharing all my personal business with you."

"And what personal business you got that I don't already know about?"

"It's personal. That means I don't want you to know." I tipped the valet and we got into the Cedes. Scorpio continued running her mouth and refused to let go of the Angela situation.

"So, tell me. What else is there to know about you, Jaylin, other than that you're a ho."

"Okay, if that's all you see in me, cool. But remember, I'm a good damn ho, baby. One of the best damn ho's you'll ever meet in St. Louis. Now, if you really want to know what I was talking about pertaining to my personal business, I was talking about my finances."

"Oh...I don't care about those. That is your business and she would be wrong for sharing that information with me. I thought you were going to tell me you and her used to mess around."

I continued looking straight and didn't say a word.

"Jaylin Rogers!"

"What? Scorpio Valentino!"

35

"Don't tell me. Are you fucking your secretary? Okay, you don't even have to answer, I can tell by that smirk on your face. No wonder she was asking me all kinds of questions about our relationship. The nerve of that bitch."

"Alright…alright. Just let it go. It was a long time ago, and since I'm such a ho, what else would you expect?"

"You're right. I wouldn't expect anything different, but how long ago is a long time ago in your vocabulary?"

"So long ago that I can't remember. I just know it's been a while. Actually, she's been exchanging juices with Boy Roy lately."

"Roy…Roy…the tall, skinny, white dude who was sitting at the table?"

"Yep."

"But he's married. And so is she. What is that matter with people these days? Do you all have some type of free-for-all at work where everybody gets a chance to screw the secretary?"

"Scorpio, just be quiet. Can I get you to shut your mouth for the rest of the way home?"

"I thought you'd never ask," she said, reaching over, and unzipping my pants. "Maybe if you put something in it…who knows, it just might shush me."

I was on cloud nine and damn near lost control over the steering wheel trying to stay focused. I held it tightly with one hand and rubbed her soft coal black hair with the other hand, as her performance was so satisfying to me. After closing my eyes a few times trying to concentrate on the feeling, I pulled over and got off at the Forest Park exit to find a quiet place to park.

Scorpio raised up and licked her lips. "Now *that* was tasty— but the park, Jaylin? This is really tacky. All kinds of crazy people be roaming through here at night. You must be out of your mind if you think I'm getting naked up in here."

"Let's just chill for a minute, okay? You don't have to get naked. All I want to do is play around for a lil bit."

I leaned over and sucked Scorpio's glossy lips into mine. Then I rolled my tongue down her neck and pecked it. I reached for the adjust button on her seat and moved it back as far as it could go. I rubbed my hands on the outside of her dress, and searched her private parts. My hands slowly crept up between her legs, and I could feel the

36

heat coming down. When I moved her lace panties over to the side, I circled my fingers inside her.

She grabbed my hands and moaned, as she pressed her head against the headrest. "Baby, can we please just go home?"

I kissed her lips again and continued working my fingers. After I slid them out, I felt her body responding. I rubbed my fingers across my lips, and licked my tongue across them to taste her.

"Okay, it's your turn," I whispered, as I placed her hand on her goodness and watched her rub her clitoris. Full of excitement after seeing it harden, I made my way down between her legs and tightened up on it with my lips. As she neared coming, she grabbed my head and opened her legs wider.

"Jaylin," she screamed. "If you don't start this damn car up and get to your place in ten minutes, the deal is off!"

I ignored her and after having the pleasure of slurping her up, I started the engine and headed home. With a true smile on her face, she eased her dress down and teased her hair with her fingers to straighten it. Not saying much to her, I got back on the highway and was home in less than fifteen minutes.

When we got out of the car, we saw Nanny B sitting in the living room reading a *Jet* magazine. We crept around to the back of the house so Nanny B and Mackenzie wouldn't know we were home.

After I removed my bow tie, ready to get down to some serious business, Scorpio caught me off guard and pushed me into the swimming pool. I tried to keep my balance, but I couldn't. The loud splash had Nanny B running outside. She slid the patio door open and stepped into the pool area.

"So, I see you two made it back," she said.

"Yeah, but we're going to chill outside for a while," I said, floating in the water.

"That's fine. Mackenzie's been asleep since nine. I'm going upstairs to watch a movie if you don't mind."

"No, not at all. We'll be up in a minute." She turned and went back into the house. I looked at Scorpio. "Uh, Miss Lady, get your butt in this pool with me."

"I don't think so. That water looks icy cold to me. Besides, I ain't got nothing to wear anyway." I hopped out dripping wet in my

37

Tuxedo. Scorpio started running because she knew I was coming to get her. I quickly caught up with her and slung her over my shoulder.

"Jaylin, you wouldn't!" She said, screaming, kicking her feet, and laughing. "Please don't throw me in the water with this dress on! It's too expensive…" I tossed her in the water and dived back in.

Scorpio's wet hair covered her entire face, and I could barely see her eyes. I made my way over to her and put my arms around her. When I moved her hair away from her face she didn't crack a smile.

"Look what you did. This dress is ruined," she pouted.

"So, so I'll buy you another one."

"My body is shivering."

"So, so is mine."

She smiled. "I want a commitment, Jaylin."

"So, so does everybody else."

"But, it's time, don't you think so?"

I gazed into her eyes. "Nope, not until I live up to your expectations of being a ho."

Before she could say anything else, I placed my lips on hers and removed her dress. It floated off into the water just as my Tux did when I took it off. Since I couldn't hit it like I wanted to while we were in the pool, I straddled Scorpio on the diving board, and as usual, had my way with her. She was exactly what I needed in my life to keep my mind off loving Nokea. Besides, Scorpio's good-ass pussy had me looking at things a little bit differently this time around, but a commitment to one woman was, without a doubt, out of the question.

NOKEA

I was so glad to be home. One week away from everybody really gave me a chance to clear my head. One thing was for sure, I wasn't going to give up on Jaylin. Some day, this all has to come together for us, and this time I was in it for the long haul. Our nine years turned to ten years. Ten years of good times and bad times, but the most important thing now is our son. Hopefully, LJ is going to bring Jaylin and I closer together, and eventually Jaylin will come around and see things for what they truly are supposed to be.

Sunday was a day that I had longed for. I woke up at five o'clock in the morning just to prepare myself for the big day. I left a message with Nanny B last night and asked her to tell Jaylin that we'd be there no later than one o'clock in the afternoon. I know he said by noon, but one extra hour wasn't going to kill him.

After I ate breakfast, I went into LJ's room and he was still sound asleep. When I checked on him earlier, he had a smile on his face like he knew he was going to see his daddy today. He was lying there peacefully, and I couldn't resist holding him. All I could think is how we really had ourselves something special. He was the cutest little baby I'd ever seen and was looking more like his daddy every day.

When Stephon and I talked, he said he'd like to continue to be a part of LJ's life, but I convinced him under the circumstances, that wouldn't be the best thing to do. He agreed, but made me promise to at least bring LJ by his barbershop sometimes to see him.

Stephon's forgiveness really had me worried. For me to walk away from him at the altar, he was handling himself extremely well. Deep down I knew he was hurt, but he was putting up a front like he really didn't care. Maybe he did understand why I couldn't go through with the wedding, or maybe he had somebody else in his life and didn't know how to break the news to me. I wasn't going to stress myself too much about it because I believe my decision worked out for all of us.

At twelve-fifteen, LJ and I were just about ready to head out. There was no sense in me calling Jaylin to let him know that we were on our way because I'm sure he was probably already having a fit since we were late.

LJ looked darling. He wore a white and blue Guess outfit with a hat to match. I found some baby Guess tennis shoes at an outlet mall when Mama and I went shopping and put those on. His soft curly hair was slightly peeking out the sides of his hat and his gray eyes, like Jaylin's, sparkled when I called his name.

We pulled in front of Jaylin's house about a quarter to one. I took LJ out of his car seat and walked to the door. I rang the doorbell and patiently waited for someone to answer. After ringing it several more times, Jaylin finally opened the door. His face lit up and he didn't even look at me, as he took LJ from my arms.

"Well, hello to you too," I said, handing LJ over to him.

"Hey, sorry, come in. I actually forgot you were coming," he said, looking like he had just woke up.

"I called last night and left a message with Nanny B. She didn't tell you?"

"No, but that's okay. I'm glad you came. Cause if you hadn't, you know I was coming for you."

I followed behind Jaylin, and we went into his office. I took a seat on the couch, and he sat in his chair lifting LJ up in the air, looking him eye to eye. "Do you know how happy your daddy is to see you, huh?" he said, talking baby talk to him. I couldn't do anything but smile after finally seeing them together. At that moment, I knew I was wrong for trying to keep them apart.

As I continued to watch him sharing precious moments with his son, I heard someone walking down the steps. I thought Jaylin was alone, but when Scorpio came into his office, I damn near died. She looked over at me. "Hi, Nokea" she said, dryly, then turned to look at Jaylin.

"Hello," I replied.

Jaylin sat LJ on his lap, then turned him around so Scorpio could see him. "Look, baby. Ain't he handsome? I bet you didn't think I could pull something off like this, did you?" he asked her.

"Yes, Jaylin. He is gorgeous, and I never said you couldn't, so be quiet." Scorpio looked over at me. "Do you mind if I hold him?"

"No, not at all," I said, knowing that I didn't want her to touch him. I cringed as she took him off Jaylin's lap and held him. When she sat down in one of his leather chairs, her silk robe slid open and showed her goods. She quickly crossed her legs, but I had already seen that she didn't have on anything underneath. Of course, with Jaylin coming to the door in his robe, I figured they were probably in the middle of screwing when I rang the doorbell. If not, I was sure they had been at it all night long.

It really wasn't like me to hate on another woman when it came to Jaylin, but after listening to him call her "baby" my feelings were hurt once again. And if that wasn't enough, Mackenzie came into the room and added to my pain. She hopped up in Jaylin's lap, and put her arms around his neck.

"Good morning, Daddy." She kissed him on the cheek and he kissed her back.

"It's not good morning, Mackenzie, it's good afternoon. And what did I tell you about speaking to guest when you see them in the house?" She laid her head against his chest.

"But I didn't see her," she said, looking at me, and putting her fingers into her mouth. She lifted her head up. "Hey, that's your wife, Daddy! That's the one who you married the other day."

Jaylin shamefully covered his face and shook his head. I smiled at Mackenzie, and Scorpio stood up and brought LJ over to me.

"You have a beautiful baby, Nokea."

"Thanks," I said, taking him from her.

"Come on, Mackenzie." Scorpio took Mackenzie by the hand. "Let's go make some of your favorite pancakes." Mackenzie pulled her hands back and wrapped them tightly around Jaylin's neck. "Mackenzie, did you hear what I said, honey? Let's go make breakfast."

"But I don't like the way you make your pancakes. I like the way Daddy makes them."

Jaylin chuckled and kissed Mackenzie on the cheek. "Baby, I'll be in there to cook you some pancakes in a minute. In the meantime, eat a big bowl of Captain Crunch, okay?" Mackenzie hopped down off his lap.

41

"Okay, Daddy, but hurry, alright." She looked over at me, "Bye Daddy's wife," she said, waving.

Scorpio and Jaylin both yelled, "She's not his/my wife, Mackenzie!"

Mackenzie and Scorpio walked out.

Jaylin got out of his chair and came over next to me. He reached for LJ again, and leaned back laying him on his chest. He removed LJ's hat, rubbed his hair, and rolled his hands up and down on LJ's back.

"He feel so good in my arms, Nokea, you just don't know. Thing is, I can't figure out if I'm upset with you for keeping him from me, or if I'm happy that you brought him over here to see me."

"Jaylin, I'm sorry, and I made a bad decision. I was wrong for keeping him from you, but at the time I thought that I was truly doing what was best for me."

"Right...right, but going forward I don't want no shit from you about him Nokea. I want to at least see him a minimum of three or four times a week. I'm willing to adjust my schedule to make sure that happens."

"Now, you know how complicated your schedule can be. Why don't you just call me on the days you're not too busy and I can bring him over? If you call ahead of time, that will make it easier for me."

"That might work. And whenever you have something to do, let me know and I'll make arrangements as well."

"Sounds like a plan to me," I said, enjoying our pleasant conversation.

"What about his expenses? How have you been handling those?"

"It's been okay. I mean, he's not wanting for much, but having a baby has put a slight hole in my pockets."

"Well, no child of mine is going to just be OKAY. After I found out he was mine, I set up several Mutual Funds for him. There are some other things I wanted to do like investing in his education, but I just haven't gotten around to doing that yet. I've been thinking about child support for him. You have my word that I will take care of him, so I don't want no damn court telling me how much I need to pay. If you don't mind I'll have my attorney put together a promissory letter that says I promise to give you…lets say $5,000 a month? Will that be enough?"

"Six sounds better," I said, jokingly.

"Okay, then six. But you better be using this money for him. Not to be buying shit for you, or getting your hair and nails done. You know how y'all women do."

"You know me better than that, and six is too much, I was just kidding. Four would most certainly suffice."

"I say five. So, I'll call my attorney tomorrow and once he puts everything in writing, I don't want you reneging on my offer."

"I won't, but honestly, you really don't have to go through all the trouble. I trust you."

"Naw, thing is, I don't trust you. I've been honest with you about almost everything in my life. You're the one who be telling lies." Jaylin gave LJ back to me and went over to his desk.

"That's not so, Jaylin, and you know it. I lied because I had to."

He pulled his calculator out and bounced his pen up and down on his desk. Then he opened this square leather burgundy book and started writing. He looked over at me.

"There are certain things that shouldn't be lied about, Nokea, like your love for someone, your credentials, and your loving children. You catch my drift?" He dropped his head and continued to write.

Shortly after, he ripped the paper out of the book, came over to me, and handed it to me. "This should financially make up for my lost time. I don't care what you do with it, but several months ago I had another responsibility. You made sacrifices, so I'd like to repay you." I took the paper out of Jaylin's hand, and it was a check for $65,000.

"Jaylin, no. You don't have to do this. I know you would have taken care of LJ had you known, and there is no need for you to give me this much money."

"Nokea, I'm not going to argue with you. There's no reason you should have a hole in your pocket and I don't. This money is petty when it comes to my son. I'll make it up in a few months anyway. So, take it. Fifty-five thousand is for LJ, and ten is for the ten

43

years of pain and suffering I caused you. If you have any problems at your bank, let me know, and I'll call mine."

Now, after breaking it down like that, I wasn't going to argue with him about the money. Every bit helps, and this was more than any court would ever offer me. Besides, I was sure Jaylin had plenty of money hidden away somewhere. The courts would never find it, and even though he never shared with anyone how much money his grandfather's estate was worth, by Jaylin's lifestyle, and many years of investing, I knew he was worth millions.

After Jaylin cooked Mackenzie her pancakes, he asked me if LJ could stay the day with him. He told me to pick him up by ten o'clock tonight, so he could get some rest before he went to work. I asked him if Scorpio was going to help him, but he said he was kicking her out too and was spending the rest of the day with his son and daughter.

This was definitely the Jaylin I'd fallen in love with. He seemed so different, but my only problem was his relationship with Scorpio. It seemed as if she wasn't going anywhere any time soon. I felt like I had the upper hand because I knew he was still in love with me. I also knew that if I didn't work fast at getting him back, she would eventually replace me. I was willing to do everything in my power to make sure that never happened.

JAYLIN

I was running around the house like a chicken with his head cut off. Trying to be hard—pretending that I could handle two kids in the house at once and I was paying for it dearly.

LJ was lying on my bed screaming at the top of his lungs, and Mackenzie was trying to get him to stop crying by giving him her Barbie dolls. When I realized that maybe he was wet, I took his diaper off only for him to piss right in my damn face. I sat on the edge of my bed laughing and thanking God these kids had mothers. I for damn sure wasn't cut out for this.

After LJ did number two and it seeped out of his diaper onto my satin Gucci sheets, I damn near died. I called Nanny B and begged for her to come back over. She said she'd already made plans, but when I pleaded with her she changed her mind and said that she was on her way.

There was no way I was calling Nokea or Scorpio for their help. After I kicked Nokea out she made me promise not to call her until it was time to pick him up. Scorpio said she was leaving anyway, and insisted that she had to finish up some homework for school.

When the doorbell rang, I rushed to it thinking it was Nanny B. Instead it was Stephon on the porch looking lost.

"Say, can I come in," he asked.

I held the door open. "Please, make it quick. I'm spending time with my kids today." I felt proud as I was holding LJ in my arms.

"Cool, I won't be long, but, uh, why haven't you returned any of my phone calls?"

"Man, I hope you didn't come all the way over here to sound like one of my women with this phone call bullshit. You know damn well why I haven't returned your phone calls. Been busy and ain't got time for snake-ass niggas in my life."

"Okay, that's cool. But I just wanted to say that I'm sorry. I made a big mistake asking Nokea to marry me, but I can't change what has already happened. If time is what you need, fine, take all the time you need. When you're ready to talk, call me or come holler at me at the shop." He turned towards the door. When I opened it to let him out, he stood there for a minute and stared at me.

"What, nigga?" I yelled. "Why in the hell are you looking at me like that?"

"Cause, Jay," he said, as his eyes watered. "I'm sorry. I tripped, cuz, and the last thing I wanted to do was hurt you."

"Well, too late for that shit. You should have thought about the consequences a long time ago."

Stephon took a hard swallow and walked out of the door. I took my foot and slammed it against the door, closing it. When I looked out of the window, Nanny B was getting out of her car. She was talking to Stephon for a while, then started laughing when she saw me open the door and standing there with LJ.

She walked up to me and took him out of my hands. "Jaylin, he's been crying because he's wet. I can feel how soaked he is just by holding him."

"Damn, I just changed him," I said, closing the door behind her. "How many times does he have to go?"

She shook her head and walked up the steps with him in her arms. I followed. Mackenzie was taking a nap in her room, so Nanny B went into one of the guestrooms. She laid LJ on the bed and started to undo his diaper.

"Aren't you going to put something underneath him? Those sheets cost me a fortune," I said.

She gave me a hard stare. "Go get a diaper, please," she said, kissing LJ on his feet. I rushed into my room and grabbed a diaper out of his diaper bag. I went back into the guestroom and gave it to her. "Did you see how you put his diaper on? It wasn't wet. He leaked through the sides because it's not taped up on him. Now, come on over here and let me show you how to do this right."

I walked over by Nanny B and looked down at LJ. "But the comforter...can't we put something underneath him so he won't mess it up. I just had to change my—"

"Jaylin! Go get a towel or something please! This anal behavior of yours has got to stop. Especially, since you have children around the house." I ignored Nanny B and ran to the closet to get a towel. She snatched it out of my hand and slid it underneath LJ's bottom. Then she showed me the correct way to put his diaper on. I

47

guess since I didn't even remove the sticky tabs on the side that could have been why the diaper wouldn't stay up on him. I thought that by pulling his pants up it would keep his diaper in place, but what did I know?

Nanny B went over to my beige leather rocker and sat down. She laid LJ on her chest, rocked back and forth a few times, and in less than five minutes he was asleep. I sat on the edge of the bed and smiled, as I was really feeling like a proud father. Didn't really know what I would do without Nanny B around, so I asked her if she would move in with me.

"There's plenty of room, Nanny B. Besides, you're here most of the time anyway."

She shook her head. "Jaylin, I don't know. Let me think about it. You really seem like a man who needs his privacy."

"I do, but I need my children in my life even more. I need proper care for them, and that means more to me than anything. So, please," I begged. "Think about it and let me know in a couple of days."

"I will," she whispered, as LJ squirmed around in her arms. "Why don't you go get some rest while Mackenzie and LJ are both asleep? You look tired. If you and Scorpio wouldn't have been up all night fooling around maybe you could have gotten some rest."

I kissed her on the cheek and left out of the room. I went past Mackenzie's room and looked in. Since I knew she probably felt neglected because LJ was around I climbed into bed with her. She woke up just long enough to put her arms around me and went back to sleep.

LJ's loud crying woke up Mackenzie and me. I hopped up and ran downstairs to the kitchen to see what all the fussing was about. Mackenzie followed. By the time we got there, Nanny B had him all taken care of. He had a bottle in his mouth and he was going at it.

"He's fine. Babies do cry, you know?" she said.

"I know, but he cries a little too much doesn't he?" Mackenzie said.

"I agree," I said, giving her five. We both laughed.

"He doesn't cry anymore than you two did when you were babies. And Mackenzie you still cry, don't you?" Mackenzie's eyes watered, and she wrapped her arms around my legs as if her feelings were hurt.

"Come on, baby," I said, rubbing her back. "Let's go upstairs and see if we can get LJ together."

I took LJ from Nanny B and we all headed upstairs. I put some old de-crusted sheets on my bed so my good ones wouldn't get messed up, and Mackenzie, LJ, and me sat up watching the *Cartoon Network Channel*.

Mackenzie's Barbies were all over the bed and LJ was staying occupied by putting them into his mouth. He was learning early, I thought, and was definitely going to have his way with the women just like I do.

Nokea came thirty minutes early. Nanny B was downstairs and opened the door for her. When she came into my bedroom and saw me sitting up in bed with my kids, she smiled.

"I knew you couldn't handle it." She put her hands on her hips. "So, don't lie. You called the nanny, didn't you?"

"Woman, please. Nanny B comes over on the weekends anyway. So, don't go talking nonsense."

"Jaylin, stop lying. She already told me you called her crying, begging, and pleading for her to come over here. You should be ashamed of yourself for lying. I thought you said earlier our child is one of the things we shouldn't lie about."

"Okay, busted. But you know I was just playing too, don't you?"

Nokea lifted LJ off the bed. "Yeah, I thought you were playing, but I also knew how much I missed my little baby today." She rubbed noses with LJ and kissed him all over his face. I was slightly jealous because he started cracking up as she talked to him. When I talked to him he just looked at me and stared. Shortly after, he started crying. I guess he probably wasn't comfortable with being around me yet.

"Hello, Mackenzie," Nokea said, as she noticed Mackenzie's sad look.

"Hi. Is LJ going home?" she asked.

I scooted Mackenzie next to me in bed. "Yes, but he'll be back with us next weekend, okay?" I said. She smiled and laid her head against me.

"Jaylin, you know you got that little girl too spoiled. She isn't going to be any good when she gets older."

"Don't go telling me how to raise my kids. If I want to spoil them, I can."

"Well, I'm letting you know now, don't come running to me when they get out of control. You have to start putting your foot down, and you can't let them run over you like Mackenzie does."

"Shut up," I said, getting angry. "Things were going cool between us, Nokea, until you come over here running your mouth trying to tell me how to raise my kids. First of all, don't say that shit in front of her. If you got something to say, pull me aside. Have a little respect, damn."

"And you have respect by cursing like that? I just think—"

"I just think you were leaving." I got off the bed, gathered LJ's things, and escorted Nokea to the door. Before she left I held LJ and kissed him again. Nanny B and Mackenzie gave their good-byes as well.

After my long nap earlier, I couldn't go back to sleep for nothing. I called Scorpio and told her Mackenzie and I was on our way. When I opened the front door, the rain was pouring. I covered Mackenzie with my jacket and we ran to the car. By the time we got in, mud covered the bottom of our shoes and messed up my damn floor mats. I thought about how bad I dissed Brashaney for the same shit and seriously thought about calling her to apologize, since it was raining that day as well. But when I thought about her trying to slap me, she was better off left where she was—Behind.

When I pulled in front of Scorpio's place, there was a nice-ass silver and blue Kawasaki motorcycle outside. Wet, but nice. I covered Mackenzie again and we ran to the door. Mackenzie knocked and Scorpio answered with a pencil in her mouth. She had on a short flimsy-ass flowered sundress that showed her shapely pretty legs and her breasts that were squeezed together showing all cleavage. Mackenzie rushed in, but I stood outside and looked her up and down.

"Are you coming in or what?" she asked fidgeting, and combing her hair back with her fingers.

"Don't you have company?"

"Yes, but he's just—"

"I'll talk to you later, alright?"

I walked off and Scorpio ran up behind me. "Jaylin, why are you tripping? It's not even like that. He's just my tutor, and he came over to help me with my homework."

"Your homework, huh? That's cool, then go do your homework. Why you out here trying to explain something to me that really ain't my business?"

"I just don't want you getting the wrong idea. But seems to me, you're a little jealous," she said, smirking.

The rain had slacked up a bit, so I had a chance to stand outside and set the record straight with her once and for all. "Scorpio, let's get something straight. Right here, and right now," I said, getting up in her face. "You are free to date any goddamn body you want to. And, so am I. So, jealous? No. Disappointed? Yes. Disappointed that I fucked you the way I did last night. You really didn't deserve it."

She looked at me in disbelief. "What? If anything, you don't deserve my loving. I'm trying to be nice and spare your fucking feelings, but you're just too much for me. If you really want to know, your dick ain't that damn good, Jaylin."

"Okay, cool. If you say so, baby. But the next time I fuck you, or if I decide to fuck you again, keep all that hollaring, moaning, and groaning...Oh, I love you so much bullshit to yourself."

"I will. And the next time we get up, it'll be my call, not yours."

When the rain picked up, I was in no mood to stand outside and continue arguing with Scorpio. And after I finished checking her ass for dissing me, I got back in my car and headed home.

The windshield wipers screeched against the window, as the rain slowed again. My mind wandered back to my amazing day with LJ and Mackenzie. They had turned my whole life around and made me feel like I could breathe again. My only problems were these damn crazy-ass women I had in my life. Nokea, Scorpio, Brashaney, and Felicia who wasn't too far gone. I couldn't figure out which one was stressing me the most. Was it Nokea for declining my proposal and denying me my son for all these months? Was it Scorpio for allowing me to support her and thinking she could bring any Tom, Dick, and Harry she wanted to home and I was paying the bills? Or, Brashaney who was just flat-out downright stupid, and couldn't look like a true lady no matter how hard she tried. Even maybe Felicia, who really wasn't stressing me at all, but I couldn't stand because we had too much in common.

I continued in deep thought about how Scorpio claimed I wasn't *that* good. The nerve. She, out of every woman that I've slept with, knew better than to let something that stupid slip out of her mouth. Every time we have sex, she's coming four and five times in less than an hour. As a matter of fact, since I met her ass, she hasn't been able to go one damn week without my dick inside of her. The only time she had been without it is when I kicked her ass out for lying to me about being a stripper. So, she can kiss my ass with that statement. She for damn sure knows it doesn't get any better than this.

I was on Wild Horse Creek Road in Chesterfield when I noticed a silver Jaguar slumped over on the side of the road. I pulled over behind it and got out of my car. As I neared the car, a young white woman, with long blonde straight hair was inside dialing out on her cell phone. She looked frightened, but when I offered to help, she seemed to relax. She opened the car door and got out as the rain started to pour down on both of us. I took my jacket off and put it over her head.

"Thank you," she said, wiping the rain away from her eyes.

"What happened?" I asked.

"My car slid. I tried to get out of the mud, but it's getting deeper. When I called for help, my cell phone went dead."

"Come get in my car. You can use my phone, or if you live close by, I can take you home." We ran to my car and got in. She wiped the rain from her face and pulled her hair back.

"Thanks again, Mr....."

"Jaylin, Jaylin Rogers. And yours?"

"Heather McDaniels." We shook hands.

"Nice to meet you Ms. McDaniels, but, uh...do you live close by?"

"Yes. Less than ten minutes away. Would you mind taking me home? I'd like to call someone to come get my car."

"Sure," I said, starting up my car. I turned the heat on to dry us off. She placed her hands against my vents and then rubbed them together. I quickly noticed a bad-ass platinum diamond ring on her finger. Had to be at least five or six karats. And the baguettes really set that motherfucker off. Somebody was lucky. I just wasn't sure if it was her husband, or her. From what I could see, though, he was the prizewinner. She was an attractive white woman. Had a nice slim body, big juicy succulent breasts, and a fairly well shaped ass. I had already peeped that when she got out of her car.

As she directed me to her house, I slowly pulled in the driveway. Good God All Mighty. That's all I could say. House was fabulous. Had to be at least a three or four million-dollar home. And there I was thinking my million-dollar home had it going on. One day, I thought, one damn day I'll be able to pull off some shit like this. If I would stop all the splurging and cut back on the material bullshit, this would be no problem for me.

"Jaylin," she said, reaching her hand out. "Thank you so much. You are definitely *the man*. I don't know what I would have done if you hadn't showed up."

"Glad to be of assistance," I said, shaking her hand back. She loosened her hand and reached into her purse. She pulled out a hundred-dollar bill and tried to give it to me.

"No, no, please, I can't take it. Like I said, glad to be of assistance to you in your time of trouble."

She put the money back into her purse. "Okay, well at least come inside for a drink. Besides, my husband is out of town on business, I could use some company anyway."

"A drink, huh?"

"Yes, whatever your heart desires. In addition, I'll show you around the place." I hesitated for a minute. "Come on, Jaylin. If my husband knew what you did for me, he'd insist. He'd actually kill me if he found out I didn't repay you."

We got out of the car and headed to the tall white double doors that opened to the entrance of the house. Nothing but beauty hit me as I walked in. In the foyer sat two baby grand pianos. A white piano was on one side and a black one was on the other. Above the pianos was a T-staircase that went from the Great Room to the Dining Room. Every piece of drapery that covered the windows was a satin white with black embroidery, and black thick tassels pulled them aside so you could see through the sheer curtains in the middle. The floors were covered with black, gray, and white swirling marble and had a shine so clear I could see a clear image of myself.

As I followed her into what they called a Bonus Room, I was sick to my stomach. It was located in a sunken room next to the Breakfast Room and had a floor made of glass where you could see the lower level. Designed like a sports bar, it had a cherry-wood bar that stretched from one end to the other, with everlasting bottles of alcohol behind it. A humongous television was built into the wall, and cherry-wood cocktail tables circled the floor. Above the tables were crystal lights that hung from the cathedral ceiling. I had seen it all. Now this is what I called straight-up motherfucking living right. As I stood there mesmerized, Heather gave me a towel.

"Jaylin?" she said, trying to get my attention.

"Aw, thanks." I took it and wiped my face and hands off. Even the towel had a feeling I had never felt before. It was soft as Charmin, had a breath taking fragrance, and had her initials on it.

"So, what do you think?" she said, drying her hair with a towel.

"I think your place got it going on, that's what I think."

"Yeah, we've put an extreme amount of money into our home to get it like this." She walked behind the bar. "So, what are you drinking?"

"Some Remy would be nice." I sat down at the bar and she picked up a bottle of Remy, then started to pour. She poured herself a glass aside of mine.

"Jaylin, while you're drinking up, I'm going upstairs to get out of these wet clothes and make a phone call. Make yourself at home. If you would like another drink, feel free to pour yourself one."

"Okay, but one will be fine. I don't want to over do it, you know what I mean?" She smiled and left the room.

Thirty minutes must have gone by when Heather returned. She came in the room with a little of nothing on. She had a soft pink lace top on with some skimpy lace shorts to match. I could clearly see the hardness in her nipples, and the nicely trimmed brown hairs covering her pussy. She definitely wasn't a true blonde. When she walked behind the bar, her bronzed tanned ass was begging me to fuck her. I dropped my head and smiled. I knew I was moments away from going where I had never dreamed of going before. White women had never been in my vocabulary, but maybe it was time for a change.

I had almost finished up the whole damn bottle of Remy by myself and was feeling woozy.

"You're quite a drinker, Mr. Rogers" she said, holding the almost empty bottle in her hand.

"No, I'm really not. I just couldn't help myself. Got kind of lonely waiting on you to return."

"Well, a handsome man such as yourself should never be lonely."

"It's okay, sometimes, but at least being by yourself gives you a chance to think things out and sort of put shit in perspective."

"I agree, but I get my share of being alone too many times." Heather took a few sips from her glass, and by the way her eyes were flirting with me, I could tell she was ready to dig into me, as I was straight-up feeling digging into her.

After talking for at least another hour, there was no doubt about it that she was lonely. Husband was a millionaire and couldn't even find the time to make love to his beautiful wife at home. Financially, she had it going on, but physically, she was deprived. So, not trying to rush the pussy, I pretended like I was getting tired and was ready to go. I stood up, stretched my arms out, and yawned.

"Well, Heather, I really must be going. Got a busy day at work tomorrow and need to get my rest."

She laughed and came from behind the bar. "Jaylin, I really enjoyed your company. You're so cute," she said, squeezing my cheek. "Maybe some day you'll invite me to your place for a drink, since you live close by."

"I just might do that." She walked in front of me and headed towards the door. My head was spinning, but not enough to keep my dick from getting hard looking at the cheeks of her ass slightly peeking through her shorts. She opened the door and held it, as I started to walk out.

"Goodnight," she said.

I stepped onto the porch. "Goodnight, Heather."

I reached in my pocket and felt for my keys. Wet again from the rain, Heather followed behind me, and grabbed my hand as I pressed down on the chirper.

"Stay," she said, tightly holding my hand, so the doors wouldn't unlock. "Besides, you shouldn't be drinking and driving anyway. I'd hate for something to happen to you."

I looked at her pretty self as the rain poured down on her body. She moved her hair behind her ears and pressed herself up against me. Then, she lifted my shirt and pulled it over my head. She rubbed her hands across the ridges of my six-pack, and placed her lips on my nipples. Getting a tingling feeling, I wiped my eyes with my hands as the rain pounded harder and I could barely see. She continued to lick my chest and I stood there thinking if this was something that I really wanted to do.

After coming to my senses, I pulled her hair back and leaned down to kiss her. Her lips were soft like melted butter, and did just that when I sucked them into my mouth. I lowered my hand and squeezed her ass, while she rubbed her hands up and down my back. Feeling horny, I ripped her shorts, then massaged her coochie with my hands.

She leaned her head back moaning, and not being able to handle my touch. "Jaylin, I'm getting so wet."

I whispered in her ear, "From the rain, or from how I'm touching you?"

"Definitely from the way you're touching me."

She moved away from me and lay down in the grass. When she opened her legs, the last thing on my mind was how dirty I was about to get by fucking her in the muddy soggy grass. I unzipped my pants, stepped out of them, and kneeled down in front of her. My knees slightly sunk in the mud, as I leaned forward and slid myself inside of her.

Trying to keep her body free from the rain, I lay over her as it fell down hard on my back. She was tight and I was only able to slide about six inches of myself inside of her. Insisting that the rest of me was too painful, she held my hips and slowed me down.

"Why are you doing this to me?" she said, painfully.

"So, what are you saying, Heather? Would you like for me to stop?"

"No, because shortly, I want you to give it all to me."

All she had to do was ask, so I prepared myself to do just that. She turned around and kneeled down in front of me, then pressed her

56

ass against my thang. I lifted her shirt over her head and massaged her breasts together. When she was good and ready, she leaned forward and allowed me to have my way. I gripped her tiny waistline from behind and slammed my nine-plus inches of goodness against her wet walls.

As mud covered our bodies, we continued rolling around on the ground fucking the shit out of each other. And after a few more minutes of intense screwing, we worked our way into the house and finished up in the foyer. She looked over at me and laughed, as we lay there with dry mud covering damn near our entire bodies.

"This is fucking crazy, Jaylin. I can't believe I let a complete stranger screw me the way you just did."

"Yeah, this was some wild shit, wasn't it? But look at it this way—just pretend that I met you at a party tonight and we're having a one-night stand. I mean, what's the difference from what we just did? People do it all the time."

"But not like this, Jaylin. I mean, you are really a satisfying man. I don't think I've ever had sex to that extreme before."

And you probably never will again, I thought. It wasn't that Heather wasn't cool to kick it with, but I already had enough on my plate. The last thing I needed was a married white woman hounding me.

Heather asked me to join her in the shower, but I declined. I told her I needed to be going and she understood. She walked me to my car, kissed me again, and said goodbye.

My car was a complete mess. Mud was everywhere and my clothes were drenched. I was pissed at myself for letting something so expensive get messed up like this. When I got home around four o'clock in the morning, I took a thirty-minute shower and scrubbed off the mud I had on my body and in my hair. I put some clean clothes on, and drove my ass to the nearest car wash. I did the best I could cleaning it considering I wasn't a professional, but most likely, I'd have to take it to a cash wash later to get the inside cleaned the right way.

By the time I finished my half-ass job, it was almost six o'clock in the morning. There was no way in hell I was going to work, so I went back home, climbed into bed, and sat up for about another hour thinking about Miss Heather. I had broken all the rules and couldn't understand why. One thing just led to another, I'd guessed. If anything, the jealousy I felt about Scorpio being with another man might have been my reasoning, but who knows. Either way, Stephon warned me a long time ago to always stick to my rules. He said if I didn't, I'd for damn sure pay for it. He left me several more messages about us discussing what happened, but I haven't quite found it in my heart to forgive him just yet. I expected a bunch of bullshit from my women, but never did I expect him to play me like he did. Soon, though, we'd have to work it out because I missed being around him like hell.

SCORPIO

I couldn't believe Jay-Baby being upset with me because I had company. If he had come inside he really would have been upset after he saw how gorgeous Shane was. Thing is, I really didn't anticipate on seeing Shane on Sunday. I asked him to come back on Tuesday after his class, but when he called Sunday and I just happened to be studying, I invited him over.

On his second visit, I started to understand Algebra a little better. The first time he came over, I think I must have been too occupied with how handsome he was and couldn't stay focused. Knowing how important it was for me to get the hang of things, I put my feelings aside and managed to learn something this time around.

Who was I fooling? I thought. Jaylin's spectacular loving the night before had me thinking about him all day long. And whether I wanted to face the truth or not, his loving had me all messed up. I couldn't let him know that, of course, but nobody could lay it down like he could. He was keeping me so satisfied that I really had no desire to go anywhere else.

Shane, however, was looking pretty damn spiffy last night. And something about the way he lifted his thick muscular legs on and off his motorcycle just did something to me. Feeling foolish about not even giving him a chance, I decided to call him. He answered with a deep, masculine voice.

"Shane?"

"Yes."

"Hi, it's Scorpio."

"I know. I mean, I recognize your voice."

To me, that meant there wasn't too many sistas calling, I thought. "Listen, I was just calling to thank you for coming over last night. Also, I wanted to be sure you made it home safely in the rain. I wanted to call last night, but it was kind of late when you left."

"Yeah, I did alright. My bike slid a few times, but I made it."

"Well…that's pretty much all I wanted," I said, trying to get my thoughts together. "Oh, by the way, Shane, you don't have to come by tomorrow since you stopped by last night. I think I'm starting to get the hang of Algebra."

"Are you sure? It gets a tad bit harder, you know."

"Yes, I'm sure it does. Unless...you'd like to have dinner tomorrow night."

"Dinner? I thought you'd never ask. Remember, I'll be a little late, though."

"That's fine. Would you like to eat in, or eat out? I mean, dine in, or dine out," I said, correcting myself.

He laughed. "I'd really like to eat out, but dining out will be better, for now anyway."

Now, this fine Negro just might have started something, "Let's say we meet at Houlihan's in the Union Station around nine?"

"Sounds perfect. I'll see you tomorrow, Scorpio."

After Shane and I hung up, I put my clothes on and got ready to leave. If anything, tomorrow would shed some light on my feelings for him. For the first time, no business between us, just strictly for entertainment purposes only.

Mackenzie was now in some type of uppity pre-school that Jaylin put her in. I was totally against her going there because there were no black children around for her to play with. I wanted her in a school that had a diversity of students. Not being in a school where she's so accustomed to being around one particular race.

After dropping her off, I was heading to school myself when I picked up my cell phone to call Jaylin at his office. First I wanted to see if he was still soaking about my company last night, then I wanted to talk to him about changing Mackenzie's school.

When Angela answered, I pretended to be someone else because I had no intentions of befriending someone that slept with the man I was in love with. When she said he was out of the office today, I hung up and called his house. When I didn't get an answer there, I turned my car around and went to his house. His car was in the driveway, so I parked next to it and went to the door.

As I stood there knocking, I could hear his shoes sliding on the floor. He opened the door, leaned against it, and looked as if he didn't want to be bothered.

"What?" he yelled. "Can a brotha get some peace around here!"

I pushed him aside and walked in. "Why didn't you take your lazy ass to work?" I looked around the room. "And where is she? I know somebody's over here."

"Scorpio, I was on the phone in my office when you knocked on the damn door. And if I do have company, that ain't your business."

"Yes it is, so stop fooling yourself thinking that it ain't. I'm sorry for interrupting your business calls, but I just stopped by to talk to you about last night, also about this pre-school you enrolled Mackenzie in."

"I'm not in the mood to talk about last night," he said, still standing by the door. "Come back some other time. Besides, I'm tired—Getting ready to take my ass back to bed."

"Now that's an interesting thought. Can I join you?"

"Nope. Ain't in the mood for that either. Anyway, didn't I just give you enough of my horrible-ass loving the other night? Besides, I'm sure your mystery man can pick up where I left off."

"I'm sure he can too," I said, walking towards him. "But, I see how you wanna play this. We only get down when you want to get down, right?"

Jaylin nodded his head. "You got that right. And since I'm kicking it down like I know I do, I say when, where, and how it happens. Thing is, if you say it's as bad as you claim it is, don't be over here begging for it."

"Beg? Never. Just remember, though, I'm not on your time Jaylin."

"Yes you are, Scorpio. So stop standing here wasting your time going through the drama. You're on my time just like everybody else is." He opened the door for me to leave. "Now, goodbye. I gotta get some rest and I'll call you later."

"Oooo…listen to you. You really think you have me under your wings, don't you? And even if you do, people and situations change all the time."

"And I expect them to change. But remember, they also change back. So, you go ahead and let your little mystery man tag that ass, and when he don't fuck you like I do, don't come running back to me. I don't work to well with leftovers anyway."

"Come on, now. All you've been dishing out is leftovers. Leftovers that should have been bagged up and thrown out like a week old piece of bread. Don't fool yourself thinking I'm some doormat you can step on whenever you want to. Lately, I've been feeling up to a challenge anyway."

"Look, well, challenge your ass out of this door." He swung the door open even wider. "I'm not in the mood for this shit, damn, I'm tired. You know how groggy I get when I tired, Scorpio, so call me later, alright? I promise you we'll talk then."

I rolled my eyes and walked out of the door. Jaylin took his hand and smacked me hard on my ass. "Do me a favor and tell the brotha, whoever he is, not to straddle you from behind. That's my work place," he winked, laughed, and slammed the door behind me.

Jaylin knew he had me wrapped around his finger. Our half-ass relationship and respect for one another was slowly, but surely, getting out of hand. Thing is, I couldn't tell if he was jealous about me seeing somebody else, or if he really didn't give a shit. The more and more I thought about it, I knew I had to put him to the test. I had to know for myself what his true feelings were for me. And even though I hated to play games with him, Shane was going to help me figure Jaylin out.

Tuesday rolled around with the quickness. Jaylin and I never had that conversation we were supposed to have. When I called him Monday night, he said that he was busy and he'd have to call me back. When he did call, he asked for Mackenzie, stayed on the phone with her for about fifteen minutes, then hung up. I wasn't going to make him talk to me, but eventually he'd want to. And whenever that time came, I was just not going to make myself available.

I sat at a table in Houlahans waiting for Shane to come. I remembered him saying he was going to be a little late, but I had a serious problem waiting on people. Especially men. I went to the ladies room for the third time tonight to make sure I was looking delightful. The mirror didn't lie. I couldn't complain about anything. My tan linen spaghetti strapped mini dress was working every curve in my body. My hair hung down on my shoulders, and was full of bouncing behaving curls. The three-inch brown leather heels I wore gave me just enough height to swish my ass from side to side as I walked. And after getting approval from the men that were staring, I went back to the table and continued to wait for Shane.

When I looked up and saw Felicia heading my way, I damn near died. She grinned as she sat at the table with me.

"Girrrrl...you know we really should stop meeting like this," she said, picking up a piece of bread from the table, and biting into it.

"Yes, we really should. Especially since we don't even like each other."

"Now, I never said I didn't like you, Scorpio. All I ever said is that Jaylin can do a hellava lot better, that's all." She took another bite of the bread.

"You think? Do you really think he can do better than me? And if so, with who? You?"

"Of course with me," she said, sitting up straight, and clinching her hands together in front of her. "You see, Scorpio, you didn't check out the way he was looking at me the other night, and you sure don't know what type of history we have together, so...if I were you, I'd be counting the days down I have left with him. And in case you haven't noticed yet, we're like two peas in a pod, they always stick together."

I rested my elbow on the table and placed my hand on the side of my face. "Felicia, I feel so sorry for you. You have one hell of an imagination. You know what," I said, sitting back, and reaching into my purse. I fumbled through my wallet and pulled out a business card. "I previously dated a psychiatrist. Here's his card. Feel free to call him any time, he could really help." I slid the card over to her. She picked it up and tapped it on the table.

"Funny, bitch, but after I call him, and screw him, that'll make two men we've shared. And when I find out how...." A voice interrupted Felicia.

"Felicia Davenport?" Shane said, as he walked up to the table. She stood up and wrapped her arms tightly around him.

"Shayneeeee Alexander. Long time no see. What are you doing here tonight?"

"I'm here to have dinner with Ms. Valentino." Shane looked down at me sitting at the table.

"Hello, Shane," I said, closing my eyes because I knew Felicia was about to eat this up. And after he leaned down and gave me a quick peck on the cheek, she went at it.

"So, you two know each other?" she asked.

"Yeah, we do. Scorpio's actually one of my students. And I take it that you two know each other as well."

"Of course. Scorpio and I go way back. We were just catching up on old times before you came."

"Well, don't let me interrupt. I'll go grab another chair, and Felicia, you can join us for dinner." Shane walked away to get a chair.

Felicia leaned down and whispered in my ear. "If you fuck him, ho, that'll be three men we've shared. He likes a woman with a deep throat so, uh, treat him well, okay. And being the experienced tramp that you are, I'm sure you won't bite." She quickly raised up, as Shane came back over to the table. It took everything that I had not to get up from the table and kick her ass. Instead, I just smiled as if I wasn't even tripping.

"Shane, I'm sorry," she said. "I really must be getting back to dinner with my bosses. I'm sure they're wondering where the heck I went." She gave Shane a pat on the back, then gave him another squeezing hug. "Shane, call me sometimes. It'll be good to catch up on old times." She looked at me, as I was still fuming. "Scorpio, tell Jaylin I said hello. Shane, you remember Jaylin don't you? Jaylin Rogers?"

"Yeah, you know I remember J.J. Rogers. How can I forget? Anyway, I haven't seen him since I moved from Atlanta."

"Well, I'm sure Scorpio can find him for you. She's got a way of sniffing him out." Felicia walked away from the table. I couldn't believe how ignorant she was. That was one bitch I wouldn't mind scratching her eyes out.

"Did I come at a bad time?" Shane asked, getting ready to sit down.

"No, actually, you came at the right time. As you can see, Felicia and I really don't get along. I used to date Jaylin and so did she. She's got a problem with letting go of the past."

"The past, huh. So, does that mean you're not seeing him anymore?"

"No, I'm not seeing him anymore. He's like a father to Mackenzie and other than that, our relationship has been on the down-low for a long time." I felt bad lying to Shane, but I wasn't really sure how well he knew Jaylin. "So what about you and Felicia? How well do you know her?"

Shane smiled. "I'd say I know her very well. We used to kick it, but, actually, she started seeing Jaylin and things got a bit complicated."

"Really?" I said, wanting to know more. "So, did the two of you fall out over her?"

"Some what, but I really didn't trip. Besides, Felicia wasn't worth the fight. She was dating one of my other boys when I met her, so we just passed her on down. I don't know what Jaylin said or did to her, but she kicked it with him for a long time. From my understanding, he was the only brotha tapping that for a while. And as promiscuous as Felicia is, that's a miracle."

Now, I for damn sure knew why, I thought. When a woman did step Jaylin's way, it was so hard to let go. I was a prime example of that. Since I wasn't really sure how to handle the news about Shane being an old friend of Jaylin's, I quickly changed the subject.

"Are you ready to order?"

"Yes, I'm starving." Shane glanced at the menu, then put it down. "Hey, tell me something," he said.

"What?"

"You don't have to answer this unless you want to, but are you in love with Jaylin?"

I hesitated for a moment because I didn't want to talk about Jaylin the entire night. So, I quickly answered and tried to move on. "Yes, but I'm working on getting him out of my system. You know what I mean?"

"Scorpio, I know what you mean, but somebody could get hurt. And this time, it's not going to be me."

"Let's hope not," I said, looking down at my menu.

Shane and I had a marvelous dinner. Jaylin's name didn't come up for the rest of the night, but Felicia's did, though. We couldn't help but talk about her. And even though he dogged her out, a part of me knew when he got home, he was going to be making a

65

phone call to her. So, with that in mind, I was going to hold off on giving myself to him a tad bit longer.

My Way Or No Way

NOKEA

L J and Jaylin's birthday was less than a month away. I called Jaylin because I wasn't sure if he'd already made plans. He suggested that we go through our normal routine and have lunch at Café Lapadero, in Clayton, then take LJ to Chuck E Cheeses. A birthday party was out of the question. I told Jaylin I wasn't up for it, but the truth was that Daddy was still upset with Jaylin and didn't want him around. I figured it was best to keep them as far away from each other as possible. And since Daddy was still barely speaking to me, I kept my distance.

Pat, LJ, and me went to the new West County Mall on Manchester to see what all the hype was about. It was so crowded; the police had to direct the incoming traffic. After roaming the parking lot for almost thirty minutes, we finally found a spot. I put LJ in his stroller and rushed through the door to spend my portion of the money Jaylin had given me.

By the time Pat and I were finished, we had a security guard help us back to the car with our packages. I bought so many outfits for LJ, and found some exquisite clothes at Nordstrom's and Lord & Taylor's for me. Pat bought shoes from damn near every shoe store in there, and insisted since her and Chad was on a budget, that shoeboxes would be easier to hide.

We laughed as we got out of the car, and sneaked into Pat's house to hide the boxes. Chad was in the living room watching TV, so we had to sneak around the back hoping that he wouldn't see us. But as soon as we came through the back door, he stood in the doorway with his arms folded. Pat quickly handed all the bags to me.

"Girl, now you know you shouldn't have bought all those damn shoes. I told you I don't have any outfits to match them," she said, trying to play it off like the shoes were mine. Chad put a piece of chicken in his mouth and smacked.

"I don't see how or why she would bring all those shoes in here if you two don't even wear the same size. It doesn't make no sense to me. How about you, Nokea? Does it make sense to you?"

I looked at Pat and smiled. "Alright, alright," she said. "Damn, I'm busted. But baby, sorry, I couldn't resist. They had some good sales out at West County Mall. You should go out there yourself."

Chad ignored Pat and left the kitchen. She told me to have a seat, while she went upstairs to put up her shoes. LJ was sound asleep in his baby seat, so I didn't want to wake him. I would have asked Jaylin to watch him, but LJ was already spending too much time with him already. I was feeling kind of neglected, and since Nanny B moved in with Jaylin, he was coming over to pick LJ up every chance he got. I didn't mind, but LJ running back and forth from both of our houses was driving me crazy. When I complained, he said I was trying to deny him time with his son and that was something I definitely wasn't trying to do, so I kept quiet.

Pat was taking forever, so I went to the refrigerator and pulled out a pitcher of lemonade. As I reached for a glass on the shelf, Chad came in and stood behind me.

"Let me get that for you, Nokea." He reached up and took a glass from the shelf.

"Thanks, Chad. So, how's the cleaning business going? Pat said it's been booming."

"Yeah, it's doing okay. She's just spending money as fast as we can make it."

"Well, you know how she is. Hasn't changed a bit since you married her."

"No, she hasn't. So, uh, how are things going with you? She told me about what happened between you and Jaylin. Sorry that it didn't work out."

"Yeah, I'm sorry too, but at least we got that little precious child over there to share," I said, pointing to LJ.

"He's adorable. I wish Pat and I could have some children. We talked about adopting, but she keep putting it off."

"Don't go giving up just yet, Chad. It might happen one day. Seems like she's seeking all options from what she's telling me."

"That might be what she's telling you, but Pat really don't want any children, Nokea. Every time I talk about having a baby she just blows me off." Looking disappointed, Chad walked over to the table and sat down. I walked over behind him, and placed my hand on his back.

"It'll be fine, Chad. If she can't have any children there are plenty of them waiting to be adopted." He dropped his head and I gently rubbed his back. "Don't be so hard on yourself. You and Pat have something really special. What's meant to be is meant to be."

Feeling sorry for Chad, I went to go pour him a glass of lemonade. He really seemed like he was going through something. I wasn't sure what—especially since Pat made everything seem all-good between them.

Shortly after I poured his lemonade, he got out of his chair and came up from behind me again. This time, he put his arms around my waist, and placed his lips on my neck. I immediately turned and pushed him back.

"Chad, what are you doing?" I yelled.

"You are so beautiful, Nokea. The way you touched me, I knew..."

"Wait a minute," I said, sharply. "What do you mean by the way I touched you?"

Just then, Pat came back into the kitchen. "What's all the fussing about? I hope y'all ain't in here arguing over those damn shoes. Listen, Chad, if it's that big of a deal, I'll take them back."

"Naw, baby, you don't have to. Nokea and I was just arguing over who LJ looks like." He looked at me and I didn't say a word. I was so stunned that he stepped to me like that, and didn't quite know what to do.

After he went back into the living room, I gathered LJ's things and hurried to go. Pat noticed my demeanor and questioned me.

"Are you okay?" she asked.

"I'm fine, Pat. I just got a severe headache all of a sudden. I'd better get home and lie down," I said, rushing.

"Okay, you do look a little flush." She felt my head. "Seems like you're running a fever too."

Pat helped me gather my things and walked me out to my car. I strapped LJ in his car seat and took off. I was sick to my stomach on the drive home, and couldn't believe Chad came on to me like that. But how was I going to tell Pat? She'd been like a sister to me. There was no way in hell I could keep something like this from her.

As I was walking through the door, my phone was ringing off the hook. I tried to put LJ down before I answered it, but whoever it was called right back. When I answered, it was Chad.

"Nokea?"

"Yes, Chad," I said, angrily.

"Sorry about tonight, but I just couldn't help myself. You're really looking good these days and I was just hoping—"

"Chad, if you ever and I mean ever, put your hands on me again, I'll tell Pat everything." I hung up. The phone rang again. "Hello," I yelled.

"You won't tell because you want me just as much as I want—" I hung up again. I covered my face and started to cry. I knew this was nothing but trouble, and when the phone rang again I quickly snatched it up.

"Listen!" I screamed. "You sorry motherfucker! Stop calling here!"

"Damn, what in the hell did I do?" It was Jaylin. I started crying even more. "Nokea? Are you okay?" he asked. "Where's LJ?"

"I'm fine." I sniffled and tried to get myself together.

"Well, you don't sound fine. I'm on my way."

"Please, don't. I said everything is fine."

He hung up.

I took the phone off the hook because I didn't want Chad calling back. I gave LJ a bath, sung him a lullaby, and he was out like a light.

When Jaylin knocked at the door, I was getting ready to take my bath. I slid my robe and house shoes on and went to the door.

"You really didn't have to come," I said. "I told you everything was fine." I walked away from the door.

"I just came by to make sure everything was cool with my son, that's all. So, where is he?"

"I just put him to bed, Jaylin. You can go check on him, if you'd like, but please don't wake him."

Jaylin went into LJ's room and I went back into mine. Moments later he came in with LJ on his shoulder.

"What did I tell you, Jaylin? You just don't listen, do you?"

He sat down on the sofa. "No, I don't listen. Especially when it comes to my son. If he wakes up I'll take him home with me."

"Do whatever. I don't even care anymore."

He leaned back and opened and closed his legs. "I know you too well, Nokea, what's ailing you?"

"Everything."

"Everything like what?"

"Everything like you, the baby, my job, Pat."

"Okay, so what about me?"

"You just seem like a different person, that's all. I really thought you would have worked things out with me..." I continued talking about us being together, but Jaylin was ignoring me, and pretending to be occupied with LJ. "Jaylin, did you hear what I said?"

"I heard you. But, I told you what was up with that. I need more time. Still hurting from what you did. Give me time to heal, alright?"

"How much time do you need? I'm feeling really lonely these days. The only thing I do is get up, go to work, and come home to be with LJ. On the weekends I at least had Pat to chill with, but I'm not sure how much longer that's going to last."

"Why? Did y'all fall out or something?"

"No, nothing like that, but Chad made a pass at me today and it upset me. When you called, I thought you were him. I don't know what to do, and if I tell Pat I'm not sure how she's going to react."

"I knew that motherfucker was up to no good. You always bragging on how he's such a good man, but I knew something wasn't right. Honestly, though, you do need to tell her. Don't keep anything like that from her. If she's a true friend, she'll understand."

"Yeah, I guess you're right. I'll tell her. I don't know when, but I will."

"I suggest you not wait like you did by not telling me about LJ. You see how much damage that's done, right?"

"Yeah, I know, but it's not going to be easy telling my best friend that her husband came on to me either."

"No it's not, but you just got to deal with it and do the right thing."

After hearing Jaylin's deep voice, LJ lifted his head off Jaylin's shoulder. Jaylin stood up and started to leave the room. "I'll take him home with me tonight. Get some rest and I'll bring him back tomorrow."

"Jaylin?" I said, softly.

"Yeah."

"Please don't go. Stay with me tonight. I don't want to be alone." My eyes watered, as I waited for him to respond. I just knew he was going to say no, but when he sat back down on the sofa, I smiled.

An hour later, Jaylin put LJ back to sleep. When he came back into my room, I had already taken my bath and was standing butt naked drying myself off.

He looked me up and down. "Hey, sorry, I didn't know you were—"

"It's okay. It's not like you haven't seen me naked before." He walked further into the room. "Here," I said, handing him some peaches & cream lotion. "Would you mind rubbing some of this on me?"

He took the lotion bottle from me, and I lay on my stomach and rested my head on my hands. Jaylin stood up for a second, then sat down on the bed next to me. He squeezed some lotion in his hands and rubbed it on my back. I just knew he was going for my ass first, but he didn't. I closed my eyes, as his hands felt like they were melting into my body.

When he did get to my ass, I was on fire. He was teasing and massaging it in a circular motion. And not being able to take his touch anymore, I rolled over and sat up.

72

"What's wrong?" he asked, looking over at my breasts.

"Nothing, nothing at all. I just…"

Before I could say anything else, I leaned him back and eased myself on top of him. Then I placed my lips on his. Surprisingly, he went with the flow and kissed me back. He bent his left leg up and moved me in the middle of his body, so I could feel his hard dick poking me through his pants.

Lying there and thinking about how badly I wanted to feel him, I looked him in the eyes. "I love you, Jaylin. God only knows how much I love you."

I reached for his shirt to take it off, but he stopped me. He pecked me a few more times on the lips, held my face in his hands, then gave me a hard stare.

"I love you too, Nokea, but I can't do this."

"Yes you can. Just let go of all your anger and make love to me, please," I begged.

He pecked me on the lips, again, and raised up. "Nokea, you don't want to be with me right about now. All I'm going to do is hurt you even more. I'm no good, baby. And making love to you is only going to complicate things. I won't be able to live with myself if I keep on hurting you."

A tear rolled down my face and I rested my head on his chest. Moments later, I lifted my head. "How can you lay here and not want to make love to me? Don't you want me anymore? Don't I even appeal to you?"

Jaylin wiped my tears. "Of course I want to make love to you. And yes, you do turn me on. But I'm saving the best for last. I'm not going to put you in this mess I'm in right now. So please, don't make me do this to you, okay?"

Disgusted, I eased over and lay on my side. Jaylin turned on his side and lay in front of me. "Nokea, you don't ever have to be lonely. Just call me, and you know I'll always be here for you. I need you to be strong for our son. Don't let anybody stop you from being there for him, not even me."

"I'm trying, but I don't understand why we just can't be together. If you love me, then why do you continue to fight this so much? Don't you see what this is doing to us?"

73

"Yeah, I do. It's making our love stronger and stronger everyday. It's making me feel as if I'm missing out on something. Like right now, our being apart is making us want each other even more. I'm not playing a game with you, Nokea, I'm just making sure when marriage presents itself again, we're both going to be ready."

Even though I disagreed with Jaylin, he wasn't giving in. After debating the issue with him, I just fell asleep in his arms. When I woke up, he was lying on the living room couch with LJ on his chest. They were knocked out and I gave them a kiss and went back into my room for the rest of the night. I was so hurt that Jaylin wouldn't make love to me, and I didn't quite understand his reasoning. Deep inside, I truly felt that he was making promises he wouldn't be able to keep. How could he promise what he did with life being so darn unpredictable? I knew his feelings for Scorpio were getting strong, and I also knew he was still making love to her. So why? I thought. Why not give me what I wanted for a change? Truly hurt, I laid my head on my pillow and cried for the rest of the night.

JAYLIN

There wasn't enough time on the weekends to do what I had to do, so I called Angela and made myself another three-day weekend. Going to work on Mondays was eventually going to become a thing of the past. Taking Mondays off would give me an extra day with LJ and Mackenzie. Nanny B was living with me now, so everything was running pretty smoothly.

I got up around seven o'clock in the morning and headed to the gym. My six- pack was slowly but surely turning into a no pack because I had slacked up on working out trying to avoid Stephon. I guess Nokea confirming her love for me gave me a little more assurance that she really never loved Stephon to begin with. So wasn't no sense in me putting off talking to him.

When I got to the gym, I didn't see Stephon anywhere in sight. Usually, he was always there before I was. I went over to a weight bench and sat down. Then I laid back and started to lift the weights somebody had already left on the bar. As I strained myself, and tried to push it back up for the tenth time, Stephon came over and put his hand in the middle of the bar, so I couldn't lift it.

"Nigga, why haven't you been returning my calls," he said, pressing down on the bar. I was pressing back and trying to lift the weights off my chest.

"Because, I don't like your motherfucking ass, that's why," I said, straining.

"Good. And I don't like your ass either."

We continued pushing the bar and after a few more minutes of intense straining, I gave up and let it rest on my chest. Stephon lifted it and put it back on the bench.

"See, that's what your ass get for not working out. I've been here everyday, and thought I would see your high-yellow ass, but I guess you'd giving up on working out too, huh?"

I sat up on the bench and stretched my back. "Naw...I've been working out. Just not at the gym. Besides, I didn't want to see your punk-ass anyway."

"So, what you want, Jay? Do you wanna fight and get this shit over with or what? You know I'll kick your ass right about now, don't you?" he said, putting me up to the challenge.

"Hell, yeah, I wanna fight! Meet me outside so I can finally get this shit off my chest." I stood up. Stephon and me headed towards the door.

"Come on you little Mighty Mouse looking motherfucker. And when I kick your ass don't go running home to your bitches crying like a little punk," he said, jokingly.

"And don't you go running home to that bitch Felicia, telling her my damn business either."

When we got outside, we continued to talk our shit. We stood there and stared each other down. "Jay, I'm gonna say this one more time and one more time only. I'm not going to kiss your ass like your women do, so this is it, man, I mean it—I'm sorry. I over stepped my boundaries and I know it. Besides that, I got straight-up love for ya, cuz, and if you can ever find it in your heart to forgive me, I'd be grateful." He put up his fist. I did the same, then slammed him in the face with my fist. He fell backwards, then sat up on his elbows and touched his mouth.

"Next time," he said. "Bring out some blood, nigga, alright." I reached my hand out and helped him get off the ground.

"Naw, next time, don't let this shit happen again. When I tell you a woman that I love is off limits, I mean it. And Nokea, she's off limits. Anybody else is fair game."

"Scorpio too? You know I've been waiting for her to shake a brotha down."

I grinned. "Hmm...talk to me about it before you do, and I'll let you know then."

We laughed, gave each other a long hug, and went back into the gym to continue our workout.

After we were finished, I was sweating and panting like it wasn't funny. Not working out for a while really set my ass back. I had gotten out of shape that damn fast. Stephon was laughing the whole time and was walking around flexing his muscles trying to make me jealous because he had kept up with his workout. He said that he wasn't going to let me, or any body else, stop him from keeping his body in shape. If anything, he said working out took his mind off his frustrations.

We went to the men's locker room and showered. I hated washing up at the gym, but there was no way I was getting my sweaty ass into the Cedes. Stephon felt the same way about his BMW, so we hung around in the locker room catching up on women talk.

"So, you still fucking Felicia, huh?" I asked.

"Yeah, man. Just hit that last night. Actually, be hitting that about three, pho, five times a week. She is wild."

"Trust me, I know. That Freak is something else. Puzzles the hell out of me why you still fucking with her though."

"Nigga, please. You kicked it with her for damn near four years and you don't know why."

I thought about it. "Okay, you got me. She is good at swallowing a brotha correctly when need be, ain't she?" We gave each other five and laughed.

"So, uh, enough about me," Stephon said. "Any new ladies on the agenda, or are you sticking it to anybody I know?"

"Naw, man, I ain't been screwing Nokea, if that's what you're asking. However, opportunity has presented itself. In the meantime, the usual: Brashaney, Scorpio, and Heather. A lil dick sucking here and there. You know, the regulars."

"Heather, huh. Heather who?"

"This, uh…chick I met several weeks ago," I said, trying not to reveal her identity.

"Where did you meet her?"

"She was a damsel in distress, and I pulled over to help out when her car was stuck on the side of the road."

"So you pulling them from the streets now, huh?"

"Naw, nothing like that. Woman needed some help, so I helped."

"Get it right, fool. Woman needed a fuck and you fucked her."

"Yep, and that I did. Very well, I might say. So well, that she sent two dozen red roses to my house the next day thanking me for my good dick. I threw them in the trash, but the thought was nice."

"Heather…and she sent roses the next day? This ain't no sista we're talking about, is it?"

I laughed. "Naw man, she's Caucasian. Bad-ass white gal too," I said, licking my lips.

"No, no, no. Haven't I taught you anything? You know we don't go there, man. Besides, you're the one who made that rule up. If I remember correctly, rule number two, right?"

"I know, man, but shit just happened so fast, I couldn't believe it myself. Got a little oil in my system, and one thing led to another."

"So?"

"So, what?"

"How was it?"

"It was wild, dog. Straight up wild. Fucked her outside in the rain. We rolled around in the mud, and I laid that pussy out. Her stuff was so tight, it had a serious choke on my dick."

Stephon and me cracked up. "You know, for a wanna be clean Negro like yourself, that does sound pretty wild. So, what's up with it? You still working with it or what?"

"Nope. The experience was cool, but I like the sistas man. Something about the way they be shaking a brotha down just make me wanna holla."

"Well, Scorpio ain't no full blown sista. And seems like she's been shaking a brotha down pretty damn good."

"Scorpio's got African American blood running through her veins. She might not be all black, but she got sista genes flowing through her body."

"You are crazy, man. But you know what we need to do? Let's go kick it this weekend. I seriously think it'll be good for the both of us. Some of the fellas at the shop been hyping up the Two STL Brothers on Natural Bridge. Let's go check it out. "

"We'll see. You know I have my kids on the weekend. If I feel up to it I'll let Nanny B see about them and I'll make arrangements to go. Call me ahead of time, though, cause I might be making plans to get into something else, you know what I mean?"

"It'll be plenty enough to get into at the club. You'll see."

"Yeah, there always is. I could probably use a new collection of women in my life any damn way."

"Cool. Just let me know and it's on."

I told Stephon I'd hollar at him before the weekend, and we left the gym on a good note. I knew we weren't going to be mad at

79

each other for long, but I also had to let him know it wasn't cool for him to betray me because of Nokea.

When I got home, there was a card stuck in the front door. I opened it and it read: *"Can't stop thinking about the other night. Hubby's out of town on business again, and it sure would be nice to see you."*

First, it fucked me up that Heather even knew where I lived. I didn't tell her, so it was obvious she looked me up in the phone book. Second, I had no intentions on going there with her again. The card and flowers were cool, but there just wasn't enough of me to go around with all these lonely-ass women in my life. Everybody wanted to get fucked. I was flattered, but damn, dick could have used a little down time. I tore Heather's card up and threw it in the trashcan just like I did the roses.

Later that day, I changed clothes and drove to the Galleria to find LJ something for his birthday. Chesterfield Mall and Plaza Frontenac were closer, but sometimes I just felt like going where I could fit in.

While I roamed the mall, I stopped at a bookstore and bought Scorpio a cookbook. She seriously needed some help with her cooking, so I was sure she would appreciate it.

I always stopped in at Victoria's Secret, to buy the ladies in my life something sexy to wear. I bought four sexy pieces of lingerie and two thongs that I envisioned Scorpio's naked ass in. It wasn't no telling when I was coming back to the mall again, so I picked up an extra pair to give to Nokea on her birthday. The sales associate neatly wrapped everything up for me. Noticing the different sizes, she gave me some extra bags just in case I needed them.

Nanny B had fired up some juicy succulent-ass baby-back-ribs, so we sat at the kitchen table and grubbed. It was so damn convenient having her around, and I was happier than ever now that I had her to help out with the kids. I think she was glad too because she had gotten just as attached to LJ and Mackenzie as I was.

After dinner I went up to my room and chilled. I called Scorpio to tell her about the cookbook and the thongs, but she wasn't at home. She was probably somewhere with her new mystery man, and I admit that I was a little jealous, but I had too much going for me to trip off something so petty.

After I lay across the chaise, and thought about him fucking her—possibly doing a better job than me—I showered and changed clothes. I told Nanny B I'd be back later, got in my car, and started driving.

Moments later, I found myself in Heather's driveway. I got out of the car with one of the Victoria's Secret bags in my hand. I stuffed some pink tissue paper inside, so she wouldn't see what was inside. After I rang the doorbell, I leaned to the side of the door and held the bag up with one finger.

She opened the door and smiled. "I'm so glad to see you, and thank you so much for thinking about me," she said, taking the bag from my hand.

"Anytime," I said, stepping into her house. "I want you to go slide into it, right now."

She pulled the tissue paper out and looked inside. "Darling, there's nothing inside of the bag." She looked puzzled.

"I know. That's what I want you to slide on for me. Nothing."

"Duhh..." she said. "Stupid me. Awesome thought, though, really it is."

She walked upstairs and I followed behind her. We went into her room and within a few minutes we were at it again. It wasn't like the pussy was all that, but I think it was the new experience that sent me back to her again. Heather, actually, was a slow rider—too slow, but I was a good teacher. Maybe, a few more times at this and she'd be able to shake a brotha down just how I wanted her to. Besides, she swallowed me a little differently from the others, so I didn't trip.

I crept into the house around one o'clock in the morning, and tried not to wake Nanny B. But when I looked in her room, she was awake watching the *Jamie Fox Show*. I let her know that I was back, then called Scorpio to see if she had made it home yet. When her answering machine came on, I left a message for her to call me.

Scorpio didn't return my call until early Friday morning while I was at work. I wanted to curse her out, but I kept my cool.

"Sorry, but I've been busy, Jaylin. I was at home when you called the other night, but I was studying," she exclaimed.

"Alone?" I asked.

"Yes, alone. And why are you asking me if I was alone? What if I wasn't?"

"No biggie, I just asked. Ain't like I care. I just don't want no naked brotha flaunting his ass around in front of Mackenzie."

"Well, don't worry because that's not going to happen. He has a nice studio apartment I can go to if I decide to get down like that."

"Ah...so, you've been to his place?"

"As a matter of fact, I haven't. I viewed the loveliness of it by looking at some pictures. So, is there anything else you'd like to know."

"Nope. And like I said before, it really ain't my business. Anytime you don't feel like answering my questions, don't. The reason for my call the other night was to tell you that I bought you a cookbook. Thought it might help you out, since you be whipping up all those messed up dishes all the time."

"For your information, Mr. Criticizer, I can cook."

"Shaat. Woman, don't go lying to yourself like that, please."

She laughed. "Whatever, but thanks. Thanks for at least thinking about me."

"I always think about you, baby. And right before you called, I was sitting here thinking about how scrumptious you're going to look tonight in one of the thongs I bought for you too."

"Damn, baby, you're being awfully nice to me. It wouldn't have anything to do with us not having sex for almost a week now, would it?"

"Six days, Scorpio, seven hours, thirty-seven minutes, and fifteen...sixteen seconds, and I'm still counting. It's been that long since I've been sexually satisfied. Tonight, you got yourself a date with the Ding-Dong man."

"Uh-uh. I got plans tonight, Mr. Ding Dong man."

"Plans with who?"

"Plans with this....oh, soooo fine, sexy, aggressive, juicy lipped, long fat dick, thick headed, and muscular tight-ass Investment Broker that be sliding that thang deeply into a sistas pussy and having it dripping we..."

"Okay, baby, that's enough. I'm at work now. You gone have me running out of the motherfucker trying to get to your ass. So, don't talk like that no more."

Scorpio laughed. "I won't. As long as you remember our routine no matter what happens between us. Three times minimum, per week. No if, ands, or buts about it."

"Bet, Ms. Porn Star. You know you should get yourself a 900 number talking shit like that. And because you had my ass over here about to explode, that's going to cost you big time tonight."

"Damn, I can't wait… but, uh, getting our minds out of the gutter, and back to the real reason for my call…I need you to meet me at Mackenzie's pre-school around one o'clock today. Her teacher called earlier, and said that she wanted to talk to us."

"Why didn't you tell me earlier? I have a lunch engagement with one of my clients today."

"Well, cancel it."

"I guess I'll just have to. Did her teacher say what she wanted?"

"No, she just said she'll talk to us when we get there."

"Okay, I'll meet you there at one."

When I got off the phone with Scorpio, I called my client to reschedule. And after I chowed down on the Chinese food Angela ordered for us, I left the office around twelve-thirty and headed to Mackenzie's pre-school.

When I pulled up, Scorpio's Corvette was already parked outside. I walked in and saw Mackenzie reading some flashcards. She ran up and gave me a squeezing tight hug.

"Hi, Daddy. What are you doing here? Am I going home with you today?"

"I'm here to talk to your teacher. And yes, if you want to, I'll pick you up when I get off work." She gave me a kiss and ran back over by the other kids to play with them.

I interrupted Scorpio and Mackenzie's teacher in her office talking. "Hello, Mr. Rogers," Ms. Franklin said, standing up, and shaking my hand. "Have a seat, please." I sat next to Scorpio and looked over at her. She turned her head and looked away like she was mad about something.

"So, what's this all about?" I asked looking back at Ms Franklin.

"Mr. Rogers, don't be alarmed. I just wanted to talk to you and Mrs. Rogers about Mackenzie's behavior."

"Let me correct you," I said, starting to get upset, and pointing to Scorpio. "This is Ms. Valentino. We are NOT married, and what in the hell do you mean by Mackenzie's behavior?"

"Well, she has a problem getting along with the other children. She's very bossy and quite controlling—"

"What do you mean by bossy and controlling?"

She took a deep breath. "I mean, she doesn't share with the other children, she tells them what to do, and when they don't, she gets angry."

Scorpio looked over at me again and rolled her eyes.

"So," I said, shrugging my shoulders. "She's supposed to have her way. And she doesn't have to share shit with anybody unless she wants to. As for telling them what to do, that's all about leadership. She's a leader, not a follower."

"Mr. Rogers, I don't think you understand…"

"No, Maam," I said, raising my voice. "I don't think you understand. I pay this school fifteen-hundred-dollars a month, and if you have to put up with a little attitude from my daughter, so damn what. Do it! Personally, I think you got a problem with the color of her skin. I'm sure you're not calling any of these white parents in here with this bullshit."

"Oh, Mr. Rogers, I'm not like that. I really like Mackenzie. I'm just—"

I quickly stood up and looked at Scorpio. "Come on, baby. Let's get the fuck out of here before I snatch her ass from behind that desk."

Scorpio looked up at me. "Jaylin, look, calm down. Ms. Franklin is just trying to tell us about Mackenzie. You act like you—"

"I don't need nobody telling me shit! And I can't believe you're sitting here listening to this nonsense." I gave Scorpio and Ms. Franklin a hard stare, then pushed the chair out of my way and walked out. I grabbed Mackenzie and left. Scorpio stayed behind and continued talking to Ms. Franklin.

By the time I got home, I was furious thinking about the whole damn ordeal. I couldn't even take my ass back to work because I was so damn mad. When I slammed my keys down on the kitchen counter, Nanny B came in.

"What's the problem, Jaylin? Why are you so angry?"

I sat down at the table and folded my leg across my knee. "Mackenzie, go upstairs to your room and let your Daddy and Nanny B have some privacy." She left and didn't say a word. I took a deep breath, "Ms. Franklin, her pre-school teacher, had a talk with Scorpio and me today. She started talking all this bullshit about Mackenzie being bossy, controlling, and even selfish. Pissed me off. I got mad and cursed her ass out."

Nanny B pulled a chair next me and held my hands together with hers. "Jaylin, I know you don't want to hear this, but Mackenzie is a splitting image of you. I've noticed it myself, but it's not my place to tell anyone how to raise their children."

"But—"

"But nothing. Just listen, please. You need to call that woman and apologize to her. It's not that she's trying to tell you what to do, but it is her job to let you know when something isn't right. Mackenzie is spoiled, rotten to the core, and she has you to thank for that. You're not a bad father, but material things just don't get it all the time. She needs for you to tell her when she's wrong, tell her when she can't have her way, and don't let her run over you like she does. I know your reasoning for giving her everything she wants is because you had a rough upbringing. But giving her what you didn't have isn't the answer, okay." She let go of my hands and folded her arms.

"Have you been talking to my mother or something? That just sounded like something she would say to me. I know you're right, but some things are just hard for me to swallow."

"No, I haven't been talking to your mother, but God puts people in your life for a reason. Good people, bad people, and ugly people. I just hope I can be of some good."

"And that you are." I kissed Nanny B on the cheek and thanked her. I told her I would call Ms. Franklin to apologize, and then make it perfectly clear to her that Mackenzie wasn't coming back any time soon.

I was taking a shower when Scorpio came into the bathroom screaming and hollering about how I embarrassed her.

"I just can't believe you reacted that way, Jaylin."

"And I can't believe you didn't have the decency to take up for your own damn daughter," I said, turning the water off, and wrapping a towel around my waist. I walked into the bedroom and sat on the bed.

She stood in front of me and folded her arms. "What in the hell has gotten into you? Your attitude is horrible. And now your little fucked-up ways have rubbed off on my daughter. I'm not having this shit, Jaylin, I mean it. "

Feeling myself getting ready to diss the hell out of Scorpio, instead, I got up, gave her the bag with her cookbook in it, and calmly asked her to leave.

"Fine, I'll leave. But please call Ms. Franklin and apologize to her."

"I am, and not because you're asking me to, but because I know it's the right thing to do." I removed the towel from around me and pulled the covers back to get in bed.

"Either way, thank you. And now that we've cleared that up," Scorpio said, crawling up between my legs, from the end of the bed, and looking me eye to eye. "I thought we had plans tonight, Mr. Ding Dong man?"

"We did, however, I just canceled them until you learn how to stand up for the ones you love. Until then, Ms. Porn Star, get the fuck off my bed, so I can go to sleep—alone."

Realizing that I wasn't joking, Scorpio got up, grabbed her cookbook and left. Disrespecting me like she did, she fucked herself right out of this good-ass dick tonight.

The Two STL Brothers wasn't no joke. Women were down to wearing a little bit of nothing. Legs, back, breasts, ass, you name it, I saw it. There were some sexy-ass women up in there, but there was also some sistas who knew damn well they shouldn't have tried to squeeze into those skimpy-ass outfits they were wearing. I felt like if your back was out, and your rolls were showing, then that wasn't the outfit for you.

This one gal had so many rolls showing that I asked Stephon if I could borrow some butter. We damn near fell to the floor laughing so hard. And Ray Ray had the nerve to ask her to dance.

When I asked Ray Ray about the OLE wife, he said they were already separated. He said he couldn't dream of being with just one woman. I definitely knew the feeling and was glad I hadn't wasted that kind of money or time on getting married.

Stephon and I were kicking our game down all damn night. We grabbed these two light skinned sistas, who were showing all titties, and asked them to dance. I was breaking it down to the flo, "Like A Pimp," and Stephon tried to go there with me.

"Hey," I said, rubbing my dance partner on her soft pretty legs. I worked my way up on the floor and held her around the waist. She placed her arms on my shoulders and worked her sexy body to my rhythm. "So, uh…what's your name?" I asked.

"Beaches."

"What?" I said, as I couldn't quite hear over the loud music.

"Beaches," she yelled a little louder.

What a peculiar name, I thought. "Say, Beaches, do you think a brotha can take you home with him tonight?"

She smiled and lifted her arms off my shoulders. "Sorry, but I don't go out like that. Besides, I'm engaged."

I immediately stopped dancing with her because it wasn't no sense in me going any further. If she was engaged, then what in the fuck was she doing up in here? I walked off the dance floor and went over to the bar. Stephon was still on the floor dancing with her sister. I'd hoped he was having better luck with her.

While at the bar, several sistas approached me and asked if I wanted to dance. Since neither one of them offered to pay for my drink, I declined. But when this thick, mocha-chocolate sista with wavy long hair slammed some money down on the bar to pay for my drink, she quickly got my attention.

"I got your back, and then some, handsome. Question is, are you ready for some serious action tonight?"

"That depends on what type of action you have in mind?"

"How about I'll show you when we get to my place."

Damn, do I look that easy, I thought? Aggressive, she was, but she was my kind of woman. "Baby, what would give you the idea that I want to go to your place tonight?"

She took my hand and eased it in between her legs. Wearing no panties, I felt the goods. And after talking to her for while, and scoping the thickness in her shiny lips, I quickly downed my drink and whispered in her ear.

"I need somewhere to lay my *head*. It would be quite nice if I could lay it in you."

She took my hand and before we left, I stopped to let Stephon know I was outtie. He was still talking to the light skinned gal with the nice breasts when I interrupted.

"Say, man, call me tomorrow," I said.

"You gone dog?" Stephon said. "I thought we were going to the Waffle House tonight?"

"Sorry, bro, waffles don't come like this," I said, looking next to me. "And please understand that plans do change, my brotha, plans most certainly do change."

Stephon checked out the loveliness I had next to me and gave me five. "Do your thang, cuz, and call me later."

"Will do," I said, winking, then leaving the club.

I rode to the club with Stephon, so the chick whose name I still hadn't gotten agreed to drive. We walked around the parking lot, searching for her car, and when she had the nerve to step to this gray beat-up raggedy-ass Lincoln, I could have died. I quickly thought about when Scorpio first came over to see me in her raggedy-ass Cadillac and tried not to judge.

No sooner had we got inside the car, she was all over me. She unzipped my pants and gagged after she tried to swallow all of me. I sat there somewhat enjoying the feeling, and trying to show her just a little satisfaction, I reached up her dress and rubbed her ass.

Feeling nothing for her, it took me forever to come. I even closed my eyes and pretended she was Scorpio, but when I felt the edges of her sharp ass teeth, I knew something wasn't right. When she finished, she raised up and started the car. The damn thing sounded like a garbage truck and shook like hell. I was so embarrassed when she sped off the parking lot, and had my ass flying out of my seat.

"Whoa…whoa…slow down, damn!" I yelled, holding onto the dashboard. "This car could really use a tune-up, you know."

She looked over at me and grinned. "It's an old car. I'm getting a new one next week."

Sure you are, I thought. A Lexus, right?

"You know, you haven't even asked me my name yet," she said, constantly taking her eyes off the road.

"That's because I don't want to know your name. Not really important to me." I was furious by the way she was driving. Bitch had my damn life in her hands and was driving like a bat out of hell trying to get home for some of this dick.

When she hit Highway 70, going one-hundred-miles, and got off near the projects, I had enough.

"Pull this raggedy-ass, piece-of-shit over, please!" I yelled.

"What?" she yelled back.

"I said, pull this son of a bitch over!"

"Why, what's wrong with you?" She slowed down and pulled over to the curb. I hopped out and slammed the door.

She tried to raise the window down but it got stuck. "You're a silly ass fool, you know that?" she said.

"And you're a non-dick-sucking, low-down, nasty-looking, dirty-ass bitch! Do you know that?"

I started walking down the street, and as she drove by, she honked the horn and gave me the finger. I pulled out my cell phone and called Stephon. He could barely hear what I was saying because of the loud music in the background. Soon after, he said that he was on his way to the restroom so he could hear me.

"Man, come pick me up," I said, laughing.

"Where are you? And what happened to that fine piece of tender you left here with?"

"Man, never ever judge a book by its cover. That fine piece of tender turned out to be a snowflake. That bitch was crazy." Stephon laughed. I told him where I was and he came for me.

We sat at the Waffle House cracking up, as I was telling him what happened. And after my experience with whatever the hell her name was, I was done messing around with women. At least for the night, anyway.

JAYLIN

I woke up around eleven o'clock in the morning almost forgetting that I told Nokea I would meet her and LJ at Café Lapadero by one o'clock in the afternoon. My little man was finally one-year-old today, and I for damn sure wasn't getting any younger myself.

I climbed out of bed and went into the bathroom to freshen up a bit. I looked in the mirror and sung a quick Happy Birthday to myself and thanked God for another year. I didn't look a day over twenty-one, and definitely wasn't feeling like the average thirty-three-year-old man. I thought it was quite odd that Mackenzie hadn't come in my bedroom yet, so I quickly brushed my teeth and splashed some water on my face. I hurried to see what was keeping her from wishing the love of her life, me, a Happy Birthday.

Seeing that she wasn't in her room, at the top of the stairs, I gathered my silk robe and tied it, then slowly jogged down the steps to find her. By the time I reached the bottom, I could see people in the living room.

"SURPRISE!" Everybody yelled. I widened my eyes and smiled because they'd caught me completely off guard. Nanny B walked up to me and placed her hands on my cheeks.

"Happy Birthday," she said, kissing me on my face. I looked into the living room where Mackenzie, Scorpio, LJ, Nokea, Stephon, and his girlfriend Mona were standing.

"Damn!" I said, walking towards them. "What's this all about?" Before anyone answered, I took LJ out of Nokea's hand, kissed him, and wished him a Happy Birthday too. Nokea smiled and wished me one as well.

Nanny B took a deep breath, "Well, I just put together a little something nice for you this morning. I know you probably have a busy day planned, but I wanted to do something special for you to show you how much we all appreciate you."

"Yeah, man," Stephon interrupted. "I almost slipped and told you about this last night, but I wanted it to be a surprise." He came over and gave me a hug. "I love you, cuz, and appreciate you like a motherfucker."

90

I embraced Stephon, then turned and looked at everyone else. My throat was aching, as I started talking. "I really don't know what to say, but thanks for thinking about me. I can't ever remember having nobody go all out like this for me on my birthday."

Somewhat feeling emotional, I sat back on the leather chaise, and sat LJ on my lap. When Mackenzie saw me close my eyes, she walked over and put her arms around my neck. I blinked a few times to clear my eyes.

"Daddy, we got you a present," she said.

"Say you did?"

"Yes. Can I give it to you now?" she asked.

Scorpio came over by us and leaned down to kiss me. "Happy Birthday, knucklehead. And Mackenzie, we'll give him his present after we eat some cake, okay."

"Cake? I get cake too," I grinned.

"Yes, Daddy. And it's your favorite."

Just then, Nanny B came into the living room with a two-tier Black Forest cake in her hands. There seemed to be enough candles on top to burn the damn house down. She said the top layer was for LJ and the bottom layer was for me. I stood up with him in my arms and everybody sung "Happy Birthday" to both of us.

I blew out the candles, and Nanny B went back into the kitchen to cut slices for everyone. It fucked me up that we were all actually in the same room talking to each other and everybody seemed to be getting along just fine. How Nanny B ever managed to get Scorpio and Nokea over here without a fuss puzzled the hell out of me. And Stephon, to bring Mona when him and Nokea were engaged before—this was, without a doubt, some crazy shit. Since nobody else seemed to be tripping, I went with the flow. The only thing I couldn't seem to get with was how jacked-up my living room was from all the cake crumbs and shoe prints on my carpet. Not being able to stand the sight, I got up and collected everybody's plates to throw in the trash.

"Jaylin!" Nanny B yelled.

"What?"

"Sit down, chile, I'll get that stuff in a minute."

"I was just trying to help, that's all."

"No, sit down and enjoy your company. Don't worry about this mess. I'll clean it up when we get finished."

I went back over to the chaise and laid back. Stephon stared at me for a few seconds, then turned to Nanny B. "Nanny B, what are you doing to this man to keep him in check like that?" He stood up with his mouth wide open. "I ain't never, and I mean never—did I say never? Never seen a woman have control over him like that."

Scorpio and Nokea looked at me and smiled. I picked up my black velvet pillow and threw it at him. "Nigga, please. Ain't nobody got control over me, fool. Nanny B said she had everything under control so, hey. No need for me to help when she's gotten everything taken care of, right," I said, looking at Stephon.

"Hey, I'm just saying I've never seen you listen to anybody without putting up a fuss." He walked over by Scorpio and nudged her on the shoulder. "How about you, Scorpio? Have you ever seen him move like that when you've demanded something from him?"

"No, can't say that I have." Scorpio folded her arms and leaned back on the couch. "Nanny B must got something I don't have." She turned to Nokea, "What about you Nokea? Does he ever listen to you, or do anything you ask?"

"You know, I really can't say that he has either. Every time I ask him to do something, he causes an up-roar. So, Nanny B, tell us. How did you ever get this man to start listening to you?" Nokea asked.

Nanny B scooted to the edge of the chair, as all eyes were on her. I quickly raised up because I had a feeling she was about to embarrass me. "Nanny B, you don't have to answer any questions. I just, uh—"

"You just what?" she said, smiling.

"Nothing," I said, leaning back, and putting my hands behind my head. There wasn't no sense in me trying to stop her because she was so ready to run her mouth.

"You know," she said, as if she was getting ready to tell a mystery story to a crowd of listeners. "I observe men extremely well. And what y'all don't seem to understand is that Jaylin likes to have control. In addition to having control, he loves confrontation. Wouldn't you all agree?" she asked. Everybody started shaking their heads. I smiled and continued to listen. "With that in mind, the only way to prevent yourself from arguing with him is to play his game and let him think he's having his way. For instance, when he got his anal butt up a minute ago, in the middle of us having a good time, and trying to clean up, I kindly—and the key is being kind and not stooping to his level—but I kindly told him I would clean up later. Then, I politely asked him to have a seat. Now, he didn't get his way because this living room is still a mess, but because my words were not on his level, he sat his butt back down over there, and didn't say a word."

Everybody cracked up because they knew Nanny B had scammed me. What they didn't know is, I had more respect for her than anybody in the whole damn room.

As they sat around still laughing about the situation the doorbell rang. I stopped Nanny B, as she was still running off at the mouth.

"Nanny B, since you're being all kind and everythang would you mind getting the door," I said, strolling over to answer it myself.

She rushed past me. "Go sit your behind down. I'm going to answer it because knowing you I might not have a job tomorrow."

"You got that right," I said, laughing, and turning back towards the living room.

When everybody stared at the front door, I quickly turned to see who it was. It was Heather. Nanny B let her in and she stood in the foyer with a maroon Chinese short dress on and some tall black heels. Her long blonde hair was pulled over to one side and laid on her shoulders. I looked down and saw a small package in her hand.

There was no way Nanny B invited Heather because they'd never met before. Trying to get my thoughts together, I cleared my throat, turned to my guest, and came up with the best lie that I could think of.

"Sorry, I forgot. This is Mr. Schmidt's daughter, Heather. He told me she was stopping by to bring over some important papers for me to sign. I didn't know he had a gift for me to."

Scorpio and Nokea looked relieved. Stephon was the only one who knew what time it was and he just grinned. I introduced everyone to Heather, and then she followed me into my office. I closed the door behind us and locked it.

"Damn, Heather, what's up?" I said, angrily, and plopping down in my chair.

After she laid her purse on the couch, she stood in front of my desk and put the bag on top of it. "I'm sorry, Jaylin, and I didn't mean to interrupt, but I wanted to give you your birthday present. I've called you several times and since you didn't return my calls, I thought you misplaced my number. Honestly, I really didn't think my coming to see you was going to be a problem."

"Well, it is. You just can't be showing up when you get good and ready to. What we have going on is my business. I don't want anybody questioning me, so please, next time call first, okay? If I don't call you back, just wait until I do."

"Well, I just don't understand why our relationship has to be such a secret. I would love to meet your friends. I really hope this has nothing to do with me being a white woman."

"No...no, I could care less about that. The biggest problem I have with you is that you're a married woman, Heather. I can't go flaunting you around like you're mine. That's ridiculous."

"Well, what do you want me to do, get a divorce? Would that please you?"

"No, Heather. The last thing I want you to do is get a divorce—trust me. I'm just saying let's keep this on the down low. I'll return your calls only if you promise not to show up again unexpected like this."

She shrugged her shoulder. "I guess, Jaylin. Whatever works for you." She picked the bag up and gave it to me. "Here. I special ordered this for you. Open it."

I reached in and pulled out a box. It was a Rolex case. I laid it down on my desk and slid it over to her.

"Thanks, but I already have three. And before this goes any further, I don't need you to buy me expensive gifts like this."

"Now, that's not fair. How can you refuse it and you haven't even seen it." She walked around my desk and placed the box in my hand. "Please, open it."

I opened the box, gazed at it, then looked up at her. The Rolex had a face filled with diamonds. It was stainless steel, trimmed in 18kt yellow gold, polished with bezel, and had an Oyster bracelet. Just taking a guess, I'd say she spent a minimum of $25,000. "You have got to be out of your mind giving me something like this. There is no way in hell I'm going to accept this from you."

"But—

"But my ass, Heather. Sorry, I'm not that kind of man. Now, I might play the fuck-me-game every once in a while, but this expensive gift-giving bullshit is not my style."

I closed the box and placed it in her hand. She shook her head. "I don't know what else to do. I thought if I bought you something nice, you'd know how much you're starting to mean to me."

"Heather you don't have to be spending that kind of money to show me how much you care. Trust me, I know how you feel. Just understand our relationship has limitations. Limitations because you're married, and honestly, I'm a playa. A playa who has no desire to be with one woman, or to take from them either."

Looking disappointed, Heather walked over by the couch to get her purse. I was watching, as her silky dress was clinging to her ass. When she turned, she noticed how mesmerized I was by looking at her. She stood in front of my desk, and tilted her head to get my attention. I grinned and snapped out of it.

"Sorry…what did you say?" I asked.

"I didn't say anything."

She put her purse back down and slowly lifted her dress. She raised it above her hips, and slid her maroon lace panties down. Having my full attention, I rested my face in my hand and watched. Shortly after, her thin model-shaped tanned legs gave me a rise. And when she leaned back on the couch, and rested one leg on the floor, I knew her insides were ready to be fulfilled.

She motioned her finger for me to come to her, "Five minutes, Jaylin," she whispered, as I was already walking in her direction. "That's all I need. I know you have guest but I—"

I placed my hand over her mouth and loosened my robe. She looked down at my goods and didn't say a word. "I need you to be extremely quiet, Heather. I know how loud you can get when we're having sex, but please, not this time."

She nodded and I removed my hands from her mouth.

I kneeled down in front of the couch, and held Heather's legs apart with my hands. She reached for my thang and put it inside of her. Seeing how difficult it was for her to keep quiet, I leaned forward and placed my lips on hers. She held me tightly around my neck, and rubbed the back of my hair with her hands. Soaking her lips with

95

mine, I was pounding her insides fast to make her come. And when I leaned her over the couch, and tagged her from behind, she was just about ready to explode. Getting straight up into it, I placed one foot on the couch, closed my eyes to concentrate, and dug deeper.

"Damn you!" she yelled. I hurried and placed my hand over her mouth. Finally, after fifteen long minutes we released our energy together.

Rushing to get back to my company, I gathered my robe and tied it. Heather eased her dress down, then took her hand and wiped my lips—I guess wiping her lipstick off. I reached for her hand and stopped her. "I don't mean to be rude, and I hate to rush you out, but you know that five minutes you asked for turned into fifteen minutes. I'd hate to keep my guest waiting."

"Oh, I understand," she said, picking up her purse so she could go. "I'll call you tomorrow…is that okay?"

"That's fine," I said, unlocking the door. "And put a smile on your face. After that, you should be grinning."

Heather laughed and followed behind me, as we walked out of my office door. All heads turned and Stephon was the only one smiling.

"Heather," I said, turning to shake her hand. "Tell your father I said thanks." I ran back into my office and grabbed the gift bag off my desk. "Here you go. I must decline his gift at this time, but please, don't forget to thank him for me."

She took the bag from me. "Sure, Jaylin. I'm sorry I took up so much of your time, but my father always teases me about rambling on and on."

I opened the door for Heather, and after she waved goodbye to everyone she left.

I closed the door, stood by the staircase, and tightened my robe again. When I looked up, everybody was staring.

"What?" I said. "I'm just getting ready to go upstairs and change into something else. It's not appropriate for my guest to see me like this, and if I had changed earlier, my boss's daughter wouldn't have seen me almost half-naked."

"Well, go put some clothes on," Scorpio said. "Why are you standing there trying to explain?"

96

A sigh of relief came over me, and I hurried upstairs to my bedroom. I grabbed a pair of jeans and a T-shirt from my closet, then took a quick shower. As I was looking in the mirror brushing my hair, Stephon stood in the doorway to my bathroom.

"Now *that* was risky," he said, folding his arms.

"What?"

"Nigga, you know what. Don't play me like a fool."

I snickered, "Was it that obvious?"

"Nope, but if she would have taken her panties with her I probably wouldn't have ever known." Stephon tossed Heather's panties to me. "I went into your office to use the phone and those were on the floor."

"Damn, man. Did anybody else see them?"

"Uh-uh. And before you ask, they don't suspect anything either. They actually down there talking about what a great boss you have, and how nice of him to send his daughter over here with a gift."

"Whew, I'm so relieved. I know it was risky, but I like doing shit like that. Besides, it's my day, and I intend on going all out."

"Nothing wrong with that," Stephon said, sitting down on my bed. He held his hands together and dropped his head. I came out of the bathroom and sat down next to him.

"Are you all right? I mean, you look as if you have something heavy on your mind."

"I'm cool. I just wonder when one of us is going to settle down and chill, man. I see how happy you are with LJ and Mackenzie and I really would like to have that type of love for somebody one day. You know what I mean?"

"Yeah. I definitely know what you mean. My kids mean everything to me. And I do mean everything. A woman will never mean more to me than they do."

"Yeah, but I wouldn't mind having some crumb snatchers around like you do. It's something about them that be having your ass glowing like a motherfucker. Hopefully, I might have something in the making right now."

I looked shocked. "Straight. So, you got a baby on the way?"

"I think. That's if she ain't lying about it."

"She...she," I said, thinking. "Aw, Mona thinks she's pregnant?"

"Nope."

"Rachelle?"

"Nope."

"Negro, I'm not going to sit here and go through all of your women. Who?" I thought deeper and looked hard at Stephon. "No! No! No!" I yelled. "Don't tell me it's Felicia!" I hopped up and grabbed my money clip off the nightstand. I counted out five-hundred-dollars and threw it on the bed. "Man, please. Whatever you do…make her have an abortion. Take the money, please!"

"Jay, it ain't even like that. You know I don't need your money. Felicia and me talked about it, and I really want her to have the baby."

I plopped back down on the bed, disgusted. "Why man? She ain't going to do nothing but cause you some serious grief. And how do you know it's yours anyway? We both know she be sleeping around like a motherfucker. I know how bad you want a child, but plan this shit out with somebody else."

"Hey, I ain't too thrilled about her being the mother of my child either, but if she's pregnant then I'm for it. Just like you were when Simone got pregnant. Remember. She was a piece of work her damn self."

"Okay, and don't go bringing that bitch up. I could kill her for taking my damn daughter away from me. Anyway, whatever you decide, you know I got your back."

"I know." He reached over and gave me five.

"Now, in the meantime…I got a question for you," I said.

"Shoot."

"Why do you keep looking at Scorpio, man? I've noticed all day how you can't keep your eyes off my woman."

Stephon laughed. "Cause man, I'm not going to lie to you no mo. But, uh, she's one woman I wouldn't mind getting down and dirty with. Just looking at that ass sends me in la la land. I sure in the hell be glad when you figure out what you're going to do with her because I am one brotha anxiously waiting."

"Well, damn. It's like that, huh? But do you straight up think she'll get down with you when she got all this to look forward to?"

"I know she will. And even while she's still kicking it with you."

98

"Nigga, please. I thought I was one confident-ass brotha, but you for damn sure got me beat. I'll bet some money on it. I got five-thousand-dollars that says she wouldn't give you the time of day."

"And I'll match your five and say that she would."

"Bet. And since you've been wanting to fuck her so badly, I'm giving you the go ahead. I'm not even going to interfere. You got one month to come back here with some evidence. I'm giving you some extra time, but if you are as confident as you seem to be, I don't think it will take you that long. And thirty-one days after today, I'm coming to collect my money. So, you'd better have it. If you don't, I'll send my hit-man out to get you."

"Fool, the only thing I'm going to be hitting is that fat ass and pussy on your woman. And when I come to you no later than the end of next week and show you some evidence, don't go drinking your life away trying to soak up the pain."

I stood up, grabbed Stephon's hand, and pulled him off the bed. Since I had a lot of faith in Scorpio, this was quite easy for me. Stephon and I laughed about the bet and we headed back downstairs.

Nanny B had already cleaned up everything, but the ladies were still sitting around chatting.

Scorpio turned and looked at Stephon and me coming towards the living room. "Just abandon your company. We don't care." She stood up and walked into the kitchen. Stephon eyes followed her, then he looked at me and winked. Trying to show him who had the upper hand, I followed her into the kitchen.

"You don't feel abandoned, baby, do you?" I asked, wrapping my arms around her.

"Sometimes, yes I do." She removed my arms and looked at me. "Do you have plans with Nokea tonight? She's been talking about this café you meet her at every year and said that you were having dinner with her tonight."

I took her hand and kissed it. "It's just dinner, Scorpio. We were supposed to meet there for lunch, but since Nanny B planned this surprise for me, I guess Nokea wants to go there for dinner."

"What about what I had planned for you? I guess I have to put my plans on hold until some other time, huh?"

"No, I didn't say that. I didn't know you had plans for us. Now that I know, let me get rid of everybody, and I'll meet you at your place. I'll schedule a late dinner with Nokea so we can spend some time together before I go. Okay?"

"No, it's not okay because I don't feel right knowing that you're going to be with her tonight. I was anticipating on you spending the night with me."

"Scorpio, look. I'm doing the best I can under the circumstances. I've been dining with Nokea at Café Lapadero on my birthday for years. Don't ask me to change something I've been doing for a long time. Work with me this time, and don't ruin my day for me."

She rolled her eyes and left the kitchen with an attitude. I followed behind her and kindly asked everybody to clear out after LJ and me opened our gifts. And when I unwrapped a beautifully framed black and white picture of Mackenzie and LJ, my heart melted. They were sitting back to back and were grinning hard like they were looking at me. Excited, I moved Mama's picture from over on the fireplace mantel and replaced it with theirs. It was perfect. Other than the Teddy bear Nokea gave me last year, this was the most touching gift I'd ever gotten.

Nokea was the last one to leave. We walked to her car and I told her I'd see her no later than nine. She complained about the time, but it was the best I could do. LJ and Mackenzie stayed at my place with Nanny B, since I had plans with Nokea and Scorpio tonight.

By five o'clock, I was looking spectacular and was ready to go. I peeked into Nanny B's room and she was in bed with Mackenzie and LJ taking a nap. I tapped her shoulder and told her I wouldn't be back until later. She told me to have a good time and reminded me to lock the door. I thanked her, then left.

When I arrived at Scorpio's condo, it was pitch black. Her car was parked outside, so I definitely knew she was there. I figured she was probably still upset with me, but at least I had the decency to show.

Seeing that the door was slightly open, I pushed it and walked in. I saw lit candles all over the living room and a chair in the middle of the floor. Figuring it was most likely my place, I strutted over to it and sat down. I loosened my tie and sat back, then called for her.

"Patience my dear," she said, whispering, and coming from her bedroom. "Good things come to brothas who wait."

Scorpio came in moving to the beat of a jazz song by Miles Davis. She knew how crazy I was about his music and moved her desirable body to the rhythm. She wore a black sheer hip length robe trimmed with fur that accented her high-yellow skin. Underneath, her breasts were visible and a silk black thong with tiny diamonds on the string line led to her ass. Much of her curly hair dangled on her shoulders and the rest was clipped on top, just how I like it. As her beautiful eyes stared me down in the candle lit room, I couldn't help but sit there and think how lucky I was. She was by far the most gorgeous woman I'd ever been with. Pussy couldn't get no better than hers, and I was out of my mind for even making such a bet with Stephon knowing that the thought of another man touching her would devastate me.

After the music stopped, she placed her foot between my legs and put my hands on her hips. I started to remove her thong, but she stopped me and straddled my lap.

"Do you love me?" she asked, looking me in the eyes. I nodded my head saying yes. "Then, I need to hear you tell me. So, again, do you love me?"

"Yes," I answered, reaching for her thong again. She held my hands so I wouldn't take it off.

"Why haven't you told me this before?" I shrugged my shoulders. She smiled and wrapped her arms around my neck. "What took you so long to tell me?" I shrugged my shoulders again, then turned and looked down at the floor. "Jaylin, if you don't talk to me. I'm going to blow these candles out and call it a night. So, for the last time, what took you so long to tell me that you love me?"

I shrugged my shoulders, "Afraid...I guess."

"Why?" she asked.

"Because."

"Because, why Jaylin? Stop beating around the bush and..."

"Because you talk too damn much." I grabbed her waist and moved her back off my lap. "Take your thong off."

"No, that's for you to do."

"I've been trying to, but you won't stop running your mouth. Besides, you do it. It arouses me when I watch—do you mind?"

"No, I don't mind, but I'll need your help." She placed her foot between my legs again, then dropped her sheer robe to the floor. I

101

touched her breasts, then closed my eyes and rubbed them. In deep thought, thinking about how much I was falling for her, I lay my head against her stomach and wrapped my arms around her. She lightly rubbed her fingers through my hair.

Having no desire to be anywhere else, I moved her back. "Would you please take those off for me like I asked you to?"

Scorpio turned in front of me, bent over and removed her thong. JAYLIN'S in black cursive letters was tattooed on her ass right above the rose that was already there. She turned her head and smiled, "So, do you like?" she asked.

I pretended not to see it. "Back up a bit so I can clearly see what it says."

She backed up and I held her ass cheeks in my hands. "Jaylin's, huh? I guess that means this is my ass, right?"

"Nobody else but yours, baby. So, Happy Birthday, and again, do you like it?"

"It's nice, but you don't have to tattoo my name on your ass when I already know it's mine."

"I just wanted to give you a little assurance. Just in case you think I might be slipping."

"Assurance, huh?" I grabbed Scorpio's waist and circled my tongue across my name. Then I rubbed it hard with my thumb to make sure it was permanent. When it didn't smear, I turned her body around so she could look at me. "Now, that is assurance. I just hope you don't expect me to do no shit like that."

"No, I don't. All I expect from you is for you to treat me like a lady, to respect me, love me, and to fuck me every damn chance you get. Everything else is totally irrelevant."

I squeezed my legs tightly together, as I could already feel how good this night was going to be. She grabbed my tie and pulled me up towards her. After she pulled it over my head, she removed my jacket and started unbuttoning my shirt. Trying to speed things along, I removed my belt and took my pants off. We stood naked and held each other.

"Why do you love me so much?" I asked.

"Because."

"Because why? And don't play games with me, Scorpio. I'm serious."

102

She laughed. "Because you are the motherfucking man, Jaylin. You keep it real like no other brotha I've ever known, and you don't have no shame in your game. Most of all, you are a man of your words. When you say something, you do it and not only that, you mean it. There's not too many brothas I can give credit to for doing that." She squeezed my ass. "In addition, let's not forget about how good you are to me. So good, that I don't want to be with anyone else. But, of course, you already know that. Now, your turn, why do you love me?"

I laughed because I did not want to answer that question for Scorpio. She pulled away from me, folded her arms, and waited for an answer. I pulled her back towards me, held her tightly in my arms, and continued to laugh.

"If you must know," I said. "And you might not like my answer, but since you love me so much for keeping it real, I'm going to be honest with you."

"Never mind. Don't even tell me. If you plan on keeping it real, I'm sure I already know."

"Okay, if you think you know then fine, I won't tell you."

"So, maybe I don't know. Just tell me. I can take it. I'm a big girl."

I smiled, "I love you because…you be fucking the shit out of me. Insides be all juicy and warm and you be on overtime working that ass like—"

She put her hand over my mouth, "Jaylin, that's okay. I told you I didn't want to know. I was hoping you would find—"

"Find another reason to love you. I just told you that was my reasoning because that's what you expected me to say. With that being said, your good loving is part of the reason, but the ultimate reason is because…Let's make love and then I'll tell you."

Scorpio backed away from me. "Would you stop messing around with me and just tell me."

"I'll tell you when I'm making love to you, okay?"

I picked her up and carried her into the bedroom. I lay her on the bed and eased in between her soft legs. We joyously made love for about two hours before she straddled herself on top and questioned me.

"So," she said, massaging my chest. "I'm waiting. We've been at this for a while and you still haven't told me why you love me."

I tickled her, and when she got into my favorite position on her stomach, I laid on top of her. I slid myself inside, and squeezed her hands tightly together with mine. She closed her eyes and turned her head to the side. I kissed her cheek, and placed the tip of my tongue into her ear. After I licked it, I whispered, "I love you because you've never betrayed me. And when I thought you did, you were doing what was best for you, not for me. You stood by me when I needed you the most, and never left my side. Not only that but," I said, closing my eyes, and trying not to come, as she was tightening up and grinding on my thang. "But I...I know you're the only woman who will do just about anything for me, and no matter what happens, you'll never let me bring you down. So," I moaned. "Along with all this good pussy, I gotta hand it to you baby, you have definitely captured my heart."

"Hmm," she said, stopping the motion. "I got it going on that much and you still don't want a committed relationship with me?"

"Not right now. But, who knows, maybe someday I will. If it's meant for us to be together, trust me, we will."

"You're starting to sound like a broken record, Jaylin. And you'd better hurry this up if you anticipate on meeting Nokea for dinner by nine."

"Don't rush me," I said, starting to move again. "I'm not quite finished with you just yet."

Within the hour, Scorpio and me finished up. The time was the last thing on my mind, but I knew Nokea was probably at home furious with me. After I put my clothes on, I went into the other room and called her. She must have seen Scorpio's number on the caller ID, and when I told her I was on my way, she just hung up the phone.

I went back into Scorpio's bedroom, and sat in bed next to her. She took my hands, and rubbed them together with hers.

"Baby, don't leave tonight. Stay. Stay not because I'm asking you to, but because you want to."

"I would love to stay, Scorpio, but remember, one thing you said you love about me is that I'm a man of my words. I told Nokea I was coming, so it would be wrong of me not to show."

She looked disappointed and took a hard swallow. "I, uh, almost hate to ask you this, but…are you planning on making love to her tonight? I mean, I'd hope you wouldn't after what we just shared but…"

I leaned forward and kissed her. "No, I don't plan on having sex with Nokea tonight. If you'd really like to know, we don't even get down like that anymore."

"Come on now, Jaylin, I know you're still a bit attracted to her. Not only that, but I know you still love her."

"Woman, please, stop stressing yourself. After that spectacular loving you just gave me, I don't have anymore juices left for anybody."

Scorpio gave me a fake smile, and before I changed my mind, I kissed her on the forehead and jetted.

Nokea's house in Barrington Downs was a thirty-minute drive from Scorpio's condo, and by the time I got there, she was standing at the door waiting. Feeling bad, I hurried out of the car and started to explain.

"I'm sorry. Time just got away from me and—"

"Whatever," she said, holding her hand up in front of my face. "Let's just go. Café Lapadero closes in about an hour, so it doesn't even make sense to go there now. Would you like to have a late dinner somewhere else?"

"Hey, it's my birthday. And you're the one paying so surprise me."

She huffed and walked to my car. I opened the door, and immediately noticed a different look about her. Dress was scrawnier and cleavage was inviting me to her. I closed the door, and rushed to the driver's side to find out what the new look was all about.

As I backed out of her driveway I kicked up a swift conversation. "Have you decided where you're taking me?"

"You're the one driving, silly. Where would you like to go?" She crossed her legs and her sexy brown thigh came peeking through the slit in her tight-fitted turquoise dress. It criss crossed in the front, and was bugging the hell out of me, since it was showing her cleavage. Classy, it was, but I was used to Nokea being a bit more conservative.

105

"You know, wherever you want to go is fine with me," I said, not being able to keep my eyes off her breasts. "But what's up with that?"

"I'd like to go to the Ritz Carlton for the night, and there's nothing up with my breasts."

"The Ritz Carlton, huh? And what do you suppose is going to happen at the Ritz Carlton?"

"Dinner, maybe. I really just want to spend some time alone with you if you don't mind."

"Okay, then, the Ritz Carlton it is."

I pulled over at the Mobil on New Halls Ferry Road and filled my tank before getting on the highway. Nokea asked me if I wanted anything, and went inside to get something to drink. Her short ass dress was still bugging me, and when I watched this man inside flirting with her I was pissed. When she came out, he held the door for her, then had the nerve to squint at her ass, as she pranced back to the car. After that, he nodded his head and gave me a thumbs-up.

I ignored him, but when he got into his pearly-white Escalade and pulled next to us, I was two seconds from going off.

He raised down his window. "Say, brotha. I'm not trying to be disrespectful, but is that your lady?"

Nokea rolled her window down and answered for me. "No, I'm not."

"Well," he said, smiling, and clearing his throat. "You are stunning. Do you think I can get your number and possibly take you to dinner sometime? It would truly be an honor."

Nokea flirted, "Only if you promise to be on time." She reached into her purse and pulled out her business card. She wrote something on the back, and stuck her hand out of the window to give it to him.

Standing there in disbelief, I took my hand off the gas pump, and rushed over to the passenger side. I snatched the card out of her hand before she could give it to him, then leaned down and looked at her.

"What in the hell is your problem? Don't you have any damn respect for me?" I tore the card up in tiny pieces and tossed them inside his car. "If you're that desperate, glue it back together and call her."

"Hey," he said. "I don't want any trouble. I thought she was just a friend." He took one last glance at Nokea, rolled up his window, and drove off.

I hopped in the car and slammed the door. Nokea jumped. "What are you so upset about?" she asked. "And how in the world did I just disrespect you?"

I jetted off and didn't say a word to Nokea until we got on Highway 270. "You disrespected me when you walked your ass out of the house with that short ass dress on. If the wind blows any harder, your ass will be showing. That's probably what that motherfucker back there was looking at."

"For your information, I like my dress. And whether I had it on or not, that man would have asked for my phone number. If you don't like it, that's too bad. I didn't wear it to entertain you."

"Please. And don't get me wrong. It's a beautiful dress, however, I DO NOT want the mother of my child in the streets with nothing like that on. Again, it's too damn revealing for someone as conservative as you are."

"Conservative or not, I like it. It's not my problem that men like you can't keep your hormones under control."

"Oh, I got control. It's going to take more than a dress like that to turn me on."

She turned her head and looked out the window, "Good. Then I guess you won't have any problems keeping your hands to yourself tonight. Besides, I'm sure Scorpio took good care of you anyway."

"If you say she did, then she did. But, now, I see why Chad came on to you like he did. If this is your new way of dressing, then don't get mad when brothas step to you like that."

"Don't even go there, Jaylin." Nokea got angry. "Pat and I are having lunch next week and I'm going to tell her what happened. Don't you go making me feel guilty about the way I look, okay?"

"Alright, I won't. Sorry if I hurt your feelings. Truth of the matter is, you look good, baby. I don't like no brothas looking at you like that, but if you want to, keep your little come-fuck-me dress on. You just might get what you ask for."

Nokea laughed and shook her head. "I swear, you are so crazy. Down-right crazy, but that's why I love your crazy butt."

I leaned over, gave her a kiss, and tried to keep my eyes on the road. "I love you too, but you messed up your loving tonight by trying to give that man your phone number."

"Darn, and just when I didn't think I had anything coming. Sorry, though, I couldn't help myself. He was really handsome."

"What? Is that what you call handsome?"

"Yes. He had that Denzel Washington look about him. You know that sexy, confident, masculine…"

"Yeah, yeah, yeah, whatever. But evidentially, you must have left your glasses at home because that brotha wasn't about nothing. Ole buckethead mother—"

"You can say what you want, or call him what you'd like but he was unquestionably a sight for sore eyes."

Deep down, my feelings were bruised. I decided not to stop and get anything to eat and didn't say much else to Nokea until we got inside the hotel room. She knew I was upset and tried to make small talk with me, but I went straight to the bathroom and closed the door. I took my clothes off and turned on the shower. As I stood there and let the water trickle down my body, I thought about my wild-ass day with Heather and Scorpio. And now, Nokea. There was no way I was going to get down with her tonight. And even though that dress was begging me to fuck her, and I'd visualized a slew of positions I wanted to put her in, my intentions were to take my ass back out there and go to sleep.

Finishing up my shower, I closed my eyes and went into a deep thought thinking about Scorpio. When I heard the door squeak open, I opened my eyes. The lights went out, and Nokea stepped into the shower and stood behind me. She rubbed up and down my back and rubbed my ass with her hands. I turned around, brought her hands up to my lips and kissed them.

"As much as I would love to, I can't do this tonight," I said.

She pulled her hands away, then took my hands and wrapped them around her. I could feel her dress dripping with water.

"There are no such words as you can't, Jaylin. Because tonight, you will." She placed her hands on my goodness and started to rub it. Worked it so good, that it surprisingly gave her some attention. I backed her up against the shower wall and untied her dress. She wasn't wearing any underclothes, and once I removed the dress there was nothing else to remove.

"Why are you making me do this to you?" I asked, holding her face in my hand, then pecking her lips with mine. "Are you sure you wouldn't want buckethead in here with you instead of me?"

"No. I think you will work out just fine. And as for making you do this to me, you're not doing anything to me that I don't want you to do."

"Yes, I am," I said, holding her wet breasts in my hands, and getting ready to suck them. "I'm going to hurt you, Nokea. I'm only being honest with—"

"Shh…be quiet. Just promise me that you'll hurt me in a good way, Jaylin."

She pushed my head down and I started sucking her breasts. A few minutes into it, she turned around like she couldn't take anymore. I pressed my naked body against hers and kissed the back of her neck. I worked myself down her back, then parted her legs when I got on my knees.

Nokea was relaxed and calm as ever. Fucked me up, though, because there was no doubt in my mind that she had been there and most certainly done this before. The thought of Stephon fucking her kept flashing before me, but I was trying hard like hell to stay focused.

Once we got out of the shower, we climbed our naked asses in bed and got busy. Nokea confessed her love for me over and over again. And as good as she had me feeling, I had no shame in telling her how much I still loved her. When she went down on me, I had a fit.

"Hold on, baby," I yelled and raised up. "What in the hell have you been doing?"

She laughed. "What do you mean?"

"I mean, you ain't been practicing with anyone, have you?"

"No, Jaylin. It's been a long time for me. Sex between you and I was long over do. I've planned this day in my mind for months, so enjoy, and please don't interrupt me again." She got back to business and I really couldn't complain. Never in a million years did I think my baby would be able to perform like she was. Stephon must have taught her well. The thought discouraged me, but there was no way that he was ever coming back her way again. I'd make sure of that. And as a matter of fact, no brotha out there was going to tap into Nokea or Scorpio again. They were mine and mine to keep.

NOKEA

When I woke up, Jaylin was still lying there asleep. I had fallen asleep between his legs, and he held me tightly in his arms all night long. I raised up a bit and took a glance at the clock. It showed one-fifteen in the afternoon. Waking up this late wasn't in the plan, but we must have been in a deep sleep.

I lay there for a while looking up at Jaylin, while he was lightly snoring with one hand resting behind his head. His head was turned and was sunken into the pillow. His hair had curled up even more from all of the sweating we did last night.

Checking out how handsome he looked, I took my fingers and rubbed them through his hair. Shortly after, I placed my lips on his and tried to wake him. He didn't budge. I straightened his thick eyebrows and rolled my fingertips across his long lashes. And still, he didn't move. But when I rubbed myself up against his thang, and slightly backed up like I was getting out of bed then he squeezed me around my waist and smiled.

"Where do you think you're going?" he whispered.

"You can stay here and sleep the day away if you'd like. I'm getting ready to go get our son."

"And how do you think you're going to get there without a car?"

"My dress is dry. I was planning on hitching a ride from someone. I'm sure somebody would be happy to pick me up."

"Well, let me get up. I sure in the hell don't want nobody picking my woman up from the street." He removed his hand from behind his head. "What time is it?"

"Almost one-thirty in the afternoon."

He put his hand back behind his head. "Shit…it's still early. I thought it was at least four or five."

"Jaylin, get up so we can go get LJ. He's been with Nanny B all night and I miss my baby."

"He's alright. I already called to check on him and Mackenzie this morning. Nanny B said she was cooking breakfast and the kids were still asleep. She said when they wake up, she's taking them to the mall, then to see her sister."

"Quit lying. You've been laying your butt in this bed knocked out since last night, snoring."

"Naw, that would be you snoring, not me. I dropped the phone when I finished talking to Nanny B and you still didn't wake up."

"Whatever, Jaylin. I, do, not, snore. Besides, I would have felt you move and heard you talking on the phone. Not only that, but I've been messing around with you all morning."

"No. You haven't been messing with me all morning. You just woke up less than thirty minutes ago. You raised up, looked at the clock, stared at me for a while, played around with my hair, straightened my eyebrows, poked me in the eyes, kissed me, and now, you're hoping that I will juice you up again."

"Now, that's not fair. Were you pretending to be asleep? You couldn't have been awake because your eyes were closed and you were snoring. As for making love to me, trust me, I've had enough for at least…two weeks."

He laughed and wrapped his legs around my body. "So what, I was pretending. But I'm not pretending when I tell you I want some more juicy-juice before we go." He placed his hand on my face and kissed me.

I backed up. "So, I see you're rejuvenated again, are you?"

He smiled. "Naw, baby. I'm just excited to have my pussy back, that's all."

After Jaylin and I messed around again, we didn't leave the Ritz Carlton until six o'clock. I stood out front and waited for him to pick me up. He got out of the car, opened the door, and shook his head when he closed it. He smirked like something was wrong.

"What?" I asked, looking at him getting into the driver's seat.

"Nothing." He drove off.

"Why do you keep smiling then?"

"Because I'm a happy ass man, Nokea. That's why."

"No, I think it's more to it than that. It's the dress, isn't it? Please don't start with me today, okay."

"I haven't said a word about it. However, I do want you to do me a favor when we get to my place."

"And what might that be?"

112

"Please, take that son of a bitch off and cut it up. I don't ever want to see you in it again. That damn thing had my ass hard as a rock. The last thing I want is another brotha to get the same ideas I have."

"No way. I paid $350 for this dress, and I'm not going home to cut it up because you brothas can't handle it."

At the stoplight, Jaylin raised up and pulled his wallet out of his pocket. He took four one-hundred-dollar bills out and laid them on my lap. "When we get to my house I'll give you something to change into, since I just bought that dress from you."

I threw the money at him and rolled my eyes. And by the time we pulled into his driveway, we were still debating the dress. Surprisingly, Scorpio was standing outside leaning against her car talking to Nanny B. Mackenzie was inside the car, and LJ was clinging onto Nanny B's leg.

Jaylin looked startled to see Scorpio and when I leaned over to kiss him, he hesitated but kissed me anyway. He got out of the car and opened the door for me. Before I could barely get out, he walked over to LJ, picked him up, and started talking baby talk to him. Mackenzie opened the car door and rushed out, as soon as she saw him. Jaylin took her by the hand, ignored everyone else, and went inside. I stood outside and talked to Nanny B and Scorpio.

"Was LJ on good behavior last night Nanny B?" I asked.

"Yes, he was Nokea. He wasn't no problem at all. He was tired from all that company yesterday."

"Well, thanks for watching him. I told Jaylin how much I miss him when he's away from me."

"I know how you feel. That's my baby too, you know. I enjoy having him and Mackenzie around. I took them to see my sister today, and she fell in love. You two really have some beautiful children. I was just telling Scorpio that before you and Jaylin came."

"Thank you. I don't know what we would do without you." I kissed Nanny B on the cheek and gave her a hug.

The whole time I was standing there talking to Nanny B I could see Scorpio checking me out. She never gave me a second look because I knew she felt as if she was more attractive than I was. True to the fact or not, I definitely had her attention today.

113

"Nokea, that is a beautiful dress you're wearing," Scorpio said, staring.

"It is pretty. I noticed it when you got out of the car. And that color really looks good on you," Nanny B added.

"Thanks." I looked at both of them. "Jaylin hated it, though. He complained about how revealing it is. We were actually just arguing about it as we were pulling up."

"Well, I like it," Nanny B insisted. "Turn around. Let me see how the back is made."

"It's nothing spectacular." I turned around. "The color is actually what makes it."

"No," Scorpio said. "I think it's your thin waistline and your petite body that makes it. And since it's one of those dresses you can't wear any panties with, I don't quite understand why Jaylin wouldn't like it."

Nanny B pulled out a cigarette from her pocket. "On that note, I'm going to take a smoke break. Don't y'all tell Jaylin I'm out here smoking because he will have a fit." She laughed and walked off.

"Listen," Scorpio said. "I didn't mean to be so bold, but it is a nice dress. If I had it, I would definitely wear it whether Jaylin likes it or not."

I smiled, thanked Scorpio for the half-ass compliment and went inside the house to get LJ. She followed. We walked upstairs to Jaylin's bedroom, and heard him loudly talking on the phone, laughing. He was lying across the bed talking to Stephon with LJ sitting on his stomach, and Mackenzie lying her head on his chest.

"Man, you are a fool," he laughed. "Let me hit you back in a lil bit, though, alright." He hung up and sat up on the bed.

"Come on, Mackenzie. Let's go," Scorpio said, holding her hand out for Mackenzie to take it. Mackenzie rolled her eyes and got off the bed.

"Why she gotta go? I'll bring her home later," Jaylin said, pulling Mackenzie towards him.

I picked LJ up because I didn't want him in the middle of an argument I truly felt was about to go down.

"Jaylin, she needs to spend some time at home too. She's over here more than she is at her own damn house." Scorpio looked at Mackenzie. "Now, go get your things and let's go."

"Just in case you didn't notice, Scorpio, this is her house too. I said I'll bring her home later."

Scorpio gave him a hard stare. "Playboy, don't argue with me right now, okay. I'm bound to say something I might regret, so it's best that you let us leave quietly."

Jaylin fell back, put his hands behind his head, and looked up. "Well, the Playboy says she stays and if you got a fucking problem with that, too bad." Before Scorpio could say anything I turned towards the door with LJ on my way out. "Nokea!" he yelled. "Put my son back down. I was playing with him, if you don't mind."

"Mackenzie go downstairs with Nanny B," Scorpio insisted, and pushed Mackenzie towards the door. I moved and let Mackenzie pass by me.

"Jaylin, look, I'm just taking LJ downstairs out of the way," I said.

"Put him on the damn bed like I told you too!" he yelled. I ignored him and headed for the door. He hurried off the bed and Scorpio stood in front of him and stopped him from moving any further. Nanny B came up the steps and took LJ out of my hands.

"What in the hell is going on up in here?" she asked. "Jaylin, I know I don't hear you yelling at these women like that."

"Hey, I was in here minding my own damn business, and they're the ones strolling in here taking my kids like I'm not even here. What kind of shit is that? So, now, fuck it! Everybody just get the hell out." He went over to his nightstand and grabbed his keys. He tossed them to Nanny B and she caught them. "Please take Nokea and LJ home for me. I don't want you burning all the gas out of your car."

"Jaylin, I'll take her home, but when I come back we need to talk. This just doesn't make any sense and you know it," Nanny B said, jiggling his keys.

Scorpio was so frustrated that she grabbed Mackenzie and left. I waited in the hallway with LJ while Nanny B went to get her purse. Jaylin yelled down the hallway from his room, "Nokea!"

"What?" I yelled back, pissed about the whole situation, then walked back into his room.

He came out of his closet with a white long Ralph Lauren shirt and some jogging pants in his hand. "Take that dress off and put this on."

I stood there and looked at him with fury in my eyes. "I will never understand how you can make love to me like you did today, tell me you love me, and then come home and act like a complete idiot."

Nanny B came into the room and took LJ from me. "We'll be in the car waiting." She walked out.

"Nokea, just take the damn dress off and put this on, would you?" He reached his hand out to give the clothes to me. I snatched them out of his hands and threw them on the floor.

"I will do no such thing. I'm one minute from losing my religion on you. Please don't make me go there."

He bent down and picked the clothes up off the floor. He held his hand out again and tried to give them to me. "You're one minute from losing your religion and I'm five seconds from snatching that motherfucker off you. So, take the damn dress off like I asked you to."

"No!" I screamed. "For the last time, Jaylin, I said no! This is my fucking dress, I like it, so the son of a bitch stays on me. If you don't like it, FUCK YOU!" I turned to walk away. By the time I reached the top of the stairs, he grabbed me from behind and pulled on the dress. The back of it ripped and he stood there holding it in his hands. Furious, I took my hand and smacked him as hard as I could on his face. He rubbed it and grinned.

"So, you got your lil smack, and I got what I wanted. Just don't touch me like that again or I'll hurt you."

Standing there half-naked, I snatched the clothes out of his hand and started putting them on.

"You are one sexy ass woman when you're mad," he said, trying to grab me around the waist.

I pulled away from him. "If you continue to bring out this sexy ass woman you think I seem to be by cursing at you, and by putting my hands on you, please leave me alone. My parents didn't raise me to disrespect the ones I love. How about yours?"

"Ouch...now, you really didn't have to go there. But if you must know, nobody taught me shit. If anything, you should know by now that when I say something, I mean it. Next time I tell you to do something, just do it. Then, all the bullshit can be avoided."

"Thanks but I already have a father, Jaylin. I'm not in the market for a new one. And if I were," I said, walking down the steps, "it for damn sure wouldn't be you." He stood at the top of the staircase and smiled at me like he truly got a kick out of the entire situation.

After Nanny B dropped us off, I gave LJ a bath and laid him down for the night. I checked my messages and everybody had called. Mama and Daddy were upset with me for not bringing LJ over yesterday, Pat was cursing me out for not calling her back, and Jaylin called about ten times apologizing. I called Mama and Daddy back and explained why I didn't come over yesterday, and then I called Pat and apologized to her. When I told her I spent the night with Jaylin, she hung up on me. She called back two minutes later and apologized and we made plans to get together for dinner next Friday. As for Jaylin, I deleted his messages. His mind needed some serious rest and I was in no mood to argue with him again.

SCORPIO

There was no doubt about it that Jay-Baby had to go. He was getting over and successfully doing so. He called and tried to apologize to me, but I wasn't having it. I let him beg and plead for forgiveness to the answering machine and had no intentions of returning his phone calls.

Going forward, all of my time was going to be focused on finishing school and taking care of Mackenzie. I wasn't going to stop him from seeing her, but as far as I was concerned, what we had is over. I know it is going to be hard for me to move on, but out of respect for myself, I have to. If I ever wanted to be with him again, I had to become some type of challenge for him. At least make him think about what he would be missing out on if he didn't get his act together. Right now, I was too easy for him to conquer and he knew it. I only hoped Nokea was thinking the same way I was. She was much easier than I was and she seemed to cope well with all the bullshit he put her through better than I did. I wanted to ask her if he made love to her the night of his birthday, but her dress said it all. I was sure that Jaylin worked her and worked her well. Besides, the look of satisfaction was written all over her face. Thing is, he didn't even care if we knew. He seemed kind of proud to be with both of us in the same night. And then to make love to me like he did, tell me he loved me for the first time, and promised me he wouldn't sleep with Nokea. Shame on me. Shame on me for letting shit go this far.

I left class on Wednesday night excited about the A I got on my Algebra test and headed to Shane's studio apartment to thank him. I called him first to make sure he was there and told him I was on my way.

When I arrived, I took the black barred elevator to the fourth floor. When I stepped off the elevator, he was sitting on a stool in the corner of the room on the telephone. He waved for me to come on back to where he was. I stepped over all the paint cans and Canvasses on the floor and headed towards him. He had a window open to clear up the paint smell and a thin white curtain was blowing as the wind was coming in. As I looked around I saw paintings all over the place.

Paintings of him, children playing, buildings, women, you name it, they were there. The hard wood floors were covered with paint blotches everywhere. There was also a king size canopy bed with black steel bars in the center of the floor. It had sheer white material draping from the top that twisted around the bars and crisp clean white cotton sheets covered the mattress.

I listened to him end his conversation, and couldn't help but hear him say Felicia's name. He hung up and asked me to have a seat on an old metal chair that had white dried paint blotches on it as well.

"No, that's okay. I'm not going to stay long. I wanted to personally come and thank you for helping me out like you did." I pulled my test paper out of my purse and flashed it in his face. "Bam! Look what I got today."

He took the paper out of my hand, looked at it, and smiled. "I told you that you could do it. Didn't I?" He leaned forward and gave me a hug. Issey Miyake was wearing him well. Had the same scent as Jaylin. I quickly let go thinking about Jaylin and took my paper out of his hand.

"You know, this calls for a celebration. Why don't you stay a while?" he asked. He walked back over to the stool and sat down. He folded his arms in front of him and I watched as his muscles bulged out of his white short-sleeved T-shirt. He had a Gucci black belt on that was holding up his dark blue wide-legged Levi jeans. He must have just come in from a motorcycle ride because he still had on his rubber boots.

"No, really, Shane, I can't stay. I promised Nanny B I would pick Mackenzie up by ten o'clock tonight."

He looked at his watch. "Hmm…it's only eight-thirty. You have time for one glass of champagne, don't you?"

He lifted his feet and kicked off his boots. Then he stood up and walked over to the small kitchen in the other corner of the room. He opened the refrigerator and pulled out a bottle of Crystal, then he grabbed two wineglasses from the shelf.

Heading back towards me, the phone rang. He put the Crystal and glasses down on a bookshelf and answered it. While talking to the caller, he leaned against the bookshelf and folded his arms.

Shane was looking worthy of my loving tonight, and by the way things were going with Jaylin, ain't no telling what I might do. I knew it was in my best interest to exit fast. Even his twisty's had been freshly done. A few strands of his baby hair were lying on his forehead and his hair was perfectly parted with twisties going neatly in the same direction. His brown skin was smooth—definitely had a shine about it and his puppy-dog eyes were begging me to get down with him tonight.

I put the test paper back inside my purse and pulled out my car keys. He heard them jiggle and quickly said goodbye to the caller.

"Sorry about that," he said, picking the Crystal and glasses up off the bookshelf. "That was one of my students. I try to make time for them whenever they call."

"Oh, I understand. But...I need to be going. Let's make plans to celebrate some other time."

"Okay. But it will only take a few minutes for me to pour us some champagne." He looked disappointed.

"Shane, next time, okay. I really should be going." I turned to walk away and he grabbed my hand. He slid my purse off my shoulder, pulled me in close to him, and wrapped his arms around me.

"Why do you keep fighting this when we get together?" He looked eye to eye with me and moved my hair away from my face. "I've thought about making love to you over and over in my mind. Wouldn't you say it's just time to do this?"

"Shane I—"

"Don't reject me, Scorpio. I know about your situation and I'm just here to help."

"What about Felicia? I heard you talking to her when I came in. Are you seeing her?"

"No," he said, still standing there holding me in his arms. "She's just a friend from the past. I'm searching for a future with a woman who don't mind letting me show her what she's been missing."

Now, with that being said, I took a deep breath and followed Shane to his bed. I kicked my heels off and scooted back on his bed. The mattress was soft and the sheets felt like cotton balls as they touched against my skin. Shane pulled his T-shirt over his head and removed his belt. He put the belt in his mouth and unzipped his pants.

I leaned back on my elbows and watched as he pulled them down. After he stood there naked, then he walked over to a dresser in front of the window and laid the belt down. He opened the drawer, pulled out a condom, then looked at me.

"Must we?" he asked.

"Yes."

"I really don't want to."

"But I'm intimate with someone else right now. You don't want to take the risk do you?"

He nodded and opened the package. I watched as his goods expanded in both directions. After he put the condom on, he kneeled down by the side of the bed and put my feet in his hands. He kissed and rubbed them, then worked his hands up between my legs. He slid my panties down, rubbed them together in his hands, and held them like he was wishing for something.

I smiled, "What are you doing?" He ignored me, laid my panties on the floor beside his bed, and stood up in front of me. He spread my legs apart, looked down between them, then lay his body in the middle. After he kissed me, he eased my dress over my head. He gave my naked body a serious stare and didn't crack a smile.

"Turn over and lay on your stomach," he asked politely. He scooted back so I could roll over on my stomach. And knowing that he probably saw Jaylin's name tattooed on my ass, he rested his body on back of mine. As he held my hands tightly in his, he whispered in my ear. "I take love making very seriously, Scorpio. I'm not going to fuck you because you don't need to be fucked. And I'm not going to talk to you because I don't talk when I'm concentrating on doing something. In addition, I must tell you that Jaylin's ass got it going on."

He loosened his fingers from mine and placed his lips on the edge of my shoulder. He raised up and swirled his fingers up and down my back. Burning hot from his touch, he lowered himself and separated my ass cheeks with his hands.

My body trembled when I felt his tongue searching deep within me. I closed my eyes and gently rubbed my hair back with my hands. When he vibrated my insides with his mouth, I completely lost control. Not being able to take the feeling anymore, I quickly rolled over on my back and screamed out loud.

121

Shane raised up, moved over in bed next to me, and pulled the cover over both of us. He kissed me on the nose and propped his head up with a pillow. Finally, he smiled. I eased over next to him and lay my head on his muscular arm.

"You had no intentions of having sex with me, did you?" I asked.

"Of course I did. And tonight I really did until you told me you were intimate with someone else. More so, something about Jaylin's name tattooed across your ass just changed the mood."

"Shane, everybody has somebody to get down with when need be. I just didn't think it was in my best interest to lie to you. And as for the tattoo, it was a birthday present. There's not much I can do about that."

"Hmm... and I appreciate your honesty. It's just that Jaylin and I got some unresolved issues. The last time we butted heads about a woman, I kind of got my feelings hurt. It wasn't that I was in love with Felicia or anything, but just to have her taken away in an instant was somewhat hurtful for me."

"But I'm not Felicia. I wouldn't do anything to purposely hurt you."

"I know you wouldn't but Jaylin has a way with women. I never figured out what it was and I just can't believe it's all about the sex. He once told me it was, but I think it takes more than just a big dick to keep a woman. Maybe I'm wrong, but this time, I refuse to let the big dick syndrome stand in my way of doing the right thing to begin with."

"So, how do you plan on doing the right thing?"

"Well, there's no doubt about it that I'm digging the hell out of you. The reason I held your panties in my hand is because you have an amazing scent about you. One that almost had me taking the risk of hurting myself again. But this time, I'm going to sit back and watch this one play itself out."

I put my head on Shane's chest, then wrapped my arms around his body. "Are you sure you don't want to change your mind. I was really feeling what you were doing to me, you know."

He laughed. "I could tell. Soon, though, the day will come when we won't be able to get enough of each other. And when it does, I'm going to be a happy man and you're going to be an overjoyed, completely fulfilled woman."

As much as I wanted Shane to fuck me I was kind of glad that he didn't. I was confused and having sex with him would only damage me even more. I drove home so impressed by him and thought about how surprisingly just his touch quickly turned me on.

In deep thought, I reached for my cell-phone and called Nanny B. She told me Jaylin had already left for my place with Mackenzie because it was almost eleven o'clock. I asked her if he was upset about me being late and she claimed he wasn't.

As I turned the corner, and saw his car parked in the front of my condo, I had a feeling something wasn't right. I parked beside his car and took a deep breath, as I slowly walked to the door. When I opened it, he was sitting in the living room chair with his legs folded, and looked enraged.

"Nice of you to finally show your ass up," he said, glancing at his watch.

I tossed my keys on the table. "You can leave now. I'm here." I went into the kitchen. The door swung and almost hit him in the face as he followed behind me.

"Classes taking all damn night now, huh?"

"No. I had something else to do."

"Something to do like what?"

"Look," I said, turning to him with attitude. "It's really none of your business." I opened the refrigerator and looked for something to eat. He pushed me away from the refrigerator and slammed the door.

"Scorpio, whether you like it or not, you are my business. I got all kinds of money tied up fucking with you, so therefore, I'm here checking up on my investment." He pulled the kitchen chair away from the table and sat down. "So, lets try this again… where have you been?"

I pulled out a chair from the table and put it right in front of him. I took his hands and held them in mine. My eyes watered as I looked at him. "Can we please end this?" A tear rolled down my face. "I'm tired, Jaylin. Truly sick and tired of your disrespect. I can't give you what you're looking for. Take this… this condo, the Corvette, the watch, the clothes, the gifts, everything. I'm leaving this relationship with what I came with and that's love for myself." I released his hands and wiped my tears. He leaned forward and placed his hand on my cheek.

"Yeah, whatever…so, where have you been? Leave me if you wish, I really don't give a damn, but I still want to know where you've been tonight?"

It finally hit me. Jaylin really didn't give a damn about me. All he cared about was if somebody was screwing me better than he was. I wiped my tears again, then put my face right in front of his. I yelled loudly, "I was out getting, my, pussy, sucked, by an old friend of yours, Shane Alexander! He sucked it so well that I couldn't help myself from coming in his mouth. It's so funny how time flies when you're having fun, ain't it?"

Jaylin didn't move. He gazed at me for a minute, then leaned back in the chair. He rubbed his goatee, which meant he was pissed, and closed his eyes.

He slowly opened them. His eyebrows raised, as he spoke calmly, "Shane Alexander, huh? That's been your mystery man all along, huh? I should have known when I saw his motorcycle outside that day." He took a deep breath. "Tomorrow, Scorpio. I want you to get the fuck out of here. I want the keys to your car and I don't ever want to see or hear from you again. As for everything else, the watch, the gifts, the clothes, the gratifying dick—keep that shit. Eventually you'll wind up selling everything for money anyway. As for Mackenzie, she's moving in with me. If you want to fight me for her you'll have to take me to court. I'll fight you with one of the best damn lawyers in St. Louis. Personally, I don't think a judge in their right mind would side with a stripper or homeless mother, and lets not give Mackenzie the opportunity to tell them how she really feels." He quickly stood up and lifted my face. "I was really starting to love you. Thinking seriously about asking you to be my wife. It's a damn shame you fucked up, though. In the meantime, if you're looking for a way out of this mess, call me tomorrow before midnight. There's always another alternative. If you don't call, your glass slipper turns into a raggedy-ass tennis shoe." He leaned down, gave me a peck on the lips, and left.

JAYLIN

That hot-ass coochie. Words couldn't express how upset I was with Scorpio. I was so frustrated that I was on my way over to Stephon's house to chat with him about the situation. It was almost one o'clock in the morning, but when I called, he told me to come over. Especially since I sounded like it was imperative that we talk.

I called Nanny B and thanked her for lying to Scorpio about Mackenzie being with me, when in reality, she was still at my house asleep. I didn't want to bring her home knowing that Scorpio and I was bound to go at it. Seems like that's all we've been doing lately. There was a time when she just went with the flow and kept her mouth shut, but I guess ole Shane Alexander had her looking at things a little differently.

He's one motherfucker who just bugs the hell out of me. Since he acted like such a little bitch when I took Felicia from his ass, I ain't had much respect for him. He claimed he didn't love her so what was the big damn deal? Women come and go all the time, so who gives a damn. Besides, ain't nobody shit safe these days, especially with a brotha like me around.

When I arrived, Stephon already had the door open for me. He yelled my name from in the kitchen and told me to come on back. I walked in and he was sitting up on the counter scraping some ice cream from a container.

"So, what's so important you had to interrupt me in the middle of the night?" He put the spoon in his mouth and licked the ice cream. I opened a drawer and pulled out a spoon to get some. When I reached for his container, he snatched it away. "Man, you better go get your own. It's some more in the fridge."

I laughed and went to the refrigerator, then pulled out a container of Ben & Jerry's Confession Obsession. I opened it and hopped up on the other side of the counter.

"Have you seen Shane Alexander lately?" I asked. I put a spoon full of ice cream in my mouth.

"No, I haven't. I heard he was back in town, though. Why are you asking?"

126

"Because that punk motherfucker is going to be a thorn in my side, that's why."

"What do you mean by a thorn in your side?"

"I mean, that nigga been sucking my woman's pussy. She's been seeing this mystery man that I haven't questioned her about and tonight she told me that it was Shane."

"Which one of your women?"

"You know which one, man, Scorpio."

"Damn! Lucky son of a bitch," Stephon shook his head and laughed.

"Man, don't play. I'm serious. Shit hurt me like hell. I was really starting to trust her and was finally feeling some love for her ass."

"Did she tell you she wanted to be with Shane or what?"

"Nope. But I know Shane. He's a persuasive brotha. Personally, I think if he even suspects I'm with Scorpio, he's going to be out for revenge."

"Why? Because of the Felicia bullshit back in the day?"

"Exactly. So, I need you to set something up for me."

"Something like what?"

"I don't know. That's why I'm here. You're a creative brotha. Throw a party or something. Send the man an invitation…do something. I want to see what's up with him."

Stephon looked like he was in deep thought. "I just thought of something. I was over Felicia's house the other day and when I came in she was on the phone. When she went to the bathroom I looked at the caller ID and it showed Alexander S. I laid it down and didn't think nothing of it."

"Do you think it was Shane?"

"Had to be. I didn't press the issue because I could care less about who Felicia talks to."

"You wouldn't have looked at the caller ID if you didn't care. And what if it's his baby she's having and not yours? Wouldn't you like to know? This big Van Dam looking nigga is going to be a problem. I can feel it."

"Yeah, you might be right. Listen, I'll get one of my boys from the shop to set something up. It won't be no party because I think just the three of us need to catch up on old times. You catch my

127

drift?" Stephon hopped down off the counter. "In the meantime, I got not one but two ladies waiting for me downstairs. I'll give you a hollar tomorrow."

"Straight. You going out like that now, huh?" I said, hopping down off the counter as well.

"Always. I'm trying to get myself in good shape for when I fuck Scorpio. Bet's still on, right."

"Hell, naw! Nigga, don't play. Bet is off! Don't you go near her, man, and I mean that shit," I said, seriously.

"As much as I would love to, I promise you I won't. Seems like you kind of got some deep feelings for her, and I will never let another woman interfere with us again. But, uh, with that being said, do you think I can get my money by tomorrow?"

"You don't give up, do you? Ain't like I believe she'll let you fuck her anyway, but since I broke the bet, and I'm a man of my words, I'll wire the money to your account in the morning."

Stephon patted me on the back. "Five thou is cool. And if you'd like to come downstairs and join the party, I'm sure the ladies would be more than happy to share."

"Naw, not tonight. Knock yourself out. My shit still sore from my birthday."

"Now, I can't believe Heather and Scorpio was too much for you."

"Let's not forget about Nokea. Worked her all night too."

"You lying. Are you working that again?"

"Fasho. And thanks for loosening everything up for me." I winked. "Makes my job a lot easier now."

"No problem. But you know I'm jealous, don't you?"

"Well, get over it. You shouldn't have been up in there to begin with."

Stephon and I laughed, then walked to the door. We hugged and I jetted.

When I got back to the house Mackenzie was still in her room asleep. I knocked on Nanny B's door and she told me to come in. She was wide-awake and was lying on her side looking at TV.

"Jaylin, sit down for a minute. I need to speak with you."

"Nanny B, can it wait until tomorrow? I'm tired. I've been running around ever since I got off work."

"This won't take long. I promise you."

I went over to a chair and sat down. I loosened my tie and kicked off my shoes. "Okay, what's up?"

"Don't you ever ask me to lie for you again. Scorpio called here looking for Mackenzie, and I had to apologize to her for lying. I don't like lying to anyone, especially when it comes to their own children."

"Okay, I'm sorry. I just didn't want Mackenzie being around us arguing, that's all. I promise you I will never ask you to lie for me again."

"Good. Because if you ever put me in a situation like that again, I'm leaving. I'm fifty-seven-years-old, and I do not want to be caught up in the middle of your games."

"That's fair. And once again, I promise you it will never happen again." I picked my shoes up off the floor and headed to the door.

"Jaylin?"

"Yes." I turned around with an attitude.

Nanny B took a deep breath. "I love you like a son. And before you go to bed tonight, call Scorpio and let her know Mackenzie is okay."

"I'll call her tomorrow. And thanks, I love you too." I walked out.

The phones at work were going crazy. Angela was trying to keep up, but I had to also be the secretary to make sure everybody got served. By one o'clock in the afternoon, I still hadn't heard from Scorpio, and was quite disappointed she hadn't called yet. Nokea called, though. She told me how scared she was about meeting with Pat on Friday and needed a little pep talk. I told her to bring LJ by on Friday, and let him spend the weekend with me, so she could relax after talking to Pat. Her meeting with Pat didn't sound like it was going to be pretty, but I at least offered her my support.

No sooner had I ended my phone call with her, Angela buzzed in and told me someone was waiting to see me. When I asked who it was, she said it was a man who insisted we had an appointment today. I checked my planner and didn't see anything scheduled, but I asked Angela to invite him in anyway.

129

She opened my door and he followed in behind her. When I looked up he was white, about six-two, had salt and pepper hair that was neatly combed back, and wore a dark black suit. Before I could ask him to have a seat, he already did, then laid a brown leather briefcase on my desk. He crossed his legs in front of him and I caught a glimpse at his expensive looking shiny deep-burgundy shoes and immediately noticed his gold cuff links with diamonds. I could smell the money on him, so I asked Angela to close the door, and then I introduced myself.

"I'm, uh, Jaylin Rogers," I said, shaking his hand. "I'm sorry, but I really don't recall making any appointments today."

He stood up and shook my hand back. "Jaylin, I'm Mr. Robert McDaniels. We didn't have an appointment today, but I'm positive that you can find time in your busy schedule to meet with me."

I strutted back over to my chair and thought hard about who in the hell this man could be. But when he opened the briefcase, it finally hit me. He was Heather's husband. He turned the briefcase around, removed a tape from inside and closed it. Inside I noticed it was full of money, but I didn't say a word. He slid the tape across my desk.

"Do you have any idea what's on this tape?" he asked.

"Nope, not a clue."

"I think you do know. But since you insist that you don't, I'm going to enlighten you." He moved my crystal framed picture of LJ and Mackenzie over to the side and propped his ass up on the edge of my desk. He picked the tape up, and shook it around in his hands. "On this tape is you having sex with my wife. That includes the mud screwing encounter, the foyer fucking bullshit, and even the one that burns me up the most. And that's when you took it up on yourself to screw her in my goddamn bed." He lifted his ass off my desk and sat back in the chair. "So, Mr. Rogers, we need to talk. Talk about how I'm going to make you disappear."

I smiled, picked up my blue crystal global ball on my desk, and rolled it around in my hands. I looked at him through it, then laid it back down. I thought about clocking his ass with it, but there was a better way of dealing with this situation.

I leaned back in my chair and bounced a pen up and down on my desk. "So, Mr. McDaniels, did you learn anything from watching the tape?"

"Yeah. I can honestly say I did."

"Really? And what might that be?"

"I learned that I have a whore for a wife, and I also learned if I have to kill someone I will do so."

"Damn," I grinned. "Sounds pretty painful. But I was hoping that you learned how to fuck your wife better, so a brotha like me wouldn't be able to step in and dick her down like I did. Or, should I say, like I do because I just tapped into that tight-ass pussy the other day. You didn't get that on tape because it occurred at my house, not yours."

"Ha," he shouted and smiled. "You are a piece of work, aren't you? But little do you know, Mr. Rogers, I know everything there is to know about you. So, let's see…as a matter of fact, you did lay my wife at your house. On your thirty-second birthday, if I can recall. Then you drove around in your fancy Mercedes Benz and found yourself some more pussy for the day because my wife just wasn't good enough. Now, I can understand why because whew…the woman whose condo you drove to that night was beau-ti-ful. And the one with the spiked short hair and short turquoise dress, wow…I gotta hand it to you Jaylin, you are definitely *the man*." He stood up and walked back over to my desk. He opened the briefcase again so I could see the money. "If my sources and calculations are correct, I'd say your net worth is about…let's say, one and a half million dollars. And that's at the most. I'm proposing half of that today, and I'm asking you to disappear as quickly as possible."

I smiled, put my hands together and clapped them, "I must say, Mr. McDaniels, you have definitely done your homework." Pissed, I massaged my goatee and stood up. I turned the briefcase around, looked at the money, and closed it. "Thirty-three, Mr. McDaniels. I turned thirty-three on my birthday, and not thirty-two. Not only that, but you forgot to do the extra-credit on your homework because you are several million dollars shy of my net worth." I picked the briefcase up, walked over to my door and opened it. "Next time you come see me, you need to come correct. I'm one Negro that can't be bought, so go home, fuck your wife, and feel free to watch the tape

131

again. You just might learn how to make that pussy talk to you like it talks to me."

He stood face to face with me and took the briefcase out of my hand. "Next time, I'm not going to be as pleasant. I'll pay you another visit in the near future, Jaylin. And when Higgins and Schmidt find out what kind of animal they have running things for them, those assets you have are going to disappear."

I laughed. "Animal, huh? I think of myself as an animal sometimes too. Not a monkey, or any animal like that, but like a panther, a Black Panther that prowls and creeps into your bed at night and fucks your wife when you're not there. And as for my assets, please. This job is playtime for me. I only come here because I don't have shit else to do. There is nothing that you, Higgins, Schmidt, or any other white motherfucker can take from me because my true money comes from my inheritance. Black folks get those too, you know? So, for the last time, get your ass out of here so I can get back to business. My message light is blinking, and I'm sure it's probably your wife on the phone begging me to fuck her."

He winked. "Jaylin, nice meeting you." He held his hand out to shake mine, and I just looked at it and grinned. "You're really going to wish that you never came in my house for a drink that night. Right about now, I'd hate to be in your shoes."

I widened the door, "Good day, Mr. McDaniels, and the next time you come, don't forget to thank me for opening up your wife's pussy. I'm sure you're mad because you're probably drowning in it now."

I gave him a hard stare and he walked out. Angela looked at me and couldn't wait to start questioning me, but I was in no mood to talk. She told me Scorpio stopped by to see me, but left after being told I was in an important meeting.

I slammed my office door and checked the messages Angela transferred to my voice mail while I talked to Mr. McDaniels. Stephon called and said that Shane was going to meet us at Freddy's Bar & Grill tonight. Scorpio called and said she would come back to see me around three. Nokea called to thank me for talking to her about the Pat situation, and Heather called asking me to come see her tonight. I took a deep breath, and hung up the phone. I leaned forward and rested my elbows on my desk. Feeling slightly under pressure, I massaged my face. I hated feeling this way, but there was no way I was going to let anything get to me.

I picked up the phone, and started to call Heather to tell her about her stupid-ass husband. There was a knock, then Scorpio cracked the door open. "Angela's not out here, so is it okay to come in?"

I laid the phone down. "Sure, I've been wanting to see you anyway. Shut the door behind you." I watched Scorpio when she came in and shut the door behind her. She was looking magnificent. Had a part down the middle of her hair, and both sides were full of long fluffy curls that hung on her shoulders. Her rosy-red pants suit had a long jacket that buttoned down the middle, and squeezed her waistline perfectly. The bottom of her pants legs were cuffed and flared out slightly over her red strapped shoes. She pulled up a chair in front of my desk and sat down. When she removed her dark DKNY glasses, I could tell by the puffiness in her eyes she had been crying.

"I guess you know I'm here to talk about this second alternative you mentioned last night," she said, putting her keys on my desk.

"You know, it's really simple. And don't go trying to make me feel sorry for you by letting me see your eyes. I have no sympathy for you."

"Good," she said, sharply. "Now, what's the alternative?"

"Are you rushing me?"

"Yes. So what's the other alternative?"

"I'm one minute from throwing you out of here with this bad-ass attitude you got, and when I tell you that today is not the day to fuck with me, you'd better believe it. So, let's start this conversation over...Are you rushing me?" I yelled.

"Yes, but that's because I can't stand the sight of you, and you can't stand the sight of me. The faster we get this over with, the better. I'm here to do whatever I have to do to keep a roof over my head, food in my mouth, and clothes on my back, until I can do better. So, for the last time, what's the alternative?"

"I never said I couldn't stand the sight of you. You actually just made my day when you walked your pretty self through the door. What I don't understand is why do you feel that way about me?"

"Jaylin, look, I don't feel that way. But who cares about how I feel? You don't. Besides, that's not the point. The point is what must I do to make this better between us?"

"That's simple. Question is, do you love me?"

She dropped her head and looked down at the floor. She took a hard swallow, then lifted her head back up. A tear rolled down her face and she wiped it. "What does that have to—"

"DO, YOU, LOVE, ME!" I yelled. "If you do, then let me hear you say it!"

Tears started pouring down her face. She shook her head. "Yes, yes I love you, but what in the hell does that have—"

"Good! And I love you too!" I picked up the phone and slammed it down in front of her. "Call this motherfucker Shane and tell him it's over! Tell him who you love and tell him you never want to see his stupid-ass again!"

She shook her head. "Jaylin, that is so petty. Shane knows who I love."

"Then he won't have a problem with you telling him again." I picked the receiver up. "What's his number?" I asked, getting ready to dial it myself. She turned the phone towards her and dialed. I laid the receiver down, and put the phone on speakerphone to make sure she wasn't playing no games with me. And just my luck, the bastard answered.

"Hello?" he said.

"Shane, hi. It's Scorpio."

"I know. Recognize your sexy voice anywhere."

I looked at Scorpio with disgust.

"Hey, I need to talk to you about something," she said.

"I hope about when, where, and how we're going to finish up what we started last night. I've been thinking…"

Scorpio hesitated and I looked at her like, get to the point. "Shane," she interrupted. "I've been thinking about last night too, but I'm afraid I'm going to have to say that you were right."

"Right about what? About us being together?"

"No. About me possibly hurting you because I'm in love with Jaylin. It was wrong for me to let things go as far as they did last night when I still have strong feelings for him. I was just calling to say I'm sorry about the whole thing, and if you don't hear from me anymore it's because—"

"Because you're afraid to let a real man love you. I felt a connection with you last night. And no matter what you say, I know you felt it too. If you're telling me that you're moving on, fine. I'll accept that and I truly wish you well." He hung up.

I turned off the speakerphone. "Now, that wasn't so bad, was it? And since you really love me, that made it a whole lot easier, didn't it?" I asked. Scorpio stood up and removed her keys from my desk. She put her glasses back on and headed to the door. "Sex tonight?" I asked. "I think we got a little something to celebrate."

"And what might that be?" she asked, turning around with an attitude. "Never mind, surprise me Jaylin. You seem to be full of surprises lately, so wait until later to tell me. I'm sure whatever it is, I'll enjoy it."

"You always do, don't you? And put on something sexy. Red is your color, but black makes me rise a bit faster."

"Black, blue, purple, green, whatever," she said, dryly. "Your shit will rise no matter who or what color it is. I don't have anything sexy to put on, so don't count on it, okay."

I reached in my pocket and pulled out a hundred-dollar bill. I bald it up and threw it at her, "Go buy yourself something sexy. Thanks to me, Saks Fifth Avenue probably knows you by name, don't they? And since you're so good at spending my money, I'm sure it won't take long for you to find something *black* that arouses me. I'll be there by nine, so don't disappoint me." Scorpio looked down at the money and left it on the floor. She rolled her eyes and walked out.

Shortly after she left, I packed my things up and left for the day. I noticed that Mr. McDaniels left the tape, so I threw it in my briefcase just in case I wanted to watch it later.

On the drive home, I called Heather's cell phone number. When she didn't answer, I left a message for her to call me. I was sure her ole hubby would probably hear it, so I spiced it up a bit and told her I was dying to fuck.

When I got home, Mackenzie and Nanny B were in the bonus room watching *Monsters, Inc.* I showered, changed clothes, and told them I would be back later. Mackenzie put up a fuss, but I promised her we would do something together on the weekend when LJ came over.

I got to Freddy's Bar & Grill around seven o'clock. Stephon was already sitting at a booth, and waved at me when I came through the door. I didn't see Shane, so I figured he hadn't made it yet.

Stephon must have had the same idea that I did because his outfit was banging. We both had on our leather pants and lizard skin boots. He had on a multi-colored sweater with zigzags on it and a hat to match. I wore a black ribbed long sleeve v-neck sweater that hugged my muscles, and matched my black leather boppy hat. My gold diamond Rolex was glistening on my wrist, as well as my thick nugget gold bracelet on the other.

"I know you didn't try and go all out for this brotha, did you?" I said, grinning, walking up to Stephon, and giving him a slamming handshake.

"I didn't try, I did. And looks like you did too."

We both laughed and sat down at a booth.

"So where this ole wishy-washy nigga at? Probably at home soaking cause I made Scorpio call him today and diss his ass."

"Whaaat…and she did it?"

"Come on, you don't have to ask, do you?"

Stephon shook his head. "Jay, you know you be playing with fire."

"Who gives a damn? I'm so mad at her ass that I could just kill her. Tonight, though, I'm gonna put a hurting on that ass."

"You need some help?"

I laughed. "Naw, man, I got it all taken care of. I'm gonna set that ass out so good tonight that when another brotha walk by she'll be afraid to even look at him."

"Well, damn. Just don't make it where she don't want to look at my black ass." "You silly, man, but, uh, I kind of got a bigger fish to fry."

"Bigger fish like what?"

"Mr. Robert McDaniels. Heather's husband. Son of a bitch came on my job today and disrespected me. He threatened me and offered me $750,000 to disappear."

"And…what did you tell him? You better not have taken the money, Jay."

"Fool, don't you know anything about me? I told him to get the fuck out of my office and damn near put my foot in his ass. Thing is, he's been watching me. Trying to find out shit about me and I don't like that. I'm a private man, and I'd like to keep it that way."

"So, do you want me to get somebody to do away with this motherfucker or what?"

"Naw, I ain't trying to go out like that cause I hope after today he realizes I ain't no poot-butt Negro he can order around."

"Well, if I were you, I wouldn't even sweat it. If he dig a little further into our family's history and find out how many relatives we got locked up for murder, he'll back off. If not, all you have to do is say the word. His ass will be the one disappearing. Just like—"

"Man, I know. Don't be talking that stuff up in here. Ain't no telling who might be listening. Besides, that punk-ass nigga Shane is on his way in. I just saw him park his car." I was looking out of the window.

"What's he driving?"

"A Lexus. Not a new one, but an older one."

Stephon and I were pretending to hold a heavy conversation when Shane came in. He looked over at us and headed our way. When he got to the booth, Stephon stood up and grinned. I didn't say shit and checked him out from head to toe.

"Whaz up, man? Ain't seen yo ass in a long time." Stephon said, then moved aside so Shane could slide into the booth next to him.

"Nothing, nothing," he said, sliding in. "Just been chillin, that's all. Teaching, tutoring, and painting my life away."

"You forgot something," I quickly said.

"Excuse me. Forgot what?"

"You forgot to mention that you've been sucking my woman's pussy, that's what."

"Ahh...so, that's what this is about. Scorpio? Well, I've been doing that too, but if that's what you two gentlemen want to talk with me about, I don't have time."

"Jaylin, man," Stephon said. "Why don't you hold it down?" He looked over at Shane who was getting ready to exit the booth. "Shane, listen, we didn't call you here to scold you or anything. We just wanted to find out the down low on a couple of females. Since

137

we're boys and everythang, I thought we might be able to sit down and talk about this like we got some sense. So, hang around for a while. Order yourself a drink and let's talk."

"Yeah, man," I said. "I apologize for coming off like that, but I'm having a bad ass day today. My lady came in the house last night, late, and then tells me that she just got off in your mouth. Now, I don't know how upset you would be if it were your woman, but I ain't too damn thrilled about it."

"Trust me," Shane said. "I understand your pain. But a few years ago, my woman came into my bedroom and told me my thang wasn't big enough. Said she found a brotha with a mega thang who liked to work it from behind, and do it in the shower. And the killing part about it was when she said it was one of my closet friends. Can you even imagine how pissed I was?"

"Of course, but why must you be out for revenge? Especially over a bitch like Felicia. If anything, I did you a favor."

"I know, Jay. And believe it or not, I'm not out for revenge. I think you have a beautiful woman and if she wasn't yours, she'd definitely be mine."

"I'm feeling you on that one," Stephon said, giving him five. "I've been saying the same damn thing for months."

"Well, I don't care what neither one of you fellas say. She's my woman, she's going to be with me, and only me." I looked over at both of them. "And even though I have a funny way of loving her, I do."

"What? Shane, did you just hear that?" Stephon asked.

"Naw, I didn't. I must have something clogged in my ears. Did he just say he was in love with someone?"

"Naw, not Jay. This is definitely some new shit to me," Stephon said.

"Shut up. Y'all playas need to be quiet. Stephon, you know I've been in love before," I said, thinking about Nokea.

"Yeah, right. With who?" Shane asked.

"My Nanny, nigga, that's who."

We all laughed.

After a few minutes of talking, Shane got up and went to the restroom. Stephon and me checked him out, as he looked spiffy his damn self with his red Ralph Lauren shirt and baggy blue jeans on.

He always was a slight bit muscular than Stephon and me, and by the looks of things, the gym was not failing him at all. I now knew why Scorpio was interested.

When Shane came back over to the table he had three drinks in his hand. He sat them on the table. "Let me see if I remember this correctly." He handed me my drink. "Remy, is your drink." He handed Stephon his. "Remy, is your drink, and Remy is also mine. With that in mind, fellas, what does that say about us?"

I looked at Stephon and he looked at me. "It says that we like the same damn drink and the same lovely ass women," I said. We laughed and clinked our glasses together.

Shane sat down. "So, straight up, Jay. I'm out of the picture. Now, that doesn't mean if I see Scorpio a year or two from now and she tells me y'all aren't together. I'm letting you know right now that she's fair game."

"What about Felicia?" Stephon asked.

Shane blew the Remy out of his mouth and laughed. "Excuse me? I'm feeling a little light-headed, but what about Felicia?"

"Nigga, don't lie. I saw your number on her caller ID."

"Stephon, you might have seen it because I finally called her back after she blew my damn cell phone up. I am not the least bit interested in her after how she played me. But what in the hell are you doing at her place? I thought she was with Jay?"

"Man, it's a long story. I've been trying to tell this knucklehead she's bad business," I said, looking at Stephon.

"Stephon, man, please listen to your cousin. She is nothing but trouble."

"Shane, Jay, mind y'all damn business. Y'all didn't say that shit when she was shaking a nigga down, so I don't want to hear it."

"He got a point now, Jay. I must admit, the brotha's got a point."

I gave Shane a slamming high-five and we cracked up. We sat at Freddy's drinking and catching Shane up on the scoop for about two hours. Heather hit me on my cell phone, but I didn't answer because I was having too much fun.

By nine-thirty I was ready to call it a night. I told Scorpio I would be there by nine and didn't want to be *that* late since she was already mad.

139

"Well, fellas, I'm outtie. I'm getting ready to stop by a flower shop, buy my woman some roses, apologize for being an asshole, and make her pay for opening up her legs to Shane."

Shane laughed. "Man, if I could change what happened last night I would. She bad, though, Jay. Baby-Girl is bad."

" I know. That's why she's with me." I stood up and tossed two dollars on the table for my four drinks, a huge plate of hot wings, onion rings, and a piece of cherry cheesecake.

"We are truly jealous about you leaving us, and going home to put it on Scorpio. But bro, what in the hell is two dollars supposed to pay for?" Stephon asked.

"I changed my mind, and now I'm thinking more like Nokea. And you did get that ten grand I wired to your account, didn't you?"

"Fasho. And thanks for the extra."

"Good. Then I'm sure it will cover the cost of my food and then some. Shane," I said, grabbing his hand. "It's been a pleasure, and keep in touch, man, alright." He agreed and I jetted.

Even though I might have been thinking about Nokea for a moment, I was on my way to see Scorpio. I was feeling kind of bad by the way I treated her, and thought about how hurt she looked in my office today.

I swerved down Olive Blvd. feeling the true effects of the alcohol. When I parked in front of her condo, her car was outside, but there were no lights on. I placed the roses in my mouth, put the key in the door, and unlocked it. I slid my boots off at the door, and walked back to her bedroom. When I turned the lights on, she wasn't there. I looked on the bed and there was a folded letter with a set of keys lying on the top. I sat down and unfolded the letter. It read: *I'm sure the bedroom is the first place you would look for me, so there's no doubt in my mind that you wouldn't find this letter. Today was a wake up call for me. You left me with little respect for myself, and I'm going as far away from you as possible to get it back. Never in my wildest dream did I think I would fall this hard for you. But my problem occurred when I started loving you more than I loved myself. You are a cruel man, Jaylin. Maybe because your life hasn't always been right, but nobody's life is perfect. I lost both of my parents at an early age and had to do without, but it never gave me the right to step on the people who God put in my life for me to love. Your watch is in the dresser drawer, your clothes are in the closet, your keys to the condo and Corvette is on the key ring, and, yes, your pussy is gone.*

I closed the letter and quickly reached for the phone to see if Mackenzie was still with Nanny B. When she told me Scorpio came to get her at eight o'clock, I slammed the phone down. Angry, I threw it against the wall and fell back on the bed.

"Damn!" I yelled out loud. "I'll be motherfucking damn!"

Brenda M. Hampton

NOKEA

Dinner plans with Pat and I had already been made. She wanted to meet at Applebee's on Lindbergh, so we could catch a movie at Jamestown Mall afterwards. I wasn't sure if she would still want to go to the movies, after I told her about Chad, but I had put off not telling her long enough.

She'd noticed my sudden distance and blamed Jaylin for coming back into my life. The truth was, I just couldn't face her after what Chad did to me. More so, I couldn't face him.

When I got to Applebee's Pat was already sitting at a table waiting for me. She smiled, as I headed towards her and stood up to hug me. As she tightly held me, I closed my eyes, hugged her back, and felt devastated about what I had to do.

"Say, Miss Thang. Good to see you," she said, sitting back down. "Have a seat so we can catch up on things since Jaylin's been taking all my time away from me."

"Pat, you know it's not even like that. I have never put Jaylin before you."

She gave me a crazy look. "Please. Yes you have and you know it. Don't make me sit here and go there."

"Okay, maybe I have. But you know I love you, don't you?"

"Of course, I do. That's why I ain't tripping." She laughed. "Anyway, how's my baby doing? I didn't even get a chance to see him on his birthday and I was crushed."

"Well, you know it was big Jaylin's birthday too. Nanny B had a get together at his house, and afterwards Jaylin and I spent the night at the Ritz."

"Yeah, I know. I remember you telling me, but how can you still sleep with him, Nokea. He is trifling. I mean down right, straight-up trif—"

"Pat, please don't talk about him like that. Jaylin has some good qualities only I know about. Besides, I didn't come here to listen to you tear him down. I came here to have a nice dinner with my best friend, and to tell you about something I've been holding back on telling you."

142

"Fine. I won't talk about the ho-bitch and please, please, please, please don't tell me you're pregnant again. I don't think I'll be as excited for you as I was the first time."

"Pat, what is up with your attitude? No. I'm not pregnant, but if I was, you'd be the last person I would tell right about now."

"Look, Nokea, I'm sorry." She took a sip of her water. "Something has been bugging Chad and he won't tell me what it is. I know my husband better than anybody, and I can sense when something ain't right. When I ask him what's wrong he just blows me off like it's nothing. Anyway, I don't want to spend the day talking about these crazy ass men. What's been on your mind, girl?"

I took a deep breath and took a few sips of my water. I put the glass back down on the table and couldn't even look her. "Has the waiter come to the table yet?"

"Yes, Nokea. But what is it? I can tell you're starting to beat around the bush."

"Did you order for us?"

"Nokea?"

"Okay. I know…but this is so hard for me to say."

"Sweetie, we've been friends for fourteen years. You have never held anything back from me, so don't start now. Whatever it is, I promise you I will not make any negative comments about it."

"You promise."

"Yes, I promise."

"Okay," I said, holding Pat's hands in mine from across the table. "The last time I was at your house, Chad came on to me. He called and told me—"

Pat released her hands from mine. "Nokea, you know how Chad is. He's always joking around with my friends, and I'm sure he didn't mean anything by it."

"No, Pat. He actually tried to kiss me. He came up from behind me and put his lips on my neck. When I got home he called and tried to tell me how much I wanted him. I wanted to tell you sooner but I…I really didn't know how."

Pat yelled angrily at the waiter, "Would you please get me another glass of water! We've been waiting forever on you to take our order." The waiter hurried over to the table and asked us what we'd like to have.

"Pat, did you hear anything I said to you? I can't sit here and order this food pretending like our conversation never took place."

"Nokea, I'm ordering right now because I don't know what else to say about you. When I'm upset, food is actually what calms my nerves. The sooner my food gets here, the faster I'll be able to respond to your selfish ass."

"Selfish? What do you mean by selfish?"

The waiter looked at us and said he'll give us another minute.

"I mean, all you ever think about is you. What you want? What you like? Who you've got to have? What you've got to have? The list goes on and on. But this time, you've crossed the line. Chad would never approach a woman like you because you're weak, Nokea. And I think Jaylin's got your mind so twisted that you're looking for anyone who gives you a little attention these days."

I tightened my eyes and tried to fight back my tears. "Pat you know I would never do or say anything to come between you and Chad's marriage. As your best friend I just wanted you to know wha—"

"As my best friend, you have stooped to an all-time low. I thought sleeping with Stephon was low, but this is crazy. I should have known I couldn't trust you then, but stupid me, always taking your side and being there for you when you needed me." Pat stood up. She picked up her glass, took a sip of the water, then splashed the remainder of it in my face. "Get that son of a bitch Jaylin to come clean up your mess. You and him seem to be good at making them, so I'm sure he'll help you clean it up." She walked off.

I grabbed a napkin, wiped my face, and then dabbed it on my silk fuchsia blouse. The waiter came over and gave me another napkin and asked if I needed help. I refused, thanked him for the offer, and left him ten dollars for being so kind.

On the drive to Jaylin's house to pick up LJ, I thought about my conversation with Pat. Not in a million years did I think she was going to respond so negatively. I finally knew how she truly felt about me and was hurting so badly inside. I didn't expect her to embrace me with open arms, but I at least thought she would talk to Chad before making any assumptions.

When I pulled up in Jaylin's driveway, his car still wasn't there. Earlier in the week we discussed LJ spending the night for the weekend, but right now I needed my baby in my arms more than anything.

Nanny B opened the door with him resting on her hip. "Nokea, I didn't think you were coming back until Sunday. Is everything okay?"

"Yes, it's fine." I walked in and took LJ from her. "Has Jaylin made it home yet?"

"No, but he's on his way. He called not too long ago and asked if LJ was here. I told him yes, so stay until he gets here. He's going to be so disappointed if he doesn't get a chance to see him."

"That's fine. We'll just go upstairs to his room and wait for him."

"Thanks, Nokea. Have you had something to eat yet? I cooked a Pot Roast, and if you'd like some you're welcome to it."

"No, that's okay," I said, walking up the steps with LJ. "Thanks though."

I turned on the light in Jaylin's room, and put LJ on the bed. When I lifted his briefcase to put it on the floor, it flew open and his papers spread out all over the floor along with a videotape. I bent down, picked the papers up, and put them back into the briefcase. Then I picked up the tape and read the label. It read: You sorry son of a bitch, in red big bold letters.

Curious, I went over by the VCR and slid the tape in. I took the remote control off the nightstand and pushed PLAY. I watched as Jaylin's car pulled into somebody's driveway, and I immediately noticed Mr. Schmidt's daughter on the passenger side. Thinking nothing of it, I pushed the fast forward button and stopped the tape when I saw her walking around the house with a lace negligee on. Jaylin seemed to be mesmerized by her as she poured him a drink. I pushed the fast forward button again, and when I saw her removing his shirt, I took a deep breath, and feared what was about to happen next.

I nervously placed my hand over my mouth as I watched them fucking. Rain was pouring down on their bodies, as they seemed to be all into it. Not trying to put myself through this again, I quickly hopped up and stopped the tape. I picked LJ up and ran out of Jaylin's room. As I was moving quickly down the steps, he opened the front door. Before he could close it, I put LJ in his arms, and jetted out to

145

my car. He yelled my name, but there was no turning back for me. I hopped in my car and took off.

I hit Highway 40 driving like a bat out of hell. And after I realized how important my life was, and how much my son needed me, I finally slowed down. I slowly pulled over and laid my head on the steering wheel. Trying to hold back my tears, I started screaming out loud. I pounded the steering wheel until the palm of my hands turned red, then placed them over my face. Over ten years of my life wasted, I thought. Wasted on a man who never wanted anything from me but security. I had been his security blanket when others failed him. I had been his security blanket when sex wasn't well within his reach, and more than anything, I had been a fool. A *serious* damn fool for love.

Sitting there for almost thirty minutes, thinking, I started my car and drove to Cardwell's in Clayton to get a bite to eat. I was drained from the Pat situation too, and needed something in my stomach to calm me.

The Maitre D asked me if I had reservations, and since I didn't, I had a short wait. I sat in the waiting area turning my head, and looking out of the window as it started to drizzle. As I dazed off thinking about what a fool I'd been, a voice interrupted.

"Say, excuse me, but haven't I seen you some where before?" he asked.

Knowing how many men use that line when they're trying to get a woman's attention, I didn't even bother to turn my head. "No," I said, dryly. "I don't think so."

"Yes, I do remember you. I remember you from the gas station several weeks back."

I quickly turned my head. And sure enough, it was buckethead. That's what Jaylin called him anyway. Thinking about it, I smiled. "Hello. How are you?" I stood up.

"I'm fine. I saw you when you came in. Are you waiting for someone?"

"No, I'm dining alone tonight."

"Well, would you like to join my business partners and I. We were just about wrapping things up, but I'd be willing to stay if you decide to join me."

"No...no, please. I'd like to have dinner alone, if you don't mind. But thanks for the offer Mr..."

"Oh, I'm sorry. Collins, Collins Jefferson. And yours?"

"Nokea Brooks," I said, smiling. Just then the Maitre D told me my table was ready. Collins took my hand, kissed it, and I thanked him again for the offer.

As I looked at the menu, I could feel Collins staring at me from across the room. He had a perfect view and was using it to his advantage. I crossed my legs to make sure he couldn't see up my short black skirt, and put the menu up high so he couldn't see my face. Feeling a bit uncomfortable, I eased the menu over a bit and noticed Collins getting ready to leave. He smiled and waved goodbye. I waved back and put the menu down on the table.

When the waiter came to take my order, he put a bottle of wine on the table and laid a business card down next to it. He said it was from the gentleman over there, but when we looked up, he said the gentleman was already gone.

Smiling, I picked the card up and it was Collins' business card. On the back he asked if we could have dinner soon and invited me to call him. I put the card in my purse and waited for my food to come.

After dinner, I got a room at the Sheraton Plaza Hotel for the night. Jaylin had been calling me like crazy trying to find out what was wrong, but I didn't return his calls. I hoped that Pat would call, but by the way things went down, I didn't expect to hear from her any time soon.

JAYLIN

I spent the entire night at Scorpio's place hoping she would come to her senses and come home. By Friday morning, I was sick to my stomach. If she took Mackenzie from me again, I thought, I was going to kill her ass. Take the pussy, that's replaceable, but my child, however, is not.

Since I told Nokea I wanted to keep LJ for the weekend, I hurried home to see him, and tried to figure out what to do about Mackenzie. This time, I didn't give a shit who got hurt. In my mind, I was willing to go to the extreme to get Mackenzie back.

Nokea's car was in the driveway, but since we talked about LJ spending the night early on in the week, I didn't understand why she was at my place. When I opened the door, she came rushing out like she was upset about something. I called her name several times, but she ignored me. Nanny B said that she had no idea what upset her, so I called Nokea on her cell phone to make sure everything went cool with her and Pat.

Since she wouldn't answer her phone, I left her at peace and went upstairs to my room. I noticed the TV buzzing, so I walked over to it and turned it off. When a tape ejected from the VCR, I pulled it out and saw it was the tape Mr. McDaniels had given me.

Nokea was angry because she saw the fucking tape. Why in the hell would she go through my things any damn way? I thought. I threw the tape on the floor and fell back on my chaise.

"Jaylin." Nanny B said, coming into my room. "What was that loud noise?"

"Nothing. I just dropped something."

"Well, be careful. I was a little worried when you didn't come home last night."

"Sorry about that, and I didn't mean to worry you. I just needed some time to clear my head."

"I know how that is. But, if you're hungry, I cooked a Pot Roast for you. In the meantime," she said, picking LJ up. "I'm going to lay LJ down for the night. He's had a busy day."

"Bring him here and let me hold him." Nanny B put LJ down on the floor and he stepped his way over to me. I smiled and applauded his walking efforts. I picked him up and lay him on my chest. "Let him chill with me tonight. I'll put him to bed a little later, okay," I said, looking at Nanny B.

"That's fine. He's your son, you know? I know sometimes I get too attached, but I can't help myself. I love him like my own."

"I know you do. And trust me, I appreciate everything you do for us. Anyway, who can help themselves from getting so attached to him."

She smiled, reached into her pocket, and pulled out a piece of paper. "Here," she said, giving it to me. "Scorpio's sister Leslie called about an hour ago. I told her you would be here shortly, so call her when you get a chance. She sounded like it was important."

"Has Scorpio called?"

"No, she hasn't."

I reached for the piece of paper and Nanny B left the room. Before calling Leslie back, I tried Nokea on her phone again. I left a message and told her I knew she had seen the tape and we needed to talk. Wasn't no telling when she would want to discuss it, but I knew it was time to put closure to our half-ass relationship.

When I called Leslie some silly asshole asked who I was, put the phone down, and left it off the receiver for about five minutes. She finally picked up and recognized my voice.

"Jaylin?"

"Yeah, it's me."

"Listen, I called you earlier to tell you that Mackenzie is with me. I know you and Scorpio had a dispute, but she asked me to make sure Mackenzie spends some time with you."

"So, Mackenzie's there with you?"

"Yes but—"

"I'm on my way. Tell her I'm on my way to get her."

"Jaylin, wait a minute. I understand how anxious you are about seeing her, but Scorpio said she only—"

"Fuck what Scorpio said! She took off, left her child behind, so fuck her! I'm on my way to get Mackenzie now."

"Hey! I'm not going to argue with you about this. I'm just trying to do what she asked me to do. And for your information she was extremely upset when she left. She just needs time alone to get her life back in order. I offered to watch Mackenzie, and out of her love for you, she asked that I made sure Mackenzie got a chance to see you. So, watch what you say about her. She's a better woman than you think she is."

"Yeah, yeah, yeah…whatever. Look, just pack Mackenzie a few things up, and tell her I'm on my way."

"Not right now. I'm on my way to the Laundromat and she has chores to do. I'll drop her off when I'm finished."

"Chores? Fuck your chores. Can't you drop her off before you go?"

"You'd better watch it, fool, or you won't see her at all. I have seven kids and they're all going to help, including Mackenzie. I'm not making any special trips to your place just because you want me to. And the only reason I'm bringing her over there to stay is because she won't stop bugging me about you. So, be patient and I'll be there when I get there."

I gave Leslie directions to my house and told her in so many words to hurry the hell up with Mackenzie. It wasn't like she didn't know where I lived because the last time she brought her ass over here, she took Mackenzie from me. Just the thought of Mackenzie helping her with her dirty-ass clothes upset me, but wasn't shit I could do.

LJ and I were lying in bed playing on my laptop, and waiting for Mackenzie to come. Finally, at one-thirty in the morning, Leslie decided to show up. I heard the doorbell and rushed downstairs to answer it. When I opened the door, Leslie was standing on the porch with Mackenzie standing next to her. Mackenzie smiled and held her arms out for me to pick her up.

"Girl, you're getting too big for me to be picking you up." I tickled her and picked her up anyway. She wrapped her arms around my neck and kissed me on the cheek. "Thanks for bringing her by, Leslie. And if you talk to Scorpio tell her to call me."

"I'll tell her, but she won't call. And I'll be back to pick up Mackenzie on Sunday night."

I looked out at the station wagon parked in front of my house with her seven kids jumping around in it acting like fools. "Leslie, please just let her stay. It looks like you already got your hands full,

151

so let her stay with me until Scorpio comes back. If Scorpio calls for her, tell her to call me. Tell her I won't question her about her whereabouts; I'll just pass the phone to Mackenzie."

"I don't know Jaylin. Let me talk to Scorpio first. I'll call you Sunday and let you know then."

She kissed Mackenzie and left.

I didn't give a fuck what she or anybody else said; Mackenzie was not going back to Leslie's house to save her soul.

I carried Mackenzie up the steps on my back, and when she laughed loudly I asked her to be quiet so she wouldn't wake up LJ. She quickly ran into her room, changed into her nightgown, and climbed into bed with us. In less than fives minutes, she was out like a light.

I couldn't sleep a wink. I had been downstairs about fifty times nibbling on the Pot Roast Nanny B cooked earlier, and cutting slices of her pineapple-upside-down cake. When I passed by her in the hallway, we laughed, as I bent down and picked up some crumbs I had dropped on the floor.

"You should be ashamed of yourself," she whispered. "Is there anymore left for me?"

"Yeah, there's plenty. But save some for tomorrow, alright."

"Please. If it's not enough, I'll make another one. Now, get your greedy butt back in bed before the children wake up."

I laughed and went back into my room. LJ was lying on his stomach with his thumb in his mouth and his butt in the air. Mackenzie was lying on her back with her curly long black hair spread out on my pillow looking beautiful like Scorpio. I kissed both of them and tried to take LJ's thumb out of his mouth. When he squirmed around, I left him alone.

I grabbed a pillow off my bed and laid it on the floor. Then I picked up the tape that Mr. McDaniels had given me and slid it into the VCR. I propped my head up with the pillow, and started to watch it.

About five minutes into it, I had a smile on my face. It was straight up wild. I had no idea that I was setting it out like that. No wonder her husband wanted me to disappear. And Heather, she was all into it, and looked as if she was enjoying every inch of my thang inside of her.

Continuing to watch the tape, my dick was starting to rise. Having no ass in sight, I stopped the tape, laid on my back, and looked up at the ceiling. Nokea had to be devastated after seeing something like that. And I knew it wasn't in my best interest to lie to her again, so I hoped she'd call back tomorrow. If not, I was determined to see her and make things right between us. As for Scorpio, I wasn't sure how I was going to deal with her. I was already missing her, but was fighting every ounce of a feeling I had for her. If time away is what she needed, then that's what I was going to give her. Eventually she'd realize what she's missing, and come back begging for forgiveness.

When I opened my eyes, LJ and Mackenzie were hanging off the edge of the bed staring at me on the floor. Knowing LJ wasn't going to keep his balance for long, I hopped up and grabbed him. Mackenzie laughed and followed us into the bathroom.

"Mackenzie, can your daddy have some privacy? Take LJ to Nanny B's room to see if she's awake yet."

She took LJ by the hand. "Come on, LJ. Let's go downstairs. I think she's in the kitchen."

"Be careful, baby. He's not good with steps yet, okay. Ask Nanny B to help you."

"Okay," she said, walking slowly with LJ, and holding his hand. Nanny B heard me and waited for them at the door. I looked at them and realized I was one lucky man. All my tedious problems on the outside couldn't overtake the love I had in my home.

I was getting out of the shower when the phone rang. I wrapped a towel around my waist and when I answered it, it was Nokea.

"Hey, where are you?" I asked.

"I'm at the Sheraton," she said, dryly. "We need to talk."

"Yes, we do. How long are you going to be there?"

"I'm on my way home. Meet me there in about an hour. And don't bring LJ with you."

"Okay. An hour it is. But I wanted to tell you how sorry—"

"Jaylin, no need to apologize. Meet me in an hour." She hung up.

I went into the closet and slid on a pair of jeans. Then I grabbed a thick brown Cashmere sweater off the hanger and put it on

153

as well. Since I'd planned to spend the entire weekend with my kids, I told Nanny B I'd be right back.

When I arrived at Nokea's house, she was already there. I stood on her porch, rubbed my hands together, and tried to keep them warm. She finally opened the door and immediately turned away. I closed the door behind me and followed her into the bedroom.

She was on the phone with her mother, so I took a seat in a chair caddy cornered from her bed. Before she ended the call, she told her mother that she loved her and sat down on the edge of the bed.

"Aren't you going to take your coat and hat off? I do have heat, you know," she said.

I edged up from the chair and removed my coat. I left my hat on because I didn't anticipate on staying long. "I know you saw the tape yesterday," I said. "Question is, why must you go through my things all the damn time, Nokea?"

"Jaylin, I didn't go through your things. Your briefcase fell open and the tape came out. I put it in the VCR wondering why the words, son of a bitch was on it."

"Curiosity killed the cat. So now you know that I fuck white women too. What's the big deal?"

"Who said it's a big deal? It doesn't matter to me if the women in your life are African American, Caucasian, Italian, Puerto Rican, Irish…who cares? It's not about them anymore; it's about you. For as long as I can remember, it's always been about you. You go through life just constantly hurting people, and the thing is, you don't even care. Is it ever going to be about someone else other than just you?"

"It is about someone else, Nokea. My children, that's who. You had your chance and you fucked up. What in the hell do you want me to do about it?" I rubbed my hands together, thinking. "You know the more and more I think about everything that's happened lately, I blame you for creating this monster in me. I was trying to get myself on the right track, and then you played me with the Stephon bullshit."

"Wait a minute," she said, angrily. "I just knew you were going to blame me for your ignorance." She stood up and went over by her nightstand. She opened the drawer and pulled out a black small pistol and held it in her hand. She aimed it at me. "Get on your knees, Jaylin" she asked, politely.

"Woman, you're crazy. I ain't—"

"Damn it, Jaylin!" she yelled. "I'm in control now! Don't argue with me, just do it! And don't think I wouldn't shoot you right now because I'm truly feeling as if I have nothing to lose."

I thought about rushing Nokea and taking the gun from her, but under the circumstances, that wasn't the best thing to do. And not knowing where her mind was, I wasn't taking any chances. I did as she asked and eased down on one knee. "Okay, so now that you have my attention, now what?"

"How does it feel letting a woman have control? For once in your life, how does it feel?" She moved in closer with the gun and aimed it directly at my face.

"Nokea, look. I'm not going to fuck around with you like this—"

"Shut up and listen! Can you do that for one time in your life?" I nodded my head, as I saw her hands shaking. "This bullshit between us is over! I don't need anymore apologies, no more of your lies, nor do I need anymore of your hand-me-down-ass dick. We have a son together and that's it. Don't call me unless it concerns him, don't touch me unless I ask you to, and don't even think about grabbing this gun because I will blow your goddamn brains out!"

"Fine. But can't we talk about this without the gun?" I asked, getting ready to get up.

"Stay there! I didn't tell you to get up yet. And no we can't talk without the gun because you won't listen to me without it."

"I promise you that if you put the gun down I'll listen. You've made your point, alright?"

Suddenly the phone rang and startled Nokea. I quickly hopped up and grabbed her around the waist. She fell back on the bed and the gun fell to the floor. She screamed and kicked, as I pressed my body weight down on her so she couldn't move.

"Calm your ass down! Would you?" I yelled and we continued to struggle. Realizing that she couldn't over power me, she chilled. I looked eye to eye with her and held her hands tightly together. "I know you don't want to hear this, but I'm sorry. I understand how upset you must be, but I can't change anything that's happened in the past. I love you, Nokea, but I'm not in love with you anymore. Every time I see you, I think of you...you making love to Stephon. Every time I touch you, I think of him touching you. I thought if you and I got married it would take away my hurt, but I now know that our marriage would have been a mistake." I raised up, as I seemed to have her attention. I pulled her next to me and held her in my arms. "Aside of that, I can't stop being who I am. I love women too much to settle down, and I'm happy with the way things are in my life."

"But what about all these years we've shared together? Don't they account for anything? Why do they have to go to waste?"

"Our years together didn't go to waste. We got a beautiful son, Nokea, and we've always had each other to depend on. I knew making love to you on my birthday was a bad idea, but I just couldn't help myself. You will always be in my heart, but now, I have to start looking at you in a different way."

"And I guess I'll have to do the same." She laid her head on my shoulder and cried. "I don't want to hurt anymore, Jaylin. I'm tired of pointing the finger at each other. Do you think we can get on with our lives in a sensible way without being together?"

"Of course I do. But if you ever put a gun on me again, I'll hurt you, Nokea. I don't take shit like that too lightly. You hear me?" I moved her away and looked at her. She could tell I wasn't playing.

"The gun wasn't loaded, stupid. I just wanted you to listen to me."

I took her arms from around my neck, then leaned over and picked up the gun. I removed the clip and it was empty. "You're a dangerous ass lil something," I said, getting up off the bed. "Where did you get this gun from anyway and where are the bullets?"

"Jaylin, LJ and I live in this big house alone. If an intruder comes up in here, I'm going to be ready. My father gave it to me and I keep the bullets in the drawer."

I went over to the drawer and opened it. I pulled the bullets out and placed them in the clip. "If an intruder comes in you can't do anything with an empty clip."

"I took the bullets out before you came because I didn't know if you would try and take the gun away from me."

"Well, don't play around like that. One of us could have gotten seriously hurt." I walked over to Nokea and pulled her off the

156

bed. "Come here," I said, holding her in my arms. "I'm sorry things didn't work out between us, but you know everything happens for a reason."

She placed her head against my chest and held me tightly. "I know. I'm a true believer in that as well, but I will never understand why they didn't."

"But in the meantime," I pushed her back and placed the gun directly on the side of her head. "This is not a good feeling, is it?" She shook her head. "I don't care how damn upset you are with me, don't ever think about doing this to me again." I pulled the trigger and she screamed loudly, then held her face in her hands.

She snatched the gun away from me. "Jaylin! There were bullets in there. You could have seriously killed me!"

"I know, but I didn't feel like it this time. Maybe next time I will." I snatched the gun back, then put it at the top of her closet. "Keep this damn thing up here. I would hate for my son to get a hold of it. Then I'd really have to kill you."

"Whatever," she said, still a bit shaken up.

Nokea packed a few things at her house and drove back to my place with me. In the car she told me how things went down with Pat, and I really felt sorry for her. Pat was the only friend she had and to lose her friendship and our relationship all in one day proved to me that she was a stronger woman than I thought she was.

When we got back to my house, Nanny B cooked us a scrumptious dinner and made another one of her pineapple-upside-down cakes. Since Heather had been calling me all week, I went into my office and finally called her back.

"Yes," I said, moody. "What's up, Heather?"

"What's up is why haven't you called me? My husband has been making all kinds of threats and I thought—"

"Well, you thought wrong. Your husband doesn't have enough courage to follow through with shit like that, Heather. And I find it quite odd that you didn't know there were cameras throughout your house."

"I didn't know. Really, you have to believe me. If I had known I never would have asked you to bring me home."

157

"That's bullshit and you know it. All I can say is if you love him, you'd better warn him. If he pays me another one of his unexpected visits, shit it going to start happening to his ass."

"Don't worry. He's a bunch of mouth and never follows through with his threats. He's threatened to kick me out and I'm still here. If he wasn't gone all the time, and sleeping around with other women, maybe sex with you and I never would have happened."

"Good to know that you used me. And I'll be happy to say that I used you too, so game is over, Heather. Have a nice life and holla at me some other time."

"Jaylin, wait. This was never a game for me. I'm feeling something for you. I haven't been happy for a long time, and being with you just makes me feel so wanted. I was thinking about having another ron-da-voo in your office again."

"Don't think so, baby. I'll pass this time, but whenever you see your husband, don't forget to tell him what I said. Again, if you love him, you'd better stop him from coming around me." I hung up.

Before the day was over, I was hoping to hear from Scorpio, since Mackenzie was with me, but she hadn't called. Leslie was supposed to pick Mackenzie up tomorrow, but she left a message and said something came up and asked if Mackenzie could stay the week with me. It didn't matter to me because Mackenzie wasn't going anywhere. I did call Leslie back to thank her, and reminded her to tell Scorpio to call me.

By eleven o'clock I was ready to shut down. Nanny B and Nokea cleaned up the kitchen, and LJ and Mackenzie were in Mackenzie's room knocked out. LJ had his own room but it was truly a waste. Either he was in with Mackenzie, or bundled up with Nanny B or me.

I could tell Nokea didn't want to go home, so I asked if she wanted to spend the night with us. She accepted my offer and thanked me for being supportive. I went to the linen closet and grabbed some extra blankets and pillows from the shelves. I handed them to Nokea and led her to one of the guestrooms.

"Sorry, but this is the only bedroom that doesn't have a TV. If you want to, you can come in my room for a while and watch TV with me. I'll be up for a while."

"Okay. I just might do that. But before I do anything, I would love to take a relaxing bath, if you don't mind."

"Well, there's six bathrooms around here. Feel free to use either one of them."

"But yours is the only one with a Jacuzzi tub. Would it be okay if I relaxed in your tub?"

"Hey, not a problem. I'll go run some bath water for you now."

I went into the bathroom and started Nokea's water. I dropped in a few flower scented fragrance balls that dissolved in the water. They were Scorpio's, but I was sure Nokea wouldn't mind. As I sat on the bed and pulled off my shoes, Nokea stood in the doorway with a towel wrapped around her.

"Is it ready?" she asked.

I looked at her smooth silky-brown legs and could only think dirty things to myself. "Yeah, it's ready. Go see if the temperature is cool. I like it hot, but maybe you don't."

She went into the bathroom and closed the door behind her. Then she poked her head out of the door. "I like it hot too, but this is scorching hot. Are you trying to burn me or something?"

"No. It's not that hot," I said, getting off the bed, and heading towards the bathroom to turn on the cold water.

She stopped me. "I can do it. Thanks, though. Just find something for me to put on when I get out. And, look through your DVD's for a good movie to watch."

"Yes ma'am," I said, saluting her. "Anything you want."

She laughed and closed the door.

I went into the closet and took one of my white long shirts off a hanger. I still had the negligee I bought from Victoria's Secret, but I thought giving it to her would be inappropriate since we agreed to keep our relationship strictly platonic. The last thing I needed was for her to get the wrong idea.

By the time Nokea came out of the bathroom, I had already changed into my pajama pants, and was forty-five minutes into watching John Q. She came out with a towel wrapped around her, and I pointed to the white long shirt that was on my chaise.

"So, you couldn't wait until I finished before you started the movie?" she asked removing the towel from around her.

159

I sucked my teeth, and gave her naked body a quick glimpse. "You took too long. I thought you drowned up in there or something."

She looked around the room. "Do you have any body lotion around here? You know, something with a feminine touch because my skin feels awfully dry."

"Yeah, I do. It's in the bathroom closet. It's not mine, it's Scorpio's. I hope you don't mind using it."

She flaunted her naked ass in front of me and went into the bathroom. She came out squeezing lotion in her hands. "I don't care whose lotion it is. My skin is calling for some moisture. And no wonder you're forever taking baths, your tub is so relaxing. That was actually my first time being in there—alone. I kind of enjoyed it." She lifted her leg on the chaise and rubbed lotion on it.

"It is comfortable, ain't it? I don't know what I would do without that tub in my life."

I continued taking quick peeks at Nokea. Horny as hell, I felt my thang rise underneath the sheets. By the way she was rubbing herself, I could tell she was teasing me, so I placed my hand on my dick to keep it down.

After Nokea finished, she turned out the lamp, and climbed in bed. My California style king-sized bed was big enough where it left plenty of room between us. She slid two pillows behind her back, and another one behind her head.

"Are you comfortable?" I asked, looking over at her.

"Yes. Very. How about you?"

"Always." I turned and looked at the TV.

Nokea yawned. "I'm tired. I think I'm going to call it a night. Besides, I've seen John Q about five times already."

"Five times? Why five times?"

She gave me a crazy look. "Duh…Denzel Washington. Need I say more."

"Aw, come on. He ain't that fine where you got to look at the damn movie five times."

"That's your opinion. And you're definitely entitled to it." She pulled the covers back and started getting out of bed. I quickly reached over and touched her hand.

"Sit back for a minute," I asked politely. She hesitated for a moment, but eased back in bed.

160

"Jaylin, I don't want any trouble out of you tonight. We said—"

I moved over closer to her and eased my body next to hers. "I know what we said earlier, but this is going to be difficult. Can we at least try to do without each other after tonight?"

She stared me in the eyes. "But I…I thought we said—"

"After tonight, okay?" I whispered and started to unbutton her shirt.

"After tonight, Jaylin?"

"Yes, baby, after tonight."

"No," she said, grabbing my hands. "We can't continue to do this."

"And we won't. After tonight, I promise you we won't." I kissed her and started to unbutton her shirt again. I removed it and cuffed her breasts in my hands. I closed my eyes and started to suck them. She leaned her head back, and opened her legs so I could get on top of her. I pecked my lips down her stomach and massaged her breasts.

She tightly gripped the cherry-oak thick pole on my headboard, and rested her thighs on my shoulders.

"After tonight," she moaned, as I slurped into her insides.

I stopped and licked the wetness off my lips. "I promise…after tonight." I leaned my head back down, and when I got ready to go at it again, she placed her hands in between her legs, then slid them off my shoulders.

"Jaylin, when are we going to stop this?" She leaned forward, put her face in front of mine, and then kissed me.

"Tomorrow. We're going to stop this tomorrow, so come on, let me finish," I said, trying to get her back into position.

"No we're not. We agreed to end this earlier, and that's what we're going to do. We just can't keep doing this to ourselves. All this back and forth, wishy-washy stuff is driving me crazy. For once, lets just stick to what we say and see how it goes."

Disappointed, I rolled over and placed my hand behind my head. I looked up at the ceiling and Nokea got out of bed.

"Goodnight," she said, smiling, and heading for the door.

"Goodnight, Nokea," I huffed, as she left the room.

After lying in bed for hours wishing I had something to get into, I finally dozed off. Around four o'clock in the morning, I crept into the kitchen to get a piece of cake. I could tell somebody had been there before me because there was a big chunk missing from it. I laughed and hurried back upstairs before Nanny B saw me. Before I went back to my room, I cracked the door to Mackenzie's room and checked on her and LJ. I noticed he was gone, so I went to the guestroom where Nokea was to see if he was in bed with her. When I called her name she sounded wide-awake.

"What?" she said, softly.

"Is LJ in bed with you?"

"No." She pulled the covers back and got out of bed. "I thought he was in Mackenzie's room."

"He was earlier." We walked down the hallway together to Nanny B's room. She was sitting in a rocking chair and reading LJ a story, while he was sleeping in her arms. She placed her finger on her lips and told us to be quiet. Then she motioned her hand for us to get out. We both smiled and closed the door. Nokea went back to the guestroom and got in bed. I leaned against the doorway and looked at her lying in the dark.

"What? Why are you standing there looking crazy? If I didn't know any better I'd think you were Freddy Krugger or somebody trying to come get me," she said.

"Ah, I want to come get you, but only in a good way."

"Jaylin, please let it go for the night. Stop trying to temp me, alright?"

"You're the one who started it. You got your naked-ass out of the tub teasing me and shit. Let me just come in and spank that ass one last time."

"Spank? Now, you know I don't get down like that."

I walked into the room and closed the door behind me. The room was pitch black and I climbed into bed with Nokea. "Well, show me how you get down. From previous experience, I know you're capable, but I'd just like to feel it right now."

Nokea took a deep breath and by mid-morning we had seriously gotten down. Gotten down on some sleep because she wasn't giving in. She was actually standing her ground and even though I was disappointed, I was glad at least one of us was sticking to the plan.

SCORPIO

As hard as I was trying not to be, I was miserable without Jaylin. It had only been one week since I'd last seen him, and there I was acting as if it had been a lifetime.

After he dissed me at his office that day, I had to get away. I called Shane later that night and apologized to him for my ignorance. He wasn't home, but I left a message on his voice mail. I wasn't trying to be his woman, but deep in my heart, I knew calling him because Jaylin wanted me to was tacky on my part. And for Jaylin to ask me to do something so immature was stupid on his.

I'd guessed their past history together was more intense than I thought. And for me to let Shane go down on me was the worst thing I could have ever done. The last thing I wanted was to give them the opportunity to sit around and talk about me.

When I left Jaylin's office that day, I went to my old boss, Jackson, and begged him to help me. He'd always been there for me when I was in dying need, so he had no problem giving me the keys to his get-away house in Denver, Colorado. Since I had very little money, he wrote me a check for $5,000 and told me to repay him later. I insisted all I needed was a few months to get myself together, and promised him I would somehow repay him his money. When he talked about sexual favors, I thanked him for his help and jetted.

I knew there was no way I could stay in St. Louis to finish school, so I had to put my career on hold until later. I wasn't too happy about doing it, but Jaylin would be a set back for me if I hung around any longer. And being away from Mackenzie was the hardest thing I had to do, but the last thing I wanted her to see was how unstable and miserable I was. I knew she would question me, and I wasn't prepared to tell her what a cruel person Jaylin had been to me, since she loved him so much. Realistically, I couldn't even offer her stability right now. Jaylin had everything in his control, including her. I had no one to blame but myself for thinking he'd have my back forever.

After I came back from Westfield Center in downtown Denver, I put a kettle of water on the white old-fashioned stove with black burners to make some tea. Jackson's get-away house turned out to be a real hole in the wall. It had one small bedroom covered with dingy flowered wallpaper and buckling hard wood floors. The bathroom had a white tub and sink with rust spots, and looked as if they hadn't been cleaned in years. The tub, itself, looked like it was about to fall through the floor, and slightly tilted to the side. Now, the kitchen wasn't too bad. Even though there was a foundation crack in the wall right next to the window, and the appliances were seriously outdated, the cabinets had been refinished with a glossy cherry-oak wood. The living room was nothing to brag about either. Especially since it was empty and was painted light green. But who was I to complain? For a person who didn't have anywhere else to go, I'd just have to cope with it.

After I tried to remove the stains in the tub, I gave up. I'd been taking wash-ups since I got here, and they were just going to have to do. By late evening, I called Leslie to check on Mackenzie. I'd wondered if she'd gotten a chance to see Jaylin, but when Leslie told me Mackenzie had been with him since Friday, I was a bit upset with her. She explained how Mackenzie lit-up when she saw him, and said there was no way she was going to take her away from him. Knowing what kind of love Mackenzie had for him, I couldn't do nothing but agree. I thanked her and called Jaylin's house.

I was praying that Nanny B answered, but when he did, I hung up. I waited a few minutes, then called back again, as I tried to get up enough courage to talk.

"Hello," he said, sharply.

"Jaylin, it's me. Where's Mackenzie?"

"Busy."

"Busy doing what?"

"Busy minding her own business."

"Kids her age don't have any business."

"Yeah, they do. She's got more business than you have, so what do you want?"

"I want to talk to my daughter, that's what I want."

"So, you didn't call to talk to me?"

"No."

"Okay, cool."

He gave the phone to Mackenzie.

She was so happy to hear my voice. I told her I had to go visit my sick cousin in Denver, and would be back soon. I asked how things were going at her new pre-school and with Jaylin and she seemed overjoyed. She told me about her new best friend, Megan, and told me LJ was already walking. When I asked her if she wanted to visit with Aunt Leslie, she said no. She begged me to let her stay with Jaylin and I told her yes.

After talking to her for at least fifteen minutes, I told her I'd see her soon, and asked her to put Jaylin on the phone. He got on the phone and continued with his attitude.

"What?" he said.

"I just wanted to say thanks for watching Mackenzie. You have no idea what it means—"

"Look, don't fool yourself. I'm not doing this for you. I'm doing this for me. Take all the time you need. Hell, take a year or two all I care, she'll be just fine."

"I don't plan on being gone that long. I just need time to sort through these feelings I—"

"Scorpio, remember, you said you didn't call to talk to me. You talked to Mackenzie, so I'll holla at you later. Besides, I'm watching the football game right now."

"Okay, well I'll call to check on her in a few days. If you need me for anything call Leslie. She knows how to get in touch with me."

Jaylin was quiet, then just hung up. I stood there with the phone in my hand and still couldn't believe him. I put the phone down and poured a cup of tea. Lonely, I went into the bedroom, pulled a blanket off the bed, and carried it back into the kitchen. I tucked it

166

underneath my arm, and stood by the old time metal heater against the wall, then banged on it. Finally feeling some heat, I wrapped myself in the blanket and sat down at the kitchen table.

Thinking about Jaylin, I folded my legs up against my chest and started to cry. I cried because this was a serious set back for me. I felt like I was finally getting ahead by at least going back to school, but now that even seemed like a thing of the past. How was I ever going to manage without him? At least I was able to keep money in my pockets before I met him, but taking my clothes off for men was something I just didn't want to start doing again. It was a last option for me, but it was still an option. Either way, I had to come up with a plan. This house was giving me the creeps, and I had to make a better life for myself if Mackenzie would ever want to be a part of it. I kind of felt like if I never came back again she wouldn't even miss me. As long as she had Jaylin, she seemed to be just fine.

Before shutting down for the night, I took a few more sips of tea and put the cup in the sink. I spread the blanket on the living room floor and lay down. I reached over and turned on the tiny black and white TV on the floor that had a hanger for an antenna. I flipped through the fuzzy channels and looked for something to watch, when the phone rang. The only people who knew how to reach me were Leslie and Jackson, but when I heard Jaylin's voice, I was shocked.

"What did you say?" I asked.

"I said the football game is off. I'm ready to talk whenever you are."

"How did you get this number? I called your house anonymously. Did Leslie give it to you?"

"Scorpio, don't play yourself, alright? You know better than I do that I have ways of finding out things when I want to. And no, Leslie didn't give it to me."

"Well, how did you get it? Jackson, right."

"Let's just say you don't cover your tracks very well. Is Denver as cold as St. Louis is? I'm sure it is, but if you want to stay cold, oh well."

"Okay, so you know where I am. Now what?"

"Nothing. Stay there. I'm just calling you back because you sounded like you wanted to talk."

"I did, but I don't feel like talking now. Besides, what I have to say doesn't matter anyway."

"You're right, it doesn't." He hung up.

I took a deep breath because the last thing I needed was Jaylin calling here with his mess. It puzzled me as to where he got his information from, so I called Leslie to find out. She didn't answer, but when I called Jackson's place to ask him, he stuttered, but said he hadn't talked to Jaylin. By the sound of Jackson's voice, I knew Jaylin must have gotten the information from him. Especially if money was involved. I yelled at him for snaking me, and told him I might as well have stayed in St. Louis if I had known he would tell my whereabouts. So, to avoid any bullshit, I promised myself not to talk to Jaylin when he called, and took the phone off the hook for the rest of the night.

The sound of the TV loudly buzzing awakened me, and I reached over to turn it off. Chilly, I lay on the floor swaddled up in a blanket. I went into the bedroom and looked at the alarm clock. It showed three twenty-five in the morning, and still tired, I plopped down on the bed, and tried to get back to sleep.

As I dozed off, I heard a soft knock at the door. I looked over at the clock again and it now showed five minutes after four. I slowly walk to the door thinking somebody was at the wrong house, but when I turned on the porch light and saw Jaylin, I couldn't believe my eyes.

"Why are you here, Jaylin?" I asked, whispering through the door.

"Just open the door. It's cold out here."

Not wanting to be bothered, I turned the porch light out, and headed back into the bedroom. Time away from him is what I needed, and that's what I intended on getting.

He banged harder for a few more minutes, and then he stopped. I closed my eyes and prayed for strength. But when I heard footsteps coming down the hallway, I sat up in bed. I could barely see because it was dark, so I quickly reached over to the lamp and turned it on. Jaylin stood in the doorway swinging a set of keys around in his hand.

"Now, I come all this way to see you and this is how you treat me, huh?"

I rolled my eyes and moved my hair away from my face. "Why are you doing this? Did Jackson give you a key too?"

"Baby, you know we brothas stick together. With some help of a little cash, he told me everything and offered me a key to get in. He said you would be difficult, and didn't want me to waste a trip down here."

Furious, I got out of bed and bumped his shoulder, as I past by him standing in the doorway. I walked into the kitchen so I could see why the heater wasn't giving off any heat. As I banged on it, Jaylin leaned against the kitchen counter with his arms folded, and stared at me. He had on a long tan Cashmere coat and tan leather pants. His v-neck cotton cream and tan ribbed sweater matched his Cashmere bobby hat that was tilted to the side, and showed his curly black hair. And the aroma he was carrying with him made me want to melt right into his arms. He was looking spectacular, and I was trying to do everything I could to avoid him. I'm sure his purpose was so I could clearly see what I was missing.

"Damn!" I said, continuing to bang on the heater. He unfolded his arms and came over by me. I was looking awful and didn't want him getting too close.

"You know you're going to break the damn thing if you keep hitting on it like that. You're probably better off buying a space heater." As soon as he said that, the heat kicked on. I went over to the kitchen table and sat down. I lay my head down on my arm and looked over at him. "Why can't you just leave me alone? Haven't you tortured me enough?" I asked

He removed his coat and put it on the back of the chair. I couldn't help but notice his big bulge in his tight ass leather pants, so I quickly looked down at the floor so I wouldn't stare. "Torture?" he said, straddling the chair after he turned it around. "Is that what you think I'm doing to you?"

I looked up. "Yes. Yes, I really do. All I'm asking for is time to get myself together, and you won't even allow me that."

"Well, I'm not here to torture you, Scorpio. I kind of missed you. Came all this way to see if you would come back with me. Christmas is coming soon and I don't want you here all by yourself."

"I'm okay. I think I'm going to stay here for a while. Maybe, even see if Jackson will let me rent this place out if I agree to fix it up

169

a bit. So, don't get too comfortable with Mackenzie being around. If things go according to plan, I'll be sending for her soon. You'll just have to visit her here."

"Really," he said, looking around at the kitchen. "This place actually needs a lot of work. Are you sure you want to bring Mackenzie to this type of environment?"

"Jaylin, she hasn't always had the finer things in life and neither have I. For me, this ain't all that bad. Especially if I fix it up like I want to. Mackenzie will just have to adjust. Like it or not, sorry, but she's going to live wherever I live."

Jaylin took his hat off and put it on the table. He picked up a toothpick and twirled it around in his mouth, then pulled it out. "Scorpio, why don't you cut the bullshit and come home with me? This ain't no way to live. It's dirty, muggy, and colder than a motherfucker in here. It really doesn't suit you at all, and if you think I'm going to allow Mackenzie to come here with you and suffer, you're sadly mistaken. If you want to fuck yourself, then do so. Don't make her suffer when she doesn't have to."

"What is so wrong with me wanting my child with me? I don't care how bad this place might look to you, but once I fix everything up, it's going to look nice. Like I said, it might not be what you're accustomed to, but Mackenzie and I will be just fine. Besides, it's about time I had something to call my own anyway. That way I don't have to worry about anybody trying to run my life. You know what I mean?"

"So, this is about your independence, huh? Trying to prove to old Jaylin you don't need any handouts from him. I'm cool with that, so let me not waste anymore of your time."

He raised up and grabbed his coat from the chair. I stood up and watched as he put it on. And as soon as he picked up his hat from the table, a roach crawled across it. He shook his hat and smiled, as he held it in his hand.

"You sure this is what you want to do?" he asked.

My eyes slowly watered. "This is not what I want to do, but this is something I have to do for me."

He pulled his coat back, reached into his pants pockets for the keys, then tossed them on the table. Immediately, he noticed me lusting at the sight of him.

"I'm not going to come back here again, so don't worry. And I'm not going to beg you to be with me, so don't worry about that either. I really thought you understood me better than anybody, but I guess I was wrong. And before I go, if you'd like to get your fuck on, just say so. Don't just stand there staring me down being all fake and shit like you don't want me." Since I didn't respond, he put both hands in his pockets and walked up to me. Then he whispered in my ear, "Are we fucking or what?"

I shook my head, "No. Not this time. I need a life absent from you, and finally I'm going to have it."

"You think so," he said, walking behind me. He reached his hands around the front of my silk robe and tried to untie it. I grabbed his hands and stopped him, but when he unzipped his pants, and pressed himself up against me, I lost it. He leaned my body on the kitchen table and held my hips from behind. After he flipped up my robe and took a look at my naked ass, I felt so ashamed. I rested my body on the table and cried as I allowed him to have his way toying with my insides. He held his dick in his hand, and circled my pussy with the thickness of his head until he had the pleasure of soaking me. And when he did, he pounded deeply in, just enough to make me think about what I was missing, then backed himself out. Continuing to torture me, he moved back and zipped his pants. Then, with the tip of his tongue, he leaned down and licked his name tattooed across my ass.

Not even finishing what he started, he straightened my robe, leaned over me, and whispered in my ear, "With a pussy that wet, you'll never be rid of me. So, stop fooling yourself and quit with the games. The only one who's going to play themselves is you." He raised up, then left the kitchen.

I fought hard trying not to go after him, but when I heard the front door open I just couldn't let him go.

"Jaylin!" I yelled from the kitchen. "Wait!"

"What's up?" he said, turning around, and holding the door open. "Have you changed your mind about coming home with me?"

"I'll come back only if you're willing to make some changes. Must you continue to do this to me? Did you come all this way just to walk in here for fifteen minutes, tease the hell out of me, and go back home? All I wanted was for you to tell me you love me, you miss me, and that you can't live without me. If not that, then share with me how much you want to make love to me. Deep in my heart I know you're feeling something for me, but I need to hear you say it. I need assurance from you that all this bullshit is going to stop. So, yes, I'm miserable without you, but I refuse to go back to the way things are."

He slammed the door. "Look, I did tell you I missed you!" he yelled. "And as for living without you, trust me, I can. There's no need for me to go through all that other bullshit when you know how I feel. I'm not going to say what you want me to say, or feel how you want me to feel. That's stupid. If coming all this way wasn't enough for you, then fuck it! It was a waste of my time and yours too. Bottom line is I love everything about me. Why in the hell should I change because you want me to? If anything, you need to adjust to dealing with my ways if we're going to be together. You've always said you would, but I guess since you got brothas out there sucking your pussy now, you want things to change. Fuck that, baby, I just can't do it."

I was in tears listening to him. "Regardless of what you say, Jaylin, sometimes we have to make changes for the ones we love. I've given up a lot for you and made plenty of sacrifices to make you happy. You haven't changed one damn thing for me. You know how much your cruel words have an impact on me, and you continue to ridicule me. Knowing how much it hurts, can you at least think about shit before you say it? Especially after knowing how much hurt it causes me."

"Once again, I'm not changing shit about me. You've always portrayed yourself to be a hard woman, so deal with it. My arrogant ways and attitude shouldn't bother you at all. None of this is new to you. It's not like I just started acting this way…"

"But…but you are different. Ever since Nokea didn't accept your proposal you have treated every woman that steps to you like shit. Including me. The only one who gets your respect is Nanny B, and that's because you ain't fucking her."

"Whatever, Scorpio." He opened the door and stepped onto the porch. "I got some business to take care of in St. Louis. Are you coming with me or not?"

I shook my head. "No. I'm not coming back until you…"

"Hey!" he yelled, loudly. "Suit yourself. I'm out of here. I'm not wasting anymore of my goddamn time!"

He walked off.

I closed the door and foolishly hoped that he would knock again. But when he didn't, I peeked out the window and watched a taxi drive down the street. I pretty much figured he wasn't coming back anytime soon, but I knew the longer he stayed away, the easier it was going to be for me to manage without him.

JAYLIN

My plane didn't touch down in the Lou until Monday at four-fifteen in the afternoon. And after being searched by security, I didn't get home until almost six o'clock that night. Nanny B said the phone had been ringing like crazy and told me which calls sounded important. When she said Nokea, I called her back first. She also mentioned Mr. Schmidt, but I decided to put him off until I got to work.

I couldn't wait to tell Mackenzie I'd seen Scorpio. I hated to pretend everything was cool, but to make her feel better I told her Scorpio would be coming home soon. I even stopped at a toy store and bought her a new Barbie doll and told her it was from Scorpio, just so Mackenzie wouldn't think her mother had forgotten about her. I was somewhat disappointed that Scorpio didn't come back with me, but I also knew what a pain in the ass she could be at times. I hated to see her living like that, but if she didn't want to come back with me, I wasn't going to make her.

When I called Jackson and asked where she was, he declined to tell me, but when I offered to pay his $5,000 back, and kicked out another grand for the phone number, he gave me all the info I needed. The key to his place in Denver cost me another grand, but I was desperate to see her. And even though I was pretending I wasn't missing her, her being that far away from me was killing me.

Before I sat down for dinner, I called Nokea. She sounded okay when she answered the phone, so I wasn't sure what the urgency was all about.

"Is everything alright?" I asked.

"Yes, Jaylin. Everything is fine. I was just calling to see if you would watch LJ on Friday night. I have an engagement that I don't want to miss."

"I thought you said it was important? You know I'll always watch my son, Nokea."

"I didn't tell Nanny B it was important. She just assumes whenever I call that it is so you'll call me back."

"Yeah, but that's cool. Stephon's card party ain't until eight o'clock Friday night, so I'll be here up until then. After I leave Nanny B will be here. And if you don't mind me asking, what kind of engagement do you have?"

She laughed. "I have dinner plans with someone."

"Who, Pat? Did you and her work things out?"

"No, we didn't. I called her several times and she refuses to talk to me."

"Damn, that's messed up. Sorry to hear that, but that's how y'all women are. Men, we can be friends forever. We might have our ups and downs, but we always stay boys. So, if you're not having dinner with Pat, then who are you having dinner with?"

"Jaylin, I'm having dinner with Buckethead."

"Who? Who in the hell is Buckethead?"

"You remember...the Denzel Washington look-a-like at the Mobil gas station we stopped at on your birthday. Actually, his name is Collins but—"

"Whoa...whoa, wait a minute. I remember who you're talking about, but you said you wasn't interested in him. And how did you get in touch with him anyway? I tore your number up when you tried to give it to him."

"Yeah, well, actually, I saw him somewhere else and I wasn't wearing that dress you hated so much either. He gave me his phone number and I called him."

"That's foul and you know it, Nokea. You said that you didn't even find him attractive. Besides, he looked a lot older than you are anyway. And I'm not going to watch LJ while you're out kicking it with this motherfucker either."

"Fine, then I'll just ask my parents to watch him. Also, I never said that he wasn't attractive, you insisted that he wasn't. Let the truth be told, he's a very attractive man and he's only forty-years-old. That's only nine years older than me."

I was truly hurt, but Nokea and I made an agreement to get on with our lives without each other. Thing is, I couldn't believe she wasn't wasting anytime. "Okay, Nokea. Sorry, but I don't want this new man of yours around my child. So, every time you and him get together, I want LJ here with me."

"Now, I won't promise you all that because I would like for him to see how handsome my baby is. When we make plans, sometimes I'll bring LJ over there, and sometimes I won't."

"Whatever, Nokea. I'll see you on Friday, and bring LJ over early. I'm going to take a half day at work so I can spend time with him before I go to Stephon's place."

"How's Stephon doing? I haven't talked to him in a while. I think I'll call him when we get off the phone. Is he at home?"

"Nokea, don't play. I know we agreed to go our separate ways, but I don't want you getting all chummy with Stephon again."

She laughed. "Chummy, huh? We got a little bit more than chummy, didn't we?" she joked.

"By the way you're setting that thang out there now, I'm sure y'all did. But don't be trying to hurt my feelings, alright? Bad enough I'm allowing you to go on this date with Buckethead."

"It's Collins. And you're not allowing me to do anything. I still love you, but if it's time for anybody to move on, it's definitely me. So, on another note, you'll have to pick LJ up over here on Friday. I'll still be at work, but Mama will be here. I'll tell her to expect you."

"Cool. And if I don't get a chance to talk to you before Friday, don't go having sex with him yet. Allow yourself a little time to get to know him. I think you might be rushing things a bit."

"Sure, *Daddy*, but I'm not that type of woman. And whenever I do decide to have sex with him, remember, that's my business, not yours."

"You're right. But, honestly, I'm not prepared to accept you sleeping with another man yet."

"Thanks for being honest, but get over it. If I can recall, I wasn't prepared for you sleeping with all the women that you slept with either. So, I'm not trying to sound harsh when I say this, but deal with it, you've made your choice."

"Goodbye, Nokea."

"Talk to you later, Jaylin."

She hung up.

This was some crazy shit. If Nokea's sleeping with this man wasn't enough to hurt me, the thought of him being a tiny part of my son's life truly was. If she was going to move on, fine, I thought. But

177

LJ definitely wasn't going to be caught up in the mix. Feeling a slight bit down on myself because Scorpio and Nokea were both trying to be out of my life, I changed clothes and took Mackenzie to the movies. She was always the one person who could pull me out of my misery and by days end, she did. We didn't get home until eleven o'clock, so I tucked her in bed and finally got some rest before going back to work. Before I dozed off, I called Jackson and thanked him for the information. I told him if Scorpio called in need for some money to give it to her and I would repay him double. After figuring out how much money he could rack up on, he joyfully agreed and we hung up.

No sooner had I walked into my office, Schmidt buzzed in for me to come see him. I asked Angela to pour me a cup of coffee and headed for his office. As I walked in, he was on the phone and whispered for me to have a seat. He seemed a little upset with the caller, and when he mentioned his wife's name, I knew exactly what he was going through. Women were created to be pains in the ass. Wives, girlfriends, whatever—they all have issues. I swear a man just can't get a break.

Schmidt slammed the phone down, then walked over to the door to close it. He sat down in his chair and started to chat with me.

"Jaylin, how's everyone doing? You know, the kids, your nanny, your girlfriends?"

"Everyone's fine, Mr. Schmidt. Why do you ask, though? You never seemed to care before."

"Oh, Jaylin, I've always cared. That's why I asked you to come see me this morning. I want to make sure you're a happy man. Because if you're not happy, I'm not happy, and that means my business is losing money."

"I'm fine, but why do you feel your business is losing money if I'm not happy?"

"Well, I got a phone call the other day. It was a call from one of my clients who makes me a very wealthy man. You might know him, Robert McDaniels. Robert simply told me if I didn't get rid of you, he would take his business elsewhere. When I asked why, he said something interesting to me. Do you know what it was?"

I shrugged my shoulders. "Yeah, I guess. He told you I fucked his wife. So what?"

"Exactly," Schmidt said, standing up, and walking over to the window looking out. "That was my point. I asked him how many men have slept with his wife, or how many times has he stepped out on her. When he couldn't answer, I made it perfectly clear to him that no matter how much business he took away from me, it could never amount to as much money that you've made for this company over the years. So, trying to replace you was out of the question. He was angry, but I'm sure he'll get over it."

"Well, I appreciate it. But, uh, I don't want to be responsible for you losing that kind of money. I'm sure that one day it will come back to haunt me, you know what I mean?"

"No, it won't. As of yet, he hasn't done anything. I've known him for over twenty years, and I think his trust for me and our friendship means more to him than he realizes. I could be wrong because he's known for being a stubborn old bastard, but my intuition tells me he's not going to do a damn thing with his investments."

"Alright, but off the record Mr. Schmidt, he needs to back off me. I have some serious plans for him if he doesn't."

"Now, don't go talking like that Jaylin. He'll back off. I'll give him a call later, and him and I will discuss this over a late dinner tonight. By the end of the day, this thing is going to be behind all of us. Personally, I don't think he's up to battling with every man that has slept with his wife. She's a beauty, but she's a fucking whore if you ask me. And let's keep that off the record. How did you get yourself involved with her anyway? Your girlfriend is one fine young woman, and there's no way I would even give Heather McDaniels a second look with someone like her."

"Experience, Mr. Schmidt. It was all about experiencing something different. I like variety. Nothing wrong with exploring every once in a while, is there?"

He smiled and put his hands in his pockets, as he continued to look out of the window. "Yeah, exploring has gotten me in trouble plenty of times. But I have a good wife. She's forgiving, and as long as I bring home my paycheck, so she can spend it, she's fine with that."

I stood up, walked over by the window, and shook Schmidt's hand. "Thanks for believing in me and recognizing my hard work. Not too many boss's out there actually know what kind of good

179

people they have working for them. Especially black people. It means a lot to me and I owe you one."

"You just get your butt back to work and don't be slacking on me like you've been doing lately. With you not being in the office on Mondays anymore, and taking all these half days it's slightly hurting the business." He put his hand on my shoulder and gripped it. "Just between you and I, Roy can not do what you can do. So, tell me, is it the money? Do I have to dish-out more money to keep you around? Tell me, what do I need to do to keep my number one producer excited?"

"I'm excited, Mr. Schmidt. It's just my personal life has changed so drastically over the past few years. I have another daughter and a son now. Honestly, been kind of thinking about retiring," I said, seriously. "Thinking about moving far, far away with my kids. And don't let me forget about my nanny. She'd definitely have to come too."

"Don't you go getting any ideas," he yelled and pointed his finger at me. "Retirement at age thirty-three is out of the question. You have too much to offer this company, and I don't ever want to hear you talk like that again. Let's just talk about how much more I can offer you to stay."

"I don't know, Mr. Schmidt. Money is not the priority here. Besides, retirement is just a thought. I'll give you notice if I decide to do so, alright?"

"No, it's not alright. I will hear no such thing. Now get out of my office, and get back to work before I fire you." We both laughed. I thanked Schmidt again and jetted.

Stephon, Shane, Ray Ray, and me kicked up a serious poker game in Stephon's basement and listened to the song that was made for me: "Pimp Juice," by Nelly.

"That is the motherfucking cut," I yelled, talking to Stephon. "Man, turn that shit up!" He picked up the remote and blasted it as we all sung the lyrics out loud. When Ray Ray started putting his own lyrics in the song, fucking it up, Stephon turned it down and we all looked at Ray Ray like he was crazy.

"Now, that's ridiculous," I said. "If I can't sit here and enjoy listening to Nelly the right way, you gotta go."

Shane and Stephon gave me five.

"Screw you, man," Ray Ray said. "Hip-Hop wouldn't be nothing without me. I invented the shit."

I took a deep breath and huffed, "Whatever, nigga. Quit imagining shit and get back to the game so I can win some of my money back."

I was two grand in the hole and Ray Ray was taking everybody else's money as well as mine.

"I'm out," Shane yelled, and slammed his cards on the table.

"Me too," Stephon said. "Motherfucker than took all of my money."

"Well, I might have a little somethin-somethin here," I said, flickering through a hand of three kings and two queens.

"Negro, whatever you got, ain't gone touch what I got," Ray Ray said, putting up five-hundred-dollars more. I met his bet and laid my cards on the table.

"Pow-dow, playa, what's up? Give me my damn money." I stood up and got ready to grab the money. Shane and Stephon laughed and smacked me on the back.

"Hold up, Pimp Daddy. You brothas know I ain't going out like Thelma and Louise, Bonnie and Clyde, Mighty Joe Young, or Kuta-Kentay. Put that shit back down and take a look at this." Ray Ray laid a hand with four aces on the table and slid all the money back his way.

"Son of a bitch," I yelled, looking disgusted. "You be cheating, man. Ain't no fucking way you got four aces." I looked at Shane and Stephon. "Y'all lets search this fool." They laughed and we picked Ray Ray's two-hundred-sixty-pound ass up by his legs and shook him. He wrestled with us, as we carried him over to the couch and tossed him.

"Now what?" he panted. "No cards anywhere you sorry bunch of sore fucking losers." He picked up a plastic cup and threw it at me. I ducked and plopped down on the leather sofa next to him completely out of breath. Shane and Stephon sat down on the other side huffing and puffing as well.

"You robbed us man. What are you gonna do with all that money?" I asked.

"Buy me some booty and pay some bills."

181

"So, you paying for your shit these days, huh?" Stephon said. "If that's the case, you should have stayed married and gotten it for free."

"I know you fellas ain't up in here talking shit like y'all don't pay for no booty. Ladies rolling around in Corvette's and shit...living up in Condo's, and wearing Rolexes. Bitches ain't gotta work a day in their lives unless they want to. So, touchy subject my brothas. Y'all fools paid up and paid out."

"That's Jay," Stephon quickly said. "I ain't giving nobody shit but this fat, long piece of goodness hanging between my legs."

"Stephon, please," I said. "Now, you know better. I can recall several times you told me you spent money for...let's see, a cruise, a Movado watch, some bikes for this chick's kids, and what about that treadmill you paid almost a grand for? Told me the woman needed to tone it up and you bought her a treadmill."

Shane and Ray Ray busted out laughing. They both fell on the floor laughing so hard.

"Ha, Ha, silly motherfuckers," Stephon said, looking at them. "Get y'all asses up. Shane, I know you ain't laughing. Felicia told me about all the shit you did for her, so get your ass up off the floor before I start talking. And if I can recall, back in the day, you were breaking the bank for some sistas. I remember you scraping up money to buy what's her name, uh, uh, Vizette, that's it...a dog. She had to have a Cocker Spaniel, or you weren't getting no booty."

"Yeah, I remember that shit," I said, giggling. "We talked about your ass bad."

"Fuck y'all," Shane said, getting up off the floor. "Personally, I was in love with the woman and wanted to do something nice. I don't mind spending money on a woman especially if she's worth it. If I had nearly as much money as Jay got, I probably would be spending money like that too. Who knows, I can't really say."

"Right...right." I shook my head and gave Shane five. "Hey, if she's worth it then why not?"

"Question is, what do you consider worth it?" Stephon asked. "I guess my idea of being worthy might be different from y'alls because I'm straight up a tight-wod. Ain't too many women getting into my pockets. That's why I don't fuck with Felicia no more. First because the bitch lied about the baby, but then she was trying to get up in my pockets. The only thing in my pockets is a pair of Scorpio's panties that I have as evidence after I boned her."

When Stephon pulled Scorpio's panties out of his pocket, I raised up. "Nigga, don't play." My heart raced when he gave them to me.

"Who in the hell's playing?" He gave me a serious look. "After her shaking a brotha down, I collected those just the other night."

Relieved, I shook my head because I now knew Stephon was lying. Just to see how far he was going to push me, I pretended to believe him. "Yep, these are most certainly her panties. I bought them myself. They even smell like her and everythang. Question is, though, how did you get them?"

He looked over at me, then looked at Shane. "This fool about to have a heart attack, man," he laughed. "Should I break it down for him before he pass out?"

"Go ahead, man," Shane said not cracking a smile. "You should tell him how much fun we both had tapping that ass and watching his name jiggle while we hit it."

"It's like that, huh," I snickered. "And both of y'all...damn. Why didn't nobody invite me to the party?"

"Cause we figured you were busy," Stephon said. "Busy shaking down that white gal you've been messing with."

"Ah, okay. But I'm never too busy to fuck Scorpio, though. Not only that," I said, standing up, "but I'd better be going before somebody gets hurt."

Stephon and Shane started laughing. "Man sit down. You know we just playing with your ass."

"Playing? Naw, brothas," I said, jumping on Stephon, and playfully choking him. "You don't play with no shit like that."

We all laughed, and after I choked him, he pretended like he was out of breath, and gagged for air.

"Whew," he said. "I'm glad I was joking. You should have seen the look on your face when I told you I had sex with her, man. That picture was worth a million dollars."

"Stephon, I knew you was lying, fool. Well, at first I didn't know, but after you said the other day, that's when you fucked up."

"Well, whenever or whatever," Ray Ray joked. "You straight up looked like you saw three ghost when you thought he tapped that ass. That was some funny shit there. I'd pay a million to see that look again my damn self."

"Fuck y'all. So, he caught me off guard. And the only reason he did that was because Scorpio and me been having some problems lately." I looked down at her panties again and moved them around in my hands. I looked at Stephon. "Without a doubt, these are her panties. The reason I know is because I bought them. Now, how in the hell did you get them?"

Shane reached over and snatched them out of my hands. "Thank you very much," he said. "But, uh, these belong to me. If memories are all I can have, I'd like to keep them."

I laughed and shook my head. "You damn right that's all you're going to have. All these fine-ass women in St. Louis and you brothas all up on my shit. I've said it once and I'll say it again—She's mine and mine only. Find somebody else to fuck y'all broke- down asses."

"Damn," Stephon said. "Broke down? That's pretty bad, Jay." He cleared his throat. "Not trying to go there but, uh, Felicia, Nokea, Sandra, Leslie, Gina, Angela, Chris, Stephanie…and all of the other women that we've shared didn't seem to think a brotha was so broke down."

"That's cause they didn't know any better, but can we please change the subject before I have to go off on your ass."

"Fine with me. But remember, you ain't the only good brotha in St. Louis shaking the sistas down correctly."

"Never said I was, but as I was saying before we got off into this other bullshit, my idea of being worth it is if she takes care of me, I take care of her. That can only mean one thing because financially, no woman can assist me with that, but if she can take care of my physical needs, meaning pop that thang how I like it, she can have just about anything she wants."

"See, mine is slightly different," Shane said. "First, I must be in love with a woman before I even start to invest my money. I'm not talking about spending money at the movies, or shit like that I'm talking about serious money. If she's intelligent, is beautiful both inside and out, and can make love to me for at least an hour, I'm

184

hooked and eventually I will fall in love. Thing is, they must come in that order. Lately, I've been finding women who give me one or the other—never the full package. So, I'm chilling. The last time I had sex was roughly over, uh…maybe, five months ago."

"Shiiit," I said. "Feel that nigga head Stephon and make sure he all right. And even though his dick ain't been in action, we for damn sure know his mouth has."

Stephon laughed, reached over to Shane, and touched his head. "He seems to feel okay, but man I would rather die than go without having sex for five months. Are you fucking gay or something?" Stephon asked.

Shane laughed. "Man, please. Now, I love me some pussy. You brotha's know that, but if it ain't right, I'd rather do without. It took me a long time to start seeing shit that way, but I got tired of throwing my dick on the table for any and every woman. Most of them be treating they shit like a piece of gold, and making a brotha go over and beyond, so what's wrong with me being particular?"

"Ain't nothing wrong with it at all. And by all means," I said, grabbing my shit. "This motherfucker here worth more than fifty pots of gold. However, I got some serious fucking needs that have to be met. Need to be met quite often, I might say. So, I'm not depriving myself for shit."

"I'm gonna have to side with Jay on that one," Ray Ray said. "You talk a good game, Shane, but ain't too many fellas looking at it like that these days. You're for damn sure a better man than me cause if she wants it, and I got a condom, she can have it."

Stephon reached over to Ray Ray and slapped his hand. "Now, that's my fucking motto. And since you brothas sitting around here talking about all this booty and shit, I'd say it's time to shake some brothas down. Time to get some ladies in the house to entertain. Mona got some bootilicious ass friends and they're at her house right now having a lingerie party."

"Well, what you waiting on?" I asked. "You didn't expect me to sit up here all damn night with no hard legs, did you?"

Stephon got up to call Mona. "Shane, are you cool with this? When I say bodacious, I mean these ladies are BO-DA-CIOUS."

"Hey, don't let me ruin the party. Y'all brothers go ahead and knock yourselves out. I'm chilling," Shane said.

Before Stephon left the room to call Mona, he pulled me aside to make sure everything was cool. I let him know I wasn't tripping off his comments, and more than anything I realized how much he and I were alike. We both always spoke our minds and definitely wanted to have the final word. When he came back he pumped up, "Right Thurr," by Chingy and said the ladies would be over in about an hour.

Shane and I went behind the bar and started making some drinks, while Ray Ray went to the bathroom.

"Jay," Shane said, handing me some glasses. "You mentioned things weren't going so well with you and Scorpio. What's up with that?"

I dropped a few ice cubes in the glasses and looked at him. "She jetted. She left me and said she needed time to sort through shit. So, I'm giving her all the time away she needs."

"I see. But, uh, I thought you might want to know that she called me the night we met up at Freddy's. She apologized for leading me on and for not telling me the truth about her feelings for you. She also told me you put her up to calling me."

"Yes, I did. I had to know who or what she really wanted."

"Well, now that you know, don't blow it man," he said, reaching into his pocket, and giving me her panties. "Stephon knew I had those from my previous encounter with her, and asked me to bring them tonight to play a joke on you. Don't take it personal, okay? If anything, I knew all along she loved you. I could see it in her eyes every time your name came up. She's a special type of woman, Jay, and you're lucky to still have her."

I tossed Scorpio's panties in the trashcan behind the bar, and told Shane how much I appreciated him for not interfering. We continued making drinks and when I looked up Ray Ray and Stephon were firing up some weed. I walked over by to the couch and laid the tray of drinks on the table.

"What the fuck is up with this shit? Naw, fellas, we don't do drugs up in here." I snatched the bag of weed out of Stephon's hand. He took a hit from his joint and blew the smoke in my face.

"Quit tripping, fool. Brotha need a little herb every once in a while to settle the mind," he said.

"Settle my ass. Don't disappoint me, cuz," I said, sternly. "We ain't going out like that. And you of all people should know better."

186

"Jay, why you tripping?" Ray Ray said. "It ain't nothing but a lil weed. Cool out, alright?"

"Man, you cool out," I said, getting loud. "Messing around with drugs has fucked up too many people in my family. I ain't about to sit around and watch nobody I care about do that shit. Smoking weed leads to other things, and you and Stephon need to put that shit out— NOW!"

"I'm with Jay this time," Shane said. "We got too much going on for ourselves to be sitting here tripping like that. Drugs are drugs. I don't care what shape, form, or fashion they come in, they all can damage the mind."

"What a terrible thing to waste," Stephon said, putting the joint out. "Y'all fellas up in my house trying to tell me what to do. Luckily, I have respect for y'all." Stephon stood up and cleared the smoke with his hands. Ray Ray helped after he put his out too.

Shane and I were sitting down on the couch playing Stephon's X-BOX when the doorbell rang. He was kicking my butt at boxing and we were acting a bit silly from drinking so much alcohol. When the ladies were coming down the steps, I nudged Ray Ray because he had fallen asleep on the couch and was snoring extremely loud. He quickly straightened up and rubbed his waves back.

Mona and her lady friends came around the couch and stood next to us. Since Stephon's leather couch circled half of the basement, there was plenty of room for everybody to sit down.

"Shane, Ray, Jaylin," Mona said. "These are my girlfriends Amber, Jeanette, Daisha, and Kennedy. They spoke to us and we spoke back. I leaned back on the couch and smiled, as I looked at Shane. He looked at me and grinned.

"Five months without no ass, bro," I whispered. "Are you pushing for six after seeing what we just saw?"

He laughed and whispered back. "It's five of them and four of us. I at least need two since it's been such a long time. Which two is the question?"

Shane and I looked over at the ladies sitting on the couch. I already had scoped the sista I wanted. Daisha. She had it straight up going on. Had on a gray leather jacket unbuttoned in the front and showed her hourglass figure. Her black sheer bra underneath showed the healthiness in her breasts and was just enough to arouse me. Most

187

of all, I was excited by the way her leather pants hugged her hips, and showed a gap between her legs that was, without a doubt, waiting to be filled. I glimpsed over to get a second look, and dug the shit out of her short neatly trimmed curly hair cut. Kind of reminded me a little of Halle Berry, but not quite.

"So, what are you thinking, Jay?" Shane whispered.

"I think I'm about to celebrate Christmas a little early. How about you?"

"Right, but, uh, with which one?"

"Daisha, man. That's who."

"Damn, that's who I was thinking. If not her, then Jeanette." Just then, Amber laughed at Stephon's joke and crossed her leg. Her dress slid over and showed her dark coffee brown legs. Shane looked at me. "Okay, Amber. Amber and Jeanette. You can have Daisha."

"What about Kennedy? She ain't short stopping," I asked.

"No, she's not but her ass is just too damn big. I like ass, but that's too much ass for me. If I can sit a drink on the top of that motherfucker while she's standing up, I don't want it." We softly giggled. "Besides, she's Ray Ray's type. He can work with that."

"What y'all brothas over there whispering and laughing about?" Ray Ray asked loudly.

"I know, Ray," Mona said. "I was thinking the same thing. I brought my friends over here to mingle and the two of them being all anti-social."

"Sorry about that," Shane said, leaning forward looking at Mona. "We didn't mean to be rude. Jay and I were just talking about how lovely your friends look. How we'd actually like to get to know them better."

"Funny," Jeanette said. "We were just talking about the same thing before Stephon started telling his crazy ass jokes."

"Alright, Jeanette," Stephon said. "Don't let me start talking about your buck-eyed mama."

"Stephon and Jeanette, please," Mona said, interrupting. "Don't start this today. The two of you get on my nerves with this joaning stuff."

Mona took Stephon's hand and escorted him upstairs. I offered to get the ladies some drinks and when I got up, I just so

188

happen to ask Daisha to help me. She smiled and got off the couch. She followed me to the bar and stood there.

"Tell me," she said, rubbing her hands together. "What can I help you with?"

I laughed because she really didn't want me to answer that question. "You can start by giving me a few of those glasses above your head." She reached up and grabbed the glasses. I looked over and Shane was sitting in between Amber and Jeanette chatting with them. Ray Ray was talking to Kennedy, and I grinned, as things seemed to be going according to the plan.

"Now what, Jaylin, right?" she asked.

"Yes, Jaylin." I looked down at her breasts. "Now, you can take your jacket off so you don't waste any alcohol on it when we get down on making these Tequilas and sour-apple Martini's."

She removed her jacket and laid it on one of the barstools. Impressed by how well she mixed class with her sexiness, I couldn't wait to get into her tonight.

"Should I take my pants off too," she joked. "I don't want to get them messed up either."

Damn, I thought, now wasn't the time or place to joke around with me. "Hey, do whatever you gotta do. I was just looking out for you when I asked you to take your jacket off. Your outfit looks kind of expensive and I'd hate to see you mess it up"

"I was just kidding, Jaylin. The jacket is off, but the pants are most certainly staying on."

What a disappointment to hear that, I thought. I turned around and grabbed a towel from the rail behind me. "Let me wrap this around you. That way if anything spills, it won't spill on your pants, okay?" She turned and I tightly tied the towel around her waist. As usual, my mind was in the gutter.

"Thanks," she said, turning back around. "Now, let's get to work."

Daisha and I fixed seven sour-apple Martini's and ten Tequilas. When we finished, she popped a cherry in my mouth and we carried the drinks over to the table. I ran upstairs to see if Stephon and Mona wanted one, but when I saw his bedroom door closed, I quietly tiptoed back downstairs.

I sat down next to Daisha, and picked up a glass along with everybody else to give a toast. "Let's drink to not letting good things go to waste," I said, somewhat thinking about Scorpio again. If not her, then Daisha.

Ray Ray put his two-cents in. "I'll drink to if she want it, and she got a condom, then she can have it."

Everybody looked at him in disbelief. Kennedy actually rolled her eyes. "Damn, I was just playing," Ray said. "Can't you people take a joke?"

"Yeah, man, that's cool, but, uh, these ladies might not have wanted to hear that," I said, looking at Ray Ray like, cool out, please. He caught my drift and chilled.

As the night went on, Daisha and I really wasn't good company for each other. She was too quiet, and when I tried to kick up a conversation, her answers were quick and sharp like she didn't want to be bothered. Sensing her coldness, I eventually stopped talking and started playing the X-BOX again.

Shane, however, was running his game and running it well. After entertaining Jeanette and Amber for about an hour, he managed to continue his conversation in another room. Even Ray Ray and Kennedy seemed like they were enjoying each other's company. So, trying to give it another try with Daisha, I put the game down and asked her if she wanted anything else to drink. She suggested a Smirnoff Ice, so I got up to get it. When I did, she followed me over to the bar, and sat down on a stool in front of it.

"Are you married or engaged—which one?" she asked.

I laughed. "Neither, but why do you ask? Do I *act* like I'm married?" I handed her a glass and a Smirnoff Ice from the refrigerator.

"Yes, you really do. Most married men are somewhat shy like you are. Kind of afraid to talk, you know what I mean?"

"Shy? No, I don't think so. I just backed off since I got a feeling that you didn't want to be bothered."

"Sorry, but it has nothing to do with you. I've been divorced for almost six months, and sometimes it's difficult trying to meet new people."

"Hmm…" I said, thinking. A divorced woman was nothing but trouble in my eyes.

190

"Yep. Things just didn't work out between us. He was headed in one direction, and I was headed in another. Really nice guy, but he just wasn't for me."

I leaned up against the counter and folded my arms while Daisha started drinking her Smirnoff. Suddenly, I was really feeling up to having sex, but didn't quite know how to break it to her just yet. When she looked over at Kennedy and Ray Ray on the couch kissing, she suggested we go into another room for privacy.

I led her to the room with a waterbed, and started taking my shirt off as soon as we hit the door.

"Wait a minute, sweetie," she said, properly. "I don't get down like that. Especially since, I don't even know anything about you."

I turned off the lights, took the drink out of her hand, and started kissing her. She kissed back, and we worked our way over to the waterbed. As I lay back, I put her body on top of mine. She stopped me again.

"Hey, Jaylin, look...I'm serious. I'd really like the opportunity to get to know you better, if that's okay with you."

"You will," I said, trying to undo her bra. She backed away from me and started to get off the bed. "Where are you going?" I asked, getting frustrated.

"Did you not understand anything I've said? I mean, I'm feeling you, but not enough to give myself to you like that. I barely know you, Jaylin, and I came in here so we could be alone and talk. If you came in here for something else, I'm sorry, but I didn't mean to mislead you."

Disgusted, I got off the bed and walked over by the stereo in the corner of the room. I turned on some Luther and got back in bed. "Can I at least hold you while we talk?" I asked. She came back over to the bed, and lay down next to me. She placed her leg over mine and placed her head on my shoulder.

"So, what is it that you want to talk about?" I asked, and not really giving a damn, since her proper-ass talking was driving me crazy.

"There's plenty for us to talk about. For starters, how old are you and what's your occupation? Do you have a Degree and if so, in what? When you're finished answering that, do you have any

191

children? If so, how many? And what do you like to do in your spare time?"

I took a deep breath because I was not up to answering a bunch of questions that really wasn't any of her business. But after we lay in bed for a while, getting to know each other, I actually found out some interesting things about Daisha. She really seemed to have it going on for herself. She was a Registered Nurse at St. Luke's Hospital, had a house in Ballwin, no children, and spoke French very well. She made me laugh a few times, as I tried to figure out what she was saying in French. I had taken a French course in college, but couldn't remember shit.

When Mona knocked on the door and asked if she was ready to go, Daisha said no and I offered to take her home. I figured Shane wasn't quite ready either because I could hear all the action going on in the room next to us. Daisha and I silently laughed a few times after we heard all the panty-popping going on, and even though I straight up wished it was me, I couldn't force Daisha to do anything she didn't feel comfortable doing.

I woke up at my usual time, four o'clock in the morning. All the alcohol I had been drinking was finally coming down. Daisha was knocked out on my chest, so I eased over and tried not to wake her. When the water shifted around, she woke up.

"Are you ready to go?" she asked, in a sleepy voice sitting up.

"Yeah, I guess. I need to go to the bathroom first, though." I turned on the lights and she quickly covered her face.

"Jaylin, that light is too bright, honey. Please turn it off."

"Can I just see how beautiful you look in the morning?"

She smiled and removed her hands. "You are a charmer. I bet you tell all the women that line, don't you?"

I laughed and headed to the bathroom. Daisha really was beautiful, and for the first time, it fucked me up that I laid in bed with a woman and didn't even fuck her. I kind of enjoyed her company too. And the best thing about her was that she didn't even snore.

I walked back towards the bedroom, and tapped on Shane's door to let him know I was outtie. He yelled for me to open it.

"What's up, man?" he asked, raising up on his elbows.

"I'm gone, dog. Give me a hollar tomorrow," I said, checking out both sistas on his side.

"Will do, my brotha. Until next time."

I sat down and waited for Daisha to put her shoes on. I looked over at Ray Ray and Kennedy and they were lying on the couch knocked out. They still had their clothes on, so I didn't suspect anything deep went down with them. Daisha grabbed her purse off the couch and we headed up stairs. As she walked in front of me, I grazed my hand on her ass just to touch it. She turned around and smiled.

"Jaylin, don't play."

"Sorry, but I couldn't help myself. You shouldn't have put all that in my face."

She moved over and I walked in front of her. And no sooner had I got to the top of the stairs, she squeezed my ass with her hands. I turned and backed her against the wall, as I stood in front of her.

"I don't like women who play games, Daisha," I said, looking her in the eyes. "If you want to, we can always finish what we started last night."

She rubbed her fingers across my lips. "Games? No, I don't play them. But when you put something like that in my face, there's no telling what I might do. And as for finishing up...oh, I intend to. Today, however, is not the day."

She pulled my face forward and placed her lips on mine. I got all into kissing her, and when I started grinding up against her, she pushed me back.

"Wait until we're alone, okay?"

"Whatever you say, Daisha," I said, backing away. "Whatever you say."

When we got upstairs Mona and Stephon were in the kitchen playing around. She had a sheet wrapped around her and he was in his boxers dripping with water.

"Are you leaving?" he asked. Mona took a cup of water and splashed it on him. "Quit playing, Mona. I'm already drenched." He opened the refrigerator and pulled out a pitcher of water. I covered Daisha with my jacket and we ran through the kitchen. Stephon tossed the water on Mona and it splashed everywhere.

"Hollar at me later, man. Bye Mona," I yelled, as we walked through the living room. Mona and Daisha waved goodbye to each other.

I drove Daisha to her house in Ballwin. From the outside it looked nice, but I was a little disappointed when she didn't invite me in. I guess inviting me in wasn't her way of doing things, so I didn't even ask. She gave me a peck on the cheek, and told me she would call me soon. I opened her car door and waited for her to get inside. When she turned off the porch light, I drove off.

Everything was cool on the home front. Mackenzie's best friend Megan had spent the night and LJ was fast asleep in Nanny B's room. I took my clothes off and lay naked in the bed. Lonely, I picked up the phone to call Scorpio, but when the number was busy I hung up. I tried a few more times when I realized she must have taken it off the hook. I was really starting to miss her. Didn't have enough guts to go see her again, so the best thing I could do was wait until she was ready to come around.

NOKEA

I had one of the best times of my life with Collins. I had no idea how handsome and classy he was until he picked me up for dinner. He had a tint of gray mixed in with his thinly trimmed beard and his gray blended well with his shiny black hair. I couldn't help but notice how well his chocolate skin meshed with his dark brown slanted eyes. His height and sliminess gave his black tailored suit the look it needed.

During dinner, Collins kept me laughing and smiling the entire time. I finally got a chance to know more about him. He's part owner of Jefferson & Assoc., a computer technology company, and has offices in St. Louis and Detroit. Most of his time is spent running back and forth making sure business is running smoothly. Then there's his eighteen-year-old son, who's a freshman in college, and an ex-wife of five years. I didn't ask why she was now an ex, but I was sure time would tell. Right about now there was nothing he could say or do that would turn me off. He was perfect for me and had come into my life at the right time. Had he come any sooner, I may not have been ready.

When he drove to his house in Ladue, I was amazed. He lived alone in a five bedroom, six bathroom house that had acres and acres of land. When I asked him if he got lonely sometimes he said yes and since his son recently left for college, he was thinking about putting his house up for sale and moving to his smaller house in Detroit. He said the house in Detroit had five bedrooms too, but it didn't have the extra living space that the one in Ladue had. Either way, he had it going on, and I was flattered to be, at the moment, a small part of his life.

Later that night, Collins and I drank wine after he lit the fireplace and he laid two square velvet pillows on the floor so we could relax. The off-white soft clean carpet covering the floor gave our bodies all the plush we needed. After he went upstairs and changed into his silk black pajama pants, he asked me if I wanted something comfortable to slip into. Insisting that he not go through all the trouble, I removed my clothes and lay naked underneath the covers close to him, while he held me in his arms.

As the night went on and we connected even more, one thing just led to another. I allowed him to make love to me and when our bodies sweated from the heated fireplace, he gently wiped my sweat off with his hands. Seeing that he was dripping wet as well, I returned the favor.

Finally, I felt like there was a light at the end of the tunnel. Collins timing couldn't be more right. One thing, I thought, for sure and that's Jaylin Rogers could become a man of the past. I had no problem moving forward with Collins because he seemed to be everything I dreamed a man to be. Not only that, but everything my parents had always wanted me to have.

Collins drove me home, and we sat in his car and smacked lips for a while. He invited LJ and me to spend a week with him in Detroit. He said that his entire family gathers there for Christmas every year and he wanted us to come along. Not really having any plans, other than to spend time with my parents, I told him we would love to and I was really looking forward to going. That is, of course, until I picked LJ up from Jaylin's house around three o'clock in the afternoon and broke the news to him.

"You have got to be out of your rabbit-ass mind, Nokea," he yelled, sitting at the kitchen table eating a sandwich.

"Jaylin, look, I could have lied to you, but I'm trying to be as open with you as possible about LJ. Allow me to be happy, please."

"You can be happy all you want. Run off with this joker you know nothing about, I don't care. But, LJ is staying right here with me. He will not be caught up with you chasing around after some dick."

"It isn't like that and you know it. Don't you know and respect anything about me? I am not the type of woman to drag my son along with me if I don't feel comfortable with the situation. If you're that bothered by Collins, why don't you meet him for yourself?"

Jaylin walked over by the dishwasher and put his plate inside. I walked over and stood next to him. Looking hurt, he glared at me. "You are asking too much of me and you know it. I got a bad ass feeling about this shit, and if you fuck me over again, Nokea, I swear—"

196

"Well, I'm not trying to mess you over Jaylin. All I would like to do is take my son with me to Detroit for one week, that's it. Please don't make me feel guilty about doing this. All I'm asking for is your support."

Upset, Jaylin turned around, moved the kitchen curtain aside, and looked out. He closed his eyes, then turned his head and stared. "You fucked him, didn't you? That's what this shit is about. And don't lie to me because I've known you long enough and can tell when you're lying."

"Believe me, this has nothing to do with—"

"Did, you, fuck, him!" he yelled loudly.

"Would you please calm yourself down? I don't want Nanny B and the kids hearing—"

"You did, didn't you?"

"Yes, we made love last night, but—"

"Get out, Nokea!"

"Jaylin, please—"

He stood face to face with me. "I said, get the fuck out of my house!"

I stared him in his eyes. "And I said, I'm not leaving without my son."

"Fine, take him." He walked towards the kitchen door. "Make sure you're ready to hear from my attorney tomorrow."

"And you make sure you're ready to hear from Collin's attorney."

He quickly turned. "What did you just say?" He rushed back over to me and put his finger in my face. "Did you just say what I think you said, Nokea?" A look I had never seen was on his face.

"Look, Jaylin," I said, trying to calm him. "I don't want—"

He grabbed my collar and leaned against me. "Bitch, if you ever bring another motherfucker up—"

Before I knew it, I smacked the shit out of him for calling me a bitch. He grabbed me tighter and lifted me up. He banged my head against the cabinet and when he let go I fell to the floor. After that, he squeezed my arm, pulled me off the floor, and shoved me into the living room. In a rage, he pushed me into a chair, straddled his arms in front of me, and leaned forward. "You're a silly-ass woman, Nokea. You need to learn how to watch your damn mouth because it's

197

liable to get you hurt. I'm so sick and tired of you putting me through this shit with LJ and I promise you, this is the last time I'm going to let you do this to me." He raised up. "So, tell your new ancient-ass man to bring it on. You are not taking my damn son home with you today, nor will you take him to Detroit. Now, get the fuck out of here like I told you to." He started to walk away.

Nanny B stood at the top of the stairs with LJ and Mackenzie. "What is going on down there?" she yelled.

"Nanny B would you bring my son to me," I asked politely, and getting up out of the chair.

Jaylin turned around and sucked his lip in. "You wanna fuck with me, Nokea?" he yelled. "I will kill you over my son!" He grabbed my neck and choked me. After he tripped me to the floor, Nanny B ran down the steps and yelled for him to stop. I squirmed around on the floor and could barely breath with his tight grip around my neck and his body weight on top of me.

"Jaylin!" Nanny B yelled. She tried to pull him off me, but he ignored her and squeezed tighter. The only thing that stopped him was when Mackenzie started crying and yelling, "Daddy, please stop!" He looked at her and LJ, as both of them stood there watching us in tears. He took a deep breath and stood up, then he walked over to the couch and sat down. Nanny B helped me off the floor, as I coughed, and tried to catch my breath. She put her arms around me and asked for my car keys. When I reached in my pocket and gave them to her, she picked LJ up and looked at Jaylin.

"I'm taking them home. This is outrageous, Jaylin. You really need to get yourself together," she said, furiously.

He didn't say a word, just laid his head back on the couch and looked up at the ceiling. Still crying, Mackenzie sat on his lap, and put her arms around his neck. And after that, Nanny B, LJ and me left.

On the drive home, I told Nanny B what happened, and she kind of sided with Jaylin. She said he was wrong for putting his hands on me, but she didn't agree with me wanting to take LJ to Detroit for Christmas. She said that she agreed with Jaylin because I really didn't know much about Collins, and explained what a disappointment it would be for them not having LJ around on Christmas day. I understood how they both felt, but he was my son too. And to get our lawyers involved would only make the situation more chaotic. Especially since I had the pleasure of seeing Mr. Frick, Jaylin's attorney, in action for him several times before. Frick was an asshole, but he definitely knew how to win a case for Jaylin. I had less than three weeks to work with before Christmas and I hoped by then Jaylin would calm down and see things my way. If not, LJ and I were going to Detroit with or without Jaylin's consent.

By late Sunday afternoon, I spoke to Collins and told him about what happened. He insisted he wasn't trying to interfere, and expressed how much he wanted LJ and me to go with him. He even suggested getting to know Jaylin better, so Jaylin would feel comfortable with LJ being around him. He then told me how he was in the exact situation with his son when his ex-wife re-married and how difficult it was for him to cope with another man trying to step in. Before we hung up, he apologized for putting me in a tough situation and was willing to do anything to make it better for me. So, we agreed to go see Jaylin at work on Tuesday and talk the situation out with him.

When I called Jaylin's house, Nanny B asked how I was doing and told me Jaylin and Mackenzie had been gone all day. She said he refused to talk about what happened last night and stayed in his room until morning. Somewhat accusing me of hurting him, I continuously reminded her of everything he had done to me, then ended our conversation. I didn't want to be disrespectful to her because she had really been there for all of us, so I later called back and apologized. More than anything, I understood that she was trying to be the typical "mother" looking out for her son.

Collins picked me up around noon on Tuesday and was looking dynamite in his tan Brooks Brothers suit. I had taken a couple days off work just so I could get this issue between Jaylin and I resolved.

On our way up the elevator in the Berkshire Building, my stomach felt queasy and I was a nervous wreck. Collins kissed my hand and told me to relax. Easy for him to say because he hadn't had the pleasure of seeing how irate Jaylin could get.

Collins was relaxed and walked with confidence as we went into the lobby. He asked Angela if Jaylin was there and when she said yes, my heart dropped. Her eyes flirted with him when she asked for his name, so I interrupted and told her to let Jaylin know I was there to see him. When she buzzed Jaylin's office, he said that he was eating lunch and asked for me to come on back. I took a deep breath and Collins took my hand, as I led the way.

When we walked through the door, Jaylin was sitting in his chair, and was on the phone laughing with someone. He was eating a lunch tray of Gourmet To Go, and his smile quickly faded when he saw Collins hand joined together with mine.

"Daisha, I'll call you back later, alright?" He hung up and cleared his throat. He looked over at me. "You just don't get enough, do you?"

"Please," I said. "I just thought it would be a good idea if you met Collins. So, Collins, this is Jaylin and Jaylin this is Collins." Collins reached out for Jaylin to shake his hand, but Jaylin just looked at it. Collins then pulled his hand back.

"Jaylin, listen," he said. "Trust me when I say that I know how you feel. The only reason I'm here today is because I was faced with the same dilemma not too long ago. My ex-wife's husband tried to be a father to my son and I wasn't having it. So, I'd like to take just a little of your time so you can get to know me better and understand that I'm not trying to replace you. From what Nokea tells me, you're a good father and there's no need for me to step in when you're handling your business."

Jaylin got out of his chair and walked over to the door. When he closed it, I noticed him and Collins eyes wonder, as they checked out each other's attire. I was glad it wasn't a contest or anything because they were running neck to neck.

"Have a seat," Jaylin said, sitting back down in his chair. Collins and I both took a seat in the chairs sitting in front of Jaylin's desk. When Collins folded his leg, Jaylin looked down at his brown leather expensive looking shoes with tassels on the flap.

"First, I'll tell the both of you that I do not like taking care of personal matters in the work place. Second, I do not like to be put on front-street by anyone. And third, Collins, I apologize for not shaking your hand when you came in here. This chaos between Nokea and I go way back, and I'm sorry you had to get caught up in the middle." Jaylin reached out and gave Collins a handshake, then looked at me and slightly rolled his eyes.

"I didn't like the idea of coming to your work place either, but sometimes these kind of places seem to work out better instead of talking things out at home. When my ex-wife's husband came to talk to me in my home, many months after the damage had been done, I was arrested for assault on the brotha. If he had come to me in the beginning and given me the opportunity to know what kind of man he was and let me know what his intentions were, the assault never would have happened. After all is said and done, we're pretty good friends now, however, I still have my moments when the situation bothers me. Especially when my son comes home from college and wants to stay with them instead of me. I have to be a man about the situation and let him decide because if I don't, it will drive him away."

Jaylin placed his hands behind his head and leaned back in his chair. "Collins, this is all very new to me. I have three beautiful children in this world, and it's like I'm fighting each and everyday to keep them in my life. My oldest child I haven't a clue where she is. I've hired detectives to find her and somehow, thanks to her mother, she's just vanished. My other daughter is now living with me, but it's just a matter of time when her mother is going to come for her and take her away—I feel it," Jaylin said, painfully. "And since I'm not her biological father I would have a tough fight keeping her with me. So, really, LJ is all I got to hang on to. If you and Nokea run off with him, I have nothing."

"But Jaylin we're not trying to run off with him," I said. "All I would like to do is take him to Detroit for one week. That's it. You act like we're talking a lifetime."

"Nokea, you say that now, but my biggest fear will be the day you call me and tell me you're moving to Detroit with Collins. Let's be realistic here, there's a possibility of that happening, so who knows. I'm letting you know now that occasionally visiting my son is not going to be enough for me. Whether you realize it or not, he needs me and I need him. So, question is, how do the both of you anticipate on working around this scenario, or have you even thought about it?"

"Jaylin," Collins said. "Honestly, my future plans do include living in Detroit. I briefly mentioned that to Nokea last night. I could actually see myself with her because she's a beautiful person, and I've longed for a woman like her." Collins reached over and touched my

201

hand. "But someday she's going to have a choice to make knowing that I probably will not support her wanting LJ to live with us because this is a personal issue for me. I truly believe that a son needs to be with his father. But remember, we're talking five or ten years from now."

"Okay," Jaylin said, resting his arms on his desk. "I have no problem with LJ going to Detroit with the both of you for Christmas, but I need something in writing from your attorney, Nokea, that says if you move to Detroit within the next five to ten years, you move alone and LJ stays with me. By then, he should be old enough to tell us what or who he wants. And at that time, if he wants to live with the both of you, so be it. I'm cool with that. But it's the best I can offer right now. These days, I have to look out for what's in my best interest."

"I'm so glad the two of you are good at predicting my future," I said. "Who says I'm moving anywhere? I know that it's stretching things a bit, but Jaylin don't you think this is taking things too far. I've only known Collins for a short time, and you're already planning my future for me."

"Nokea, I like to prepare myself ahead of time for things. The unexpected is what hurts. Just a few months ago I never thought I would be sitting here having this conversation with you and Collins. And vice versa, I would assume. So, if you want my consent, you're gonna have to work with me on this."

Collins and I looked at each other. "I'd probably be asking for the same thing, baby," Collins said. "I don't like the idea of getting your attorney involved, but sometimes it's for the best. Just know that I will never make you choose between your son and me. If this situation ever occurs we will work together to do what's right."

I seriously had a problem with giving Jaylin some papers that said if I ever left St. Louis he could have full custody of LJ. It wasn't like leaving St. Louis was in my plans, however, you just never know. Either way, I agreed to it and after Jaylin seemed cool with the arrangements, we got ready to go.

Jaylin and Collins shook hands again, but before we left, I asked Collins if I could talk to Jaylin alone. He agreed and left out. I closed the door behind him and stood in front of it.

"You have to know that I never wanted to hurt you," I said. "I'm sorry for the way all this has turned out, but I do have to move on."

He stood in front of me. "I know. And I'm going to try hard to accept that. Collins seems like a really nice man, Nokea. I'm a little jealous, but you deserve someone like him. And before I forget, I'm sorry for cursing you the other day, I'm sorry for putting my hands on you, and uh, I'm even sorry that it had to end like this between us."

"I am to." I opened my arms for him to hug me. He leaned forward and squeezed me tightly in his arms. After he let go, I squeezed his left cheek and kissed it. When I saw how much lipstick I put on it, I wiped it off.

"Jaylin," I said.

"Yes."

"Who's Daisha?"

"What?" he said grinning and grabbing my hand.

"You heard me. Who's Daisha? The female you were talking to when we walked in."

"She's just a friend, Nokea."

"Really? What kind of friend?"

"Nokea..."

"Okay, I won't pry, but I just want to make sure you're happy."

"I am. Really, I am. If not, then one day I will be." He reached for the door and opened it. "Hey, have you talked to Pat yet?"

"No," I said, walking out. "She won't talk to me. She got her number changed and everything. When I call her at work, she never comes to the phone, so I gave up."

"Well, don't. All friendships can be mended no matter what. Especially when you wasn't the one at fault."

I gave Jaylin another hug and he walked me out to the lobby. Collins was standing there looking at Jaylin's awards on the wall.

"Man, you got it going on, don't you?" Collins said, looking at Jaylin.

"I'd like to think so. I got plenty more of those at home," he bragged.

"Well, why don't you give me a call." Collins pulled out his business card and handed it to Jaylin. "I have my money invested elsewhere, but if I can switch everything successfully and keep it in the family, I will do so." He nudged Jaylin.

"And I will make sure that I call you," Jaylin said.

We waved goodbye and Jaylin stood by Angela's desk and talked to her. As Collins and I waited for the elevator, he leaned over and kissed me. He hugged me and we rocked back and forth together, as I thanked him for handling his business with Jaylin so maturely.

Before I stepped onto the elevator, I looked over at Jaylin again and he smiled, then nodded his head. The last time I saw him do that was when I was walking down the aisle about to marry Stephon. This time, I felt as if he was finally giving me the go ahead to move on with my life.

SCORPIO

I had really jazzed up the place since Jay-Baby left and went back to St. Louis. I called Jackson and cursed him out again for giving Jaylin the phone number and key. And when I finished chewing him out, he apologized. He said he'd make it up to me by sending me some more money so I could fix the place up like I wanted to. He told me to do whatever I wanted to do to it, and sent me another check for $10,000 to get things started.

Trying to make the place feel like home, I went on a shopping spree. There was hella work to be done and by the time I finished, it finally felt kind of livable. I bought a new sofa-bed for the living room, an entertainment center, two space heaters to warm the place up, white paint for the dingy walls, and even had a plumber come over today to replace the old vanity, sink and tub in the bathroom.

As for the bedroom, I covered up the old wallpaper with light blue and yellow flower print wallpaper and it looked much better. I finally had a feeling that I was here, and here to stay.

I had even gotten myself a job at Stars Cafe around the corner. It was close by and I needed the money to pay Jackson back the fifteen-grand he'd already given me.

Being away for almost a month now, I talked to Mackenzie every day around three-thirty in the afternoon while Jaylin was at work. After I got off the phone with her, I normally took it off the hook because I didn't want him calling me. I had a feeling he was trying to call because I knew he was missing me as much as I was missing him. But until he was willing to make some changes, I was staying right here.

After work, I walked down the blistering cold streets of downtown Denver and made my way home. When I got in, I made some hot chocolate and called Jaylin's house to talk to Mackenzie. I was so glad when she picked up.

"Hi, sweetie," I said, happy to hear her voice.

"Hi, Mommy. When are you coming home?" she asked.

"Soon. Is everything okay?"

"Yes. Nanny B and me are in the kitchen making some cookies."

"You are? Will you save me some?"

"I guess...that's if Nanny B doesn't eat them all up," she whispered.

"Well, put a few of them in your room for me, okay?"

"No. Daddy said food in the room causes bugs, so I'll keep them in my coat pocket."

"Thanks, honey. So, are you still coming to see me in a few weeks? Mommy can pick you up at the airport and we'll spend Christmas together."

She hesitated. "I guess. Can Daddy come along too?"

"Not this time, Mackenzie. We need to have a little girl talk and Daddy can't hear it."

"Okay. But, Mommy, he's really been bad lately. He cried after he beat-up his *wife* the other day. I was scared and I cried too." I heard Nanny B say something to Mackenzie in the background, and then Mackenzie gave the phone to her.

"Hello, Scorpio," she said.

"Hi, Nanny B. How's everything going?"

"Fine, just fine. I picked Mackenzie up from school and we're in the kitchen making cookies. Her friend Megan is spending the night tomorrow, so I'm trying to get things ready."

"Thank you so much Nanny B. You are an angel sent from heaven. I don't know what we would do without you."

"Well, I enjoy living here. Mackenzie and LJ have brought new joy to my life. I don't have much of a family anyway so I enjoy their company. Jaylin's too. Don't let me forget about him."

"Nanny B, what was Mackenzie saying about him and Nokea fighting? Is everything okay?"

"Yes, it's fine. They got into an argument over the baby and Jaylin got upset. You know how he can get at times. Especially when it comes to these kids. And by the way, have you mentioned to him that Mackenzie is spending Christmas with you?"

"No, I haven't. I was going to ask my sister to fly to Denver with Mackenzie. I'll call him the week before and tell him then."

"No, I think you should tell him today. Honestly, I don't like the way you and Nokea handle things. He's been a good father to these children, and you all have to learn how to communicate things to him instead of telling him what you're going to do. Now, this leaves both of us with no one to share Christmas with. I guess I'll just have to go over to my sister's house and visit with her."

"I'm sorry, Nanny B, but I miss my child. We have never spent the holidays apart and we're not going to start now. Besides, Mackenzie wants to come see me. I know she misses me just as much as I'm missing her."

"I understand, but please let Jaylin know ahead of time. Don't throw this on him at the last minute and ruin his holiday. It just doesn't make sense to do that."

"Sure, I'll call him tonight. If you get a chance, tell him I'll call him later."

"Thank you," she said, giving the phone back to Mackenzie.

Mackenzie and I talked for another ten minutes and before we hung up I told her how much I love her and how anxious I was to see her. She seemed excited about seeing me too, but I wasn't sure how long it was going to last without Jaylin being around. The last thing I wanted was to invite him to stay with us because one thing would lead to another, and I would be right back where I started. So, him coming here with her was out of the question.

After I got off the phone with Mackenzie, I called the Exterminator. He came over in a flash and sprayed the entire house. When he asked for a kiss, instead of payment, I laughed and quickly pushed him out the door. As fine as he was, and as horny as I was, I thought about breaking the brotha down, but men were just not on my agenda right now. The last mistake I made was with Shane, and I didn't intend on making anymore.

Later that night, I stripped butt naked and pulled the sofa bed out in the living room. The heat was kicking up and I was sweating like hell. I lay down and grabbed the phone to call Jaylin. When he answered, he asked me to hold on because he was on the other end talking. He sounded perky, so I figured it was Stephon, but when he left me on hold for damn near five minutes, I figured it must have been a female. Finally, he clicked back over.

"Yeah, what's up?" he asked.

"Nothing much. I just called to talk to you about Christmas."

"What about it?"

207

"I'd like Mackenzie to spend Christmas with me. I know you probably have plans, but Jaylin, I'm really missing her."

He sounded like he was smacking on something. "Well, come spend Christmas here with us. Why does she have to come to that rat-trap with you?"

"Because I want to spend Christmas with her alone. And I'm fixing this rat-trap up just in case you want to know."

"Really?" he said, smacking harder. "Let me guess, Jackson gave you some money, didn't he?"

"Yes, but I intend on repaying him every dime. I'm working at a cafe around the corner so I can do so."

"Um…interesting. But, uh, I talked to Mackenzie earlier, after Nanny B told me about your plans. I'll bring her to Denver myself. I promise you I won't stay, but I'll expect to have her back with me by New Years."

"Did she say she wanted to come back by New Years?"

"Yes, and she also said that she wanted me to stay with her. But knowing how you don't want me around, I told her it's best that she spends some time with you." He smacked again.

"What in the hell are you eating?"

"I wish it were your pussy, but these strawberries just have to do."

"Some things you say are just ridiculous, Jaylin." I closed my legs tight and wished for the same thing. There wasn't anything I wanted more than to feel him inside me.

"Ridiculous? What's ridiculous is you being in Denver depriving the both of us from being together. But go ahead, baby, and keep up with the bullshit. You're going to miss out on a good thing. And by the way, have you been taking your phone off the hook? I've tried calling a few times and couldn't get through."

"Yes, because I don't want you calling here persuading me to do something I don't want to do. I'm doing just fine and I'd like to keep it that way."

His phone clicked. "Hold on," he said, then clicked over. He clicked back. "Say, I'll see you late Sunday night before Christmas. I already called to make reservations and because of the rush, I prefer to leave out on Sunday."

"That's fine, but why are you rushing me off the phone. You don't waste any time meeting people, do you?"

"And why are you assuming that it's a female on the other end?"

"Because I know you Jaylin. When you're upset, you think with your dick and not with your brains."

He laughed. "You are getting really good at this, Scorpio. Besides, I'd hate to persuade you to do anything you don't want to do. So, chow, gotta go."

He hung up.

I flipped through the channels, and tried to find something to watch. Unable to focus, I got frustrated thinking about Jaylin being with someone else. Normally, I was there to keep his mind occupied, but without me around there wasn't no telling how much trouble he was getting into.

I fell asleep thinking about him, and woke up in a sweat after dreaming he was fucking me so well. Trying to calm myself, I got in my new tub and fantasized about him being in there with me. No matter how hard I tried, the thought of him just wouldn't shake my mind. I wanted him so badly I rushed out of the tub and called his house. I let the phone ring two times, and as I was about to hang up he answered sounding asleep.

"Jaylin?" I whispered.

"What?" he said. Who is this?"

"It's me, Scorpio."

"Do you know what time it is?"

"Yes, but...I just needed to hear your voice."

"Okay, so now that you've heard it, goodbye."

He hung up.

I took a deep breath and closed my eyes. How stupid of me to call him—like he really was going to come all this way and make love to me, and tell me he was going to change. I was out of my mind. But as I was getting ready to get back into the tub the phone rang. I rushed to it knowing it was him.

"Hello," I said, softly.

"Say," he said.

"What?"

"I'm lonely."

"So am I. That's why I called you."

"Then come home."

"I will when you change your ways."

"No can do."

"Not even for me?"

"No, not even for you. I love who I am and I'm hoping that you figure out a way to accept me."

"As much as I want to, I can't."

"Then I can't put my life on hold for you any longer. Goodnight, Scorpio. Maybe next time."

"Yeah, maybe so."

I hung up.

JAYLIN

I was up all night thinking about Scorpio. I called that punk-ass Jackson and told him don't get carried away with the money giving bullshit. With him sending her $10,000 that meant I was already $20,000 in debt with him. And that doesn't even include the money I already paid his slick ass. I also told him that he better not take any money from Scorpio and if he did, the deal was off.

Since I couldn't get back to sleep, I got up and took an early morning drive to the Waffle House and ate breakfast. Knowing that Daisha was getting off work at six o'clock in the morning from the hospital, I called her on my cell phone to see if she wanted some company. When she told me to meet her at her place, I was all smiles. I called Angela's voice mail and told her I was not coming in today.

Being able to read females so damn well, unbelievably, I really couldn't figure out what kind of game Daisha was playing. She seemed to be digging the shit out of me, but whenever I mentioned sex, she always changed the subject. We had been on the phone more than anything, and as much as I was enjoying our conversations, I was ready for her to shake a brotha down. Especially since it had been a while since I'd last had sex. Wasn't like I couldn't get no ass, but right about now I had to have a certain kind of pussy. Any woman just wasn't going to do, and the ones who could satisfy me were straight up bullshitting. Nokea was off with her new man and probably wasn't even thinking about my black ass. Scorpio was holding back, playing games, knowing that she damn well wanted some of this, and Daisha, I wasn't sure if she could please me or not, but I was dying to find out.

I pulled in front of Daisha's house and she was getting out of the car. She was trying to pull a huge duffel bag out of her trunk, and I rushed out of my car to help. I took it from her and put it on my shoulder.

"Thank you," she said, slamming the trunk down. She walked in front of me, and once again, I had the opportunity to check her out from behind. Ass was perfect. I couldn't wait for the opportunity to see how well that motherfucker could move.

After we entered the house, she took the bag off my shoulder and told me to have a seat in the living room. I was thinking more like the bedroom, but I settled for the living room.

I sat down in a burgundy executive-style leather chair, and looked around the room. It was decorated with old-fashioned furniture and was spotless. She had magazines neatly laid out on a glass round table that sat on a green rug, and covered the shiny hardwood floors. As I continued looking around, I noticed her wedding picture on the fireplace mantel and stood up to go check out the groom. He looked okay, but she seemed much too pretty to be with someone like him. I heard her coming down the stairs, and I eased back over to the chair and sat down. She leaned down on the steps, and invited me upstairs to her bedroom.

"I was getting ready to take a shower, but I didn't want to leave you downstairs all alone," she said, walking up the steps. She sat on the edge of her bed, and kicked her shoes off. I stood in the doorway with my hands in my pockets.

"You can come in," she said. "I promise you I won't bite."

I laughed and wished that she would. Then sat on the bed next to her. "So, are you tired? I know you probably had a long night at the hospital, and you sounded pretty tired when you called me last night."

"Exhausted more like it. Normally, I come in, take a shower, and I'm out until three or four o'clock in the afternoon."

"Well, if you want to get some rest, I can come back later."

"No, that's okay. I can rest with you here, can't I?" She walked into the closet and came out with a few pieces of clothing in her hand.

"I can use some rest myself," I said, falling back on the bed, and putting my hands behind my head.

"Then we'll rest together." She went into the bathroom and closed the door. I took my jacket, shoes, and hat off and scooted back on her comfortable ass king-sized bed. Her room was very feminine: dressed with light-purple, pink, and an eggshell white, had flower shaped purple pillows all over the place, white wicker chairs sat in front of a bay window, and her room smelled like peaches. What I admired about the whole damn house was the cleanliness about it. A clean house was a must for me, and Daisha had no clue that she was already my kind of woman.

213

I lay my head on her pillow and waited for her to come out of the bathroom. When she did, she had a towel wrapped around her head and had her pink cotton pajamas on. She removed the towel and teased her short hair around with her fingers. Extremely pretty, I thought, and could pass for my sister quite easily—if I had one.

She pulled the covers back and climbed in bed next to me. She lay on her back and closed her eyes. I moved over next to her.

"Are you falling asleep already?" I asked.

"Shh...I'm praying."

"I'm sorry," I said, then moving back over.

She opened her eyes. "It's okay. I just like to thank God for the wonderful day He's already planned for me, that's all."

"Nothing wrong with that. Did you thank him for me too?"

"I thanked him for you yesterday, but if you're asking me if I thanked him for allowing you another day, you need to do that."

"Okay, I will." I closed my eyes and thanked Him. "There, done deal."

She smiled, turned to her side, and looked at me. "You are an interesting man, Jaylin."

"And why do you say that?" I turned to my side as well.

"Because, I've heard some crazy things about you. Mona and I were talking the other day, and the things she said about you, I'm having a hard time believing."

"Damn! What did she tell you?"

"Bottom line, she said that you were a serious ho."

"Really? Not just a ho, but a *serious* ho?"

"Yes. She also told me you have several lady friends and you treat them like shit."

"Keep going," I said. "This could get pretty ugly. Tell me more, please."

She laughed. "Anyway, I told her the same thing about Stephon. I also told her I saw more in you than just that and we squashed it. So, tell me, is she right, or am I wrong?"

"Depends."

"Depends on what?"

"Depends on what you see in me that she doesn't see."

"I see an arrogant, confident, classy, well put together, educated, aggressive, controlling, wealthy, handsome, persuasive-ass man who loves to have sex with women."

"Now, *that*, was a mouthful."

"So, now, am I wrong, or am I right?"

"Depends."

"Depends on what, Jaylin," she said, smiling.

"Depends on if this arrogant, confident, classy, well put together, educated, aggressive, controlling, wealthy, fine-ass man is going to persuade you to make love to him this morning."

"No."

"Well, then, you're wrong and she's right."

"No she's not," Daisha said, playfully pushing me back.

"Yes she is. Because that's how women perceive a man like me to be. Forget all the wonderful things about me, nobody ever looks at that. It's always the bottom line and that's I'm a *serious* ho. Truth of the matter is, I love myself more than anything in the world. I do what makes me happy and if that's being with more than one woman, so be it. Eventually everybody settles down, I just haven't found the right person to settle down with."

"Are you looking for someone to settle down with?"

"No. I'm never looking. See, men are different. Most of the time, love for us comes totally unexpected. We don't actually go around looking for a woman to marry. A woman has to catch us off guard, kind of slip into our hearts for us to settle down. Sometimes we don't even know the feeling is there until she's gone, and that's when we have to learn from our mistakes and move on."

"Sounds like you've been there and done that before. Question is, are you learning from your mistakes?"

"Nope. Can't honestly say I have. That's because I don't mind making mistakes. I believe everything happens for a reason, and if I make a hundred mistakes in my lifetime, I won't sweat it. When God connects me with the woman He made for me, those mistakes will not be happening."

"Jaylin, I agree, but you have to draw the line somewhere. Especially when you keep hurting women in the process. One day, those mistakes are going to cost you big-time, if they already haven't. The days of finding a good sister are just about over because we are

215

getting tired of the, excuse my French, but the bullshit. Men are losing out right now and don't even know it. So, anytime a good woman comes your way you'd better hold on to her and I mean tight. If you don't wake up, you're going to find yourself being without."

"You're a smart woman, Daisha. And I honestly appreciate your opinion, but I'll never be without."

"Well, you're going to be without this conversation because I am getting tired. Come over here and hold me so we can get some sleep."

Daisha turned around and I eased over behind her and held her. She placed her hand on top of mine and turned up her cheek for me to kiss it. I kissed it and breathe in her fresh smelling body. As I continued kissing down her neck, she turned back around and lifted my face.

"Jaylin, I recently ended a marriage that I wanted so desperately to work. And even though I come off being hard on you, I have needs just like everyone else does. Don't hurt me, please. I've been hurt enough. More so, don't make me regret making love to you this morning, okay?"

She raised my shirt over my head and I leaned forward to kiss her. Immediately thinking about my unfinished business with Scorpio, I started concentrating hard on fucking Daisha. I unbuttoned her pajama top, looked at her succulent breasts, and cleared my mind. And when she took her pajama pants off there was no turning back for me. Her ass was just as I had imagined it, smooth and plump enough for me to work it how I wanted to. She placed her head on the pillow, and I stood up and took my pants off. I looked at her naked body and stood there trying to figure out where to adventure first. When she gave me a hint and widened her legs, I crawled in between them and slid my dick deeply in. Being sexually deprived for weeks, I felt myself quickly wanting to come, but I held back so I could make it last.

Daisha felt good. The way she softly moaned and touched my ass, as we rocked our bodies together seriously turned me on. And when she came, she was calm about it. She took my head and placed it between her breasts and squeezed her legs tightly around my waist. When her moment was finished, and no questions asked, she rolled over and let me love her from behind. I remained gentle with my strokes until she raised up on her knees. And after having the pleasure of watching her ass shake, I had to let go.

"Now, you know better," I said, tightly holding her hips.

"Jaylin," she said, softly. "Don't you dare. Especially when I'm so into you right now."

I definitely couldn't disappoint her, so I took a deep breath, and pressed my body up against hers, as she lay down on her stomach. On the rise, I slid myself back inside of her, and was thinking about how bad I wanted to feel her for at least another hour. Enjoying myself, I gripped her hands together with mine.

"Are you okay now?" I whispered, as I expanded inside of her.

"Uhm...more than okay," she mumbled. I went in deeper. "Okay," she moaned, "Better, oh, so much better."

"Better than this?" I said, rolling her over backwards on top of me, spreading her legs, and massaging her clitoris with one hand, and her breast with the other.

"No, uh, uh. Never better than this," she trembled. "Never in my entire lifetime better than this."

I kept stroking Daisha at a slow pace, while she was still on top of me, so neither one of us would come. She was grinding down on me and wasn't cutting a brotha no slack. When I heard her pussy clack, and that being my cue, I picked up the pace.

"Daisha?" I whispered in her ear.

"Yes, Jaylin," she whispered back.

"I'm getting ready to make you come. This time, I want to feel it. Not only that, but I want to hear you say how much you enjoyed this, okay."

"Stop talking so damn much and just do it," she yelled.

I slammed myself further in, and rubbed my head up against her clit on my exits. Feeling every bit of me, she tried raising up, but I held her hips down tightly with my hands.

She took deep breaths. "Okay, now I see," she said, rocking faster with me, as I was starting to feel her come. "I truly see what the big fuss—" she screamed my name.

"Yes?" I said, kissing her on the back of her head.

She rolled over and looked at me. "That's a shame."

"What...what did I do?" I smiled.

"*That* was not supposed to be that good."

"And neither were you. So, I'm sorry, and I'll take it back."

"No, you can't have it back."

"So, it's yours for keeps."

"Yes, it is. Only if you'll let me keep it."

"Whenever," I gave her a peck on the lips, then eased over next to her. "However," I circled my tongue around her nipples. "And wherever," I leaned down, and licked her between the legs.

"Come here," she said, laughing. "I have to be honest with you about something."

"What?" I said, lying next to her again.

"I didn't intend on having sex with you, and I hope I didn't come off too easy because when I have my head on straight, I'm not."

"Daisha, I truly believe that. I just hope you don't have any regrets. Especially after how we just got down."

"No regrets, Jaylin. You have no idea how much I needed, or should I say, wanted to feel like that."

"Tell me about it. It's been a long time for me too."

"Really? Well, it's been almost one year for me. I stop sleeping with my husband months before the marriage was over. And honestly, he never made me feel like that. Anyway, come over here and hold me so we can get that rest we talked about earlier."

"Rest my ass. I'd say lets make up for some of this lost time you and I seem to have had."

She looked at me. "Where do you get all your energy from? Are you serious?"

"Serious as serious can get." I opened her legs with my foot and eased in between them.

"You are going to find yourself in trouble messing with a woman like me—you handsome devil."

"I love trouble, baby, bring it on."

Daisha didn't lie. After messing around with her for a while my ass was in trouble. I was drained and she was going full force. She talked bad about me, but still told me how much she enjoyed herself. I enjoyed myself as well. Every time I thought you couldn't teach an old dog new tricks, a different woman would come along and show me something new. On a good day, Daisha could actually outlast me. Thing is, I was going to enjoy every moment of competing with her.

When I woke up and looked for Daisha she wasn't there. I looked at my watch and it showed almost six o'clock in the evening. Damn, where did the time go? I thought. I pulled the covers back and slid into my boxers.

After hearing Daisha downstairs on the phone, I went down there to see why she let me sleep so long. I was coming down the steps, and could see her sitting in the living room with her legs folded up in a chair. She was gazing at the fire burning in the fireplace and running her mouth on the phone. When she heard me step down onto the hardwood floors, she turned her head.

"Mona, I'll call you back later, okay?" she whispered, then looked at me. "Hey, sleepy head."

I walked over by her and sat down on the floor in front of her. She put her legs on the floor and I lay my head against them. As she rubbed her hands in my hair like Scorpio does, I started to think about her. And when Daisha noticed how quiet I was she snapped me out of it.

"A penny for your thoughts," she asked.

"Naw, a nickel for your kiss," I said. She leaned down and kissed me. "I'm just thinking about what a wonderful day I had with you Daisha. Usually, I'm anxious to leave, but for some reason I feel a sense of peace when I'm with you."

"Good. And I hope you continue to feel that way. I wish I could stay here with you all night, but I have to be at work by nine. If you want to, you can stay the night. I won't be back until at least six or seven o'clock in the morning."

"That won't be necessary. I'm getting ready to go home. I, uh, need to spend some time with my son before he goes to Detroit and with my daughter before she goes to Denver. The next few weeks are going to be tough for me, so please don't be offended if you don't hear from me, and by all means, don't take it personal. When I'm upset, sometimes I prefer to be alone."

"Well, you shouldn't be alone on Christmas. I have plans to go to Florida where my parents live, but I was just there on Thanksgiving. If you'd like, I can cook dinner for us and we can celebrate Christmas and New Years together."

"That's nice, but we'll see. I'll let you know next week."

Daisha headed for work and I headed for home. There was something different about her, but I just couldn't quite put my finger on it. Maybe it was how good the sex was between us, but that might have been because I haven't had any for a while.

Either way, she could really be a set back for me, especially when I thought I was feeling something special for Scorpio. And trying not to think about her so much, I focused my mind elsewhere and sped up to get home.

Mackenzie's best friend Megan was staying a few days with us because her parents were out of town on vacation and asked if she could stay. Nanny B cleared it with me last week, and I said it was fine as long as it was cool with her.

No sooner had I walked through the door, Mackenzie and Megan were running around the house like they were outside on a playground, and making all kinds of noise. Having a slight headache, I asked them to be quiet. Mackenzie yelled back and told me to shut up.

"What did you say?" I asked in total disbelief, while standing in the foyer with the mail in my hands.

She put her hands on her hips. "I said don't raise your voice at me!" She screamed.

Nanny B came out of the kitchen. "Mackenzie, I heard you all the way—"

"Naw, that's all right, Nanny B, I got this one here." I took my belt off my pants. "Get your butt upstairs right now Mackenzie! Go to your room!"

She handed Megan her doll and stomped upstairs to her room. Nanny B took Megan into the kitchen and came back out before I started up the steps.

"Jaylin, don't you hit her and I mean it. I know she can get out of hand sometimes, but she's just a kid. Don't blame her for learning all that bossy stuff from those kids she go to school with."

"Nanny B stop making excuses for her. I don't care where she's learning that stuff from. First me, and now the school. Bottom line is she will not disrespect me and I mean it." I ignored Nanny B and went right upstairs to Mackenzie's room. She was lying across the bed crying like somebody was killing her.

220

"Get up off the bed," I said, angrily. She ignored me and continued to cry. "Mackenzie, did you hear what I said?" I yelled.

She stood up with tears pouring down her face and was barely able to catch her breath. She looked at me and rubbed her beautiful eyes. "I want my Mommy," she burst out. She ran up to me and hugged me around the waist. "Daddy, please, don't hit me. I want my Mommy."

I closed my eyes and hugged her back. "I want her too, sweetheart. In due time, though, alright? I promise you, in due time."

I sat down on her bed, put her on my lap, then wiped her tears. "Mackenzie, I will never hit you, but you are not allowed to speak to me in such manner. Do you understand?" She nodded. "I don't care how your other friends talk to their parents, we don't talk like that in this house, okay." She nodded again. "Why would you talk to me like that anyway? I thought you loved me."

"I do love you Daddy, but…I'm afraid of you."

"What? Since when did you become afraid of me?"

"Since you tried to kill your wife downstairs. I told my friends about you choking her and they said you're a murderer."

Damn stupid kids, I thought. "Mackenzie, you can't be telling your friends things like that. And you tell them your daddy is not a murderer. I would never do anything to hurt anyone—it was all a big mistake, baby. My *wife* knows I wouldn't do anything to purposely hurt her."

"But she was crying."

"And so was I. But that's because we don't enjoy hurting one another like that. Please don't be afraid of me. I love you and I will never hurt you."

She hopped down off my lap and wiped her eyes. "Can I go downstairs now to play with Megan?"

"Yes, Mackenzie. But let's go call Mommy before you do and tell her we're coming to see her."

"But I thought we were going to see her on Christmas."

"I know, but let's surprise her and go see her earlier."

Mackenzie and I called Scorpio but the number was busy. I called reservations and made arrangements for us to leave Thursday night instead of Sunday before Christmas. And even though I lost my money for the tickets, Mackenzie needed to see Scorpio and so did I.

221

It was time for me to change my game plan because Mackenzie was watching my every move. I truly believed her bad behavior was from her missing Scorpio.

Our plane touched down in Denver around ten o'clock late Thursday night. Mackenzie was all bundled up in her new pink and white coat that I bought. And her long fluffy hair was hanging out of her hat. She looked adorable and I knew Scorpio was going to be glad to see her. I bought her a puppy for Christmas, but I wasn't going to pick him up until she came back home.

When the rental car assistant pulled up with our rental car, we were well on our way. Before I'd left St. Louis, I stopped by Jackson's place and paid him his money. He showed me another check that he sent her for $5,000, so I knocked that one out too. He claimed the only reason he sent the money is because she made it clear to him that she was never coming back to St. Louis. I guess by the way she was spending money to fix the place up maybe, just maybe, she was there to stay. I made him promise to never tell Scorpio about the money because she would be furious with me if she knew I was taking care of her expenses in Denver as well.

We pulled in front of Jackson's house and Mackenzie rushed to open the car door. I reached in my pocket for the second key Jackson gave me before I left. I put the key in the door and whispered for Mackenzie to be very quiet. When we walked in, the TV was blasted. Scorpio was lying naked on her stomach across the sofa bed. She was asleep and held a body pillow close, with her legs wrapped around it. I guessed she thought it was me.

I told Mackenzie to go back into the bedroom, so she could surprise Scorpio when I woke her. Mackenzie quietly tiptoed down the hallway.

I moved in closer to Scorpio, and looked at how pretty she was, as her long hair spread out over the pillow. She actually had a white silk thong on and my imagination took me to where the string was lying. I couldn't see her breasts because she held them closely to the body pillow. I swore that if it wasn't for Mackenzie being with me, I would have torn into her right then and there.

Instead, I spit on my hands, rubbed them together until they felt nice and warm, then I smacked her on her ass as hard as I could. Panicking, she hopped up and quickly reached for her robe.

"What are you doing?" she yelled. "That shit is not funny." She put her robe on and gave me a crazy look. "Why are you here, Jaylin?"

"Damn! Happy to see you too Scorpio."

She pulled her hair back, rolled her eyes, and got up. Abruptly walking to the kitchen, I followed behind her. "Where's my child?" she asked while standing against the refrigerator.

"Where's my hug?"

"You don't get one after scaring the shit out of me and hitting me on my ass like that."

"Couldn't resist."

"Well, it's not made for smacking. Just in case you can't remember."

"I know, it's made for me, right?" I walked up to her and put my arms around her. "Can I at least have a kiss?" I rubbed my hands on the cheek of her ass to cool it off. "Sorry about that and I promise I'll make it up to your ass later."

She pecked me on the lips and removed my arms from around her. "No, thanks. Where's my child, Jaylin? Did you come here without her?"

I took Scorpio's hand and walked her back into the bedroom where Mackenzie was. Mackenzie had even hid by the side of the bed. When we walked in she jumped up and yelled for Scorpio. They kissed and hugged each other, and even though I was happy to see them together, I couldn't believe that a small part of me was actually kind of jealous.

Trying to allow them some time together, I went back into the kitchen. Thinking about LJ, I pulled out my cell phone to call Nokea. I knew they were heading out on Monday, so I called to make sure she was bringing him over to spend the weekend with me before they left.

"I'll drop him off before I go to my hair appointment early Saturday morning. Is that okay?" she asked.

"Yeah, that's fine. Anyway, how are things going? Every time you bring LJ by I hardly get a chance to talk to you anymore."

"Everything is fine, Jaylin. Actually, couldn't be better. You don't sound too good, though. Is everything okay with you?"

"Yeah, I'm cool. I'm dreading being alone without my children on Christmas, but I'm cool."

"What about Mackenzie? Is she going somewhere too?"

"Yeah, I'm in Denver now, bringing her to see Scorpio."

"Oh...I didn't know, but I'm sorry. You're welcome to come to Detroit with us. Collins wanted me to ask you the other day, but I knew you would probably say no."

"Thanks, but you know that is out of the question. I'm not that comfortable with the situation yet."

"Well, what about Stephon and Ray Ray?"

"Nokea, they have their own lives. Don't worry, I'll be fine. I'll do something to keep myself occupied."

"Darn, Jaylin, I feel so bad. Look, if you want LJ to stay with you, that's fine. I'll take him some other time with Collins and me."

"I will consider no such thing. I told you that I'm cool. Take him with you and Collins. You'd better take me up on my offer because it might be your last chance."

"Are you sure?"

"Yes, Nokea. Look, I'll see you soon. I gotta go, okay."

"Alright...I love you."

"Love you too."

I hung up.

Nobody knew my true pain but me. All my life I had a serious fear of being alone. My fear came from spending those two years in an orphanage and having no one to come see me but Nokea and her mother, on occasion. I guess when my grandfather passed away he must have felt guilty, and that's why he left me so much money. It was probably his way of making up for lost time, and for betraying his deceased daughter, my mother.

After sitting in the kitchen for about an hour, thinking, I got up to check on Scorpio and Mackenzie. When I walked back into the bedroom, Mackenzie was cuddled up in Scorpio's arms sound asleep. Scorpio kissed Mackenzie and whispered for me to be quiet, as she slid out of bed. As she walked down the hallway, I followed her into the living room. She sat on the sofa bed, placed her hands over her face, and cried.

"Thank you so much Jaylin. You have no idea how much I've missed her. And for you to ask me to let her come back with you, I can't. There is no way, I'm sorry."

I sat down next to her. "Look, don't stress yourself out about it. I'm not going to fight you over this anymore. She's your child and I know more than anything how much she means to you. I'm just sorry you won't come back and work this out with me."

"Not right now, I can't." She wiped her eyes. "Did you see what I've done to this place?"

"Yeah, I have. It doesn't look too bad either. I kind of like it."

"Like it enough to live here yourself."

I laughed. "No...I don't like it that much."

"I'm sure you don't. I guess you wouldn't trade in your mansion for a place like this anyway."

"No, I wouldn't. But it says a lot about a woman's character that would. Especially for the sake of her own happiness." I raised up off the sofa and went into the kitchen to get my coat. Scorpio followed.

"Are you leaving already?"

"Yes, I think it's best. Especially while Mackenzie's still asleep."

"Okay. When she wakes up I'll tell her you said goodbye." Scorpio reached over and hugged me. I held her tight and didn't want to let go. When I did, I took a deep breath and walked to the door.

"Can I have my key?" she asked.

"No, no way. This key is worth a lot of money to me. Trust me, you don't want to know."

"If you paid Jackson more than ten dollars for it, you're a fool. He's a serious money hustler and will do anything to make a dime."

"I'm sure he would, but whatever, my loss—I guess."

"So, if you're keeping the key, that must mean you're coming back, right?"

"One day, maybe I will. Who knows?" I winked and opened the door. Scorpio stopped me.

"I love you, Jaylin. And thanks again for bringing Mackenzie."

"Ditto. And anything to make you happy."

No sooner had I got to the car, Mackenzie stood on the porch looking at me. When I waved she started hysterically crying. I got out of the car and pulled her back into the house because it was freezing outside.

"Why are you crying, Mackenzie? I'll be back to get you." Seeing her cry was really starting to work my nerves. I kneeled down to calm her, but she hugged me and wouldn't let go. I looked up at Scorpio. "Why don't you just come home? This is just down right ridiculous for us to be apart like this."

Mackenzie continued to hold me tightly around the neck, crying. "Oooo, Daddy, don't go. Please don't leave me. I'll be good, I promise. I don't want to stay if you don't stay."

"Mackenzie, I can't stay. You said you wanted to spend time with your Mommy, so please, I'll be back." My eyes watered.

Scorpio leaned down next to Mackenzie and me. "Mackenzie, if you don't want to stay with me, you don't have to. You can go home with your Daddy." Scorpio looked disappointed.

Mackenzie grabbed Scorpio around the neck too. "I want to stay with you Mommy, but I want Daddy to stay with us too. Why can't he stay? Please let him stay," she begged.

"I can't stay, Mackenzie. I promise you I'll be back." I kissed her on the cheek and stood up. I tightened my coat in the front, quickly opened the door, and didn't look back. Mackenzie yelled and screamed my name, but I just kept on walking.

I couldn't take the pressure anymore. It was killing me not knowing if she was going to be a part of my life forever. And by the time I reached the end of the street, I pulled the car over and broke down. Pain was rushing all through my body and I couldn't stop it. Why did life have to be so damn difficult? I thought. First Jasmine, then LJ and now Mackenzie. How much more of this can a brotha take?

After sitting there soaking for a while, and trying to get myself together, I started the car. I wanted to go back for Mackenzie, but I couldn't. Instead, I drove back to the airport and waited for my plane back to St. Louis.

On the plane ride home, this very attractive Stewardess tried to entertain me, but I wasn't interested. She had given me her phone number, and when I got to Lambert Airport I threw it in the trash.

226

At home, Nanny B hired some fellows to put up a twelve-foot Christmas Tree and they decorated it with off-white and gold trimmings. When she told me they were coming to put it up, I had no idea it was going to look so magnificent. She left a note on the table with some cookies and said she went to her sister's house and wouldn't be back until the day after Christmas. She left a number where I could reach her, and left a present for me on the table with a card on top.

I lay back on the chaise looking at the white lights on the tree, as they were flashing on me in the dark. Then I opened Nanny B's card and started to read: *Merry Christmas, my dear. I wanted to give this to you personally, but I wasn't sure when you would be back. Save me a slice of the pineapple-upside-down cake, and I'll see you when I return, Love You, Bertha. P.S. Christmas dinner is in the refrigerator and the house is spotless just how you like it.*

I smiled because I thought her name was Brenda. When I asked her she would always tell me to call her Nanny B, so I just assumed the B was for Brenda. Maybe because it was an old girlfriend of mine name.

I opened the box and there was a silver and gold photo album laced with black velvet cloth. An old black and white picture of mama and me, when I was a baby was on the front. On the inside were pictures of my grandfather, Stephon when he was a baby, my Aunt Betty, my cousins, and even a picture of my father was in the far back. After I saw a picture of LJ and Mackenzie, there were some blank pages and the last page was a photo of Nanny B and my grandfather. I pulled it out, looked at the back, and it read Anthony Jerome Rogers & Bertha Marie White married June 1953.

Well, I'd be damn, I thought. She was my grandmother? What I vaguely remembered about my grandmother, she didn't look anything like Nanny B. I knew very little about my family's history, but there was no way in hell that she was my grandmother.

Curious, I got up and ran downstairs to look through an old cedar chest I kept hidden away in a closet. When I opened it, I could tell someone had been rummaging through it because the pictures weren't as neat as I had had them. I looked through them one by one until I found a wedding picture of my grandparents on their wedding day. The picture was of the grandmother I'd remembered, and when I

227

looked on the back, it said married May 1971. I was only two-years-old, so that's why I couldn't remember. Nanny B was married to him before he married my grandmother. Question is, which one of them was my mother's mother, I thought. Had to be Nanny B because my mother was already twenty-one when my grandfather re-married in 1971.

After I put the pictures next to each other, Nanny B didn't look like my mother, the other woman did. Still confused, I grabbed all the pictures and ran back up stairs. I thought I was losing my damn mind, but when I thought about who introduced me to Nanny B to begin with, it started to all make sense. Stephon's mother, my Aunt Betty, did. She told me about a nanny who did a superb job cleaning, and told me how much I could trust her.

I wanted to call Nanny B at her sister's house first, but instead, I called Stephon to see how much of this he knew about. It was early in the morning, but I desperately wanted some answers.

"Yeah," he said, sounding asleep.

"Man, wake up."

"Nigga, I'm tired. What's up?"

"Do you know who my nanny is?"

"Jay, you ain't sleeping with your nanny, are you?"

"Naw, fool. I mean, have you ever seen her besides her being over here?"

"Uh-uh, why?"

"Because I think she's our grandmother."

"Fool, what you over there smoking? Our grandparents were killed in a car accident, remember? Jay, I hope you ain't smoking that shit man."

"Naw, listen, I'm serious. Nanny B gave me a picture of her and Grandpa for my Christmas present. Well, the picture was in a photo album she gave me. Anyway, on the back, it said they were married in June of 1953. But then, there's another picture of him with our grandmother that says they were married in 1971."

"Sounds like the apple doesn't fall far from the tree. Sounds to me like Grandpa had his mack on."

"Could be...definitely could be. But, uh, you've never seen Nanny B before? Especially since your mother hooked me up with her."

"Man, I really can't say that I have. Let me think about it for a while and if something comes up, I'll call you back. Anyway, why is this so important to you?"

"Please, Stephon. How can you ask me that? If she's our grandmother, then that explains everything."

"Everything like what?"

"Her attachment to me. To Mackenzie, to LJ...everything."

"My love for you. My understanding you," she said. I turned around and Nanny B was standing behind me.

My heart dropped and I yelled, "Turn the fucking lights on! Now! Jesus Christ!" Nanny B turned the lights on.

"Jay!" Stephon yelled. "You alright, man?"

"I'll call you back," I said, and quickly hung up on Stephon. I angrily looked at Nanny B. "Tell me...what in the fuck is going on? Who in the hell are you?"

"Sit down, Jaylin," she asked, sitting down on the couch.

"I ain't sitting no where until I find out what the fuck is going on?"

She looked serious. "Please, sit down. I'll tell you everything, just have a seat." My heart was racing, as I walked over to the couch and sat down. She placed her hand on my leg. "I was close to my sister's place, and I turned the car around thinking about how important it was for me to come back here and tell you my story."

"What story, Nanny B, damn it what story?"

"I'm not your blood grandmother, but I was married to your grandfather in 1953. When I met him he had two beautiful daughters, and a son, like you. He was much older than I was, but I loved him and his children more than life itself. Your grandmother had run off with some other man and left your grandfather and her kids behind. So, when he met me, I gave them all the love I could muster, and they finally had someone they could look up to even though I was only eighteen-years-old at the time. Your mother was my favorite. She was the oldest and was twelve-years-old when I met your grandfather. She was by far the prettiest child I'd ever seen."

"Was she as pretty as me?" I asked, smiling.

"Yes, a lot prettier. Anyway, when your real grandmother decided to come back your grandfather asked me for a divorce to marry her. I was devastated. I had given up everything for him, and I do mean everything. But there wasn't nothing I could do. He was still in love with her and I was out. When your mother and Aunt Betty had you and Stephon they would bring y'all by my house so I could see y'all, but even that soon stopped. Your grandfather threw a fit about me keeping in touch and cut off all ties."

"Was he that mean, Nanny B?"

"Stubborn," she looked at me and smiled. "Just like you."

"So, anyway, when I found out your mother had been killed, I cried for months. Lord knows I was hurt, and since I couldn't have any children she was like my child. All three of them were. But when I showed up at her funeral, your grandfather turned me away. He said I needed to stop interfering and move on with my life. So, that's what I did. I kept in touch with your Aunt Betty for a while, but mostly by phone. When she got herself on drugs, and I found out she lied to me about getting you out of that orphanage, I really didn't want anything to do with her. Then, one day she called and told me you were looking for a nanny. She made me promise to never tell you the truth, and begged me to look out for you like I looked out for them."

"No, not Aunt Betty, Nanny B. She hated me. The things she used to do and say to me I never understood."

"Baby, she didn't mean to hurt you. Those drugs made her a totally different person. But she was very jealous of your mother. Like Stephon is of you. They loved each other, though. Nothing could keep them apart. Your mother's death is actually what sent her over the edge."

"But why didn't you just tell me all this before? Why tell me all of this now?"

"Because I was afraid to tell you. If I had told you along time ago, you would have turned me away, Jaylin. You would have found no purpose for me. Now, you know what my purpose is. It's to love you, to take care of you, and to make sure you do the right things when it comes to your children."

Thinking about how much Nanny B knew about me, I shamefully stood up, walked over by the tree, and looked at her. "Have I disappointed you? Do you think my mother is proud of me?"

"Yes and No. You and Stephon are a splitting image of your grandfather. I watch the two of you with all these women and how disrespectful y'all can be and I just shake my head. But the love that

230

you have for your children is what I'm proud of. I know your mother is proud of that too. Being in that orphanage might have hurt you, but it helped you in some ways too. It helped you open up to children in a way you probably never would have been able to."

"You're right. I never want any child to have to suffer like I did." Nanny B stood up, and came over by me, as she could tell I was about to lose it. She took my hand. "Nanny B," I said, looking at her. "Why did Grandpa leave me his money, though? Why not Stephon, or my other cousins? More so, why not his own son?"

"Jonathan, that's your uncle, moved away years ago. He married some white woman in Kentucky and nobody's heard from him since. When your grandfather died, he left 11.5 million dollars to me in his WILL. I was shocked and didn't know what to do with the money. I truly didn't want one dime after what he put me through. So, I got a lawyer, decided which one of his grandchildren I wanted to give the money to and since I loved your mother so much, I didn't have a difficult choice to make."

There was silence. "But I only got 9.5 million. Where's the other two?"

"Well, the lawyer suggested that I take a little something for my pain and suffering, so I did." She laughed. "But, Jaylin, I never wanted a dime. That money is growing in a mutual fund right now untouched. I'd like for you to put it up for your children. All I ever wanted was to be a part of this family and if my being a nanny got me here, so be it."

Nanny B and I tightly hugged each other. "Nanny B, I got one more question for you. How old are you? You told me you were fifty-seven, but if my calculations are correct, you're actually sixty-seven."

She laughed. "How old do I look? Can't I pass for fifty-seven or even forty-seven?"

"You really could, but I'm worried about all the things you do around here. All the driving and everything you do for the kids. And the cigarettes, those can't be good for you."

"I'm a blessed healthy young woman, Jaylin, that's all you need to know. But how did you know about my cigarettes? I only smoke them every once in a while and when I do, I go outside."

"Mackenzie told me. I didn't believe her, but when I checked your pockets, I saw them."

231

We laughed and when the doorbell rang we looked at each other like who in the hell that could be at this time in the morning. When she opened the door Stephon came rushing in.

"What's going on, man? Why did you hang up on me?"

I looked at my watch; it was way over an hour after I'd talked to him. "You can't move no faster than that? I could have been over here dying or something," I said.

He plopped down on the couch. "I had to get dressed. Damn. But what's all this crazy talk about Nanny B?"

I was getting ready to tell him, but Nanny B stood behind him and shook her head telling me not to. "Nothing, dog. It was a joke. She was messing around with me because she knew how upset I was about Christmas."

"But since the both of you are here, why don't I whip y'all up some breakfast? Besides, I'm hungry myself." Nanny B said.

"Sounds like a plan to me," Stephon said. Nanny B went into the kitchen and started breakfast. "Man, you straight up lucked up on a good ass nanny. You just can't find them like that these days."

"I know, man. Deep in my heart I truly know."

Nanny B cooked a scrumptious breakfast for us: cheese eggs, grits, bacon, sausage, toast & jelly, and some buttermilk pancakes. Shit was off the hook. After Stephon left she told me not to tell him the truth because she didn't want him being hurt by her decision to give the money to me.

I talked to her about my situation with Mackenzie and she advised me to back down. She told me to allow Scorpio and Mackenzie time together and assured me Mackenzie would be coming back soon.

Nokea dropped LJ off early Saturday morning and headed to her hair appointment. I was feeling a slight bit better and she could tell when she finally came in to talk to me this time. Her whole attitude and outlook on life had changed. I was seeing a different side of her, one that I admired and respected more than anything. I was sure Collins was the reason, but I was kind of disappointed in myself for being with her all those years and not bringing out the best in her like Collins did.

I spent the entire weekend alone with my son. Nanny B had even left for her sister's house yesterday, after spending most of the day with LJ and me. We really couldn't do much, but I showed him how to play cards, how to use the remote control, and even how to make investments transactions on my laptop computer. He loved being in the water, so I let him splash around in the tub after I filled it with bubbles.

Late Sunday night, we bundled up and went outside to hoop. Of course, he won but it was considered cheating since I had to lift him up to make the ball go in.

Nokea called around ten o'clock that night and said she was tied up at her parents' house and would send Collins over to pick up LJ. When I accused her of having a shitty excuse, she laughed and said she wanted me to be comfortable with Collins and the more time we spent getting to know each other, the better. Slightly pissed about being forced into this situation, I went with the flow.

Collins was there by ten-thirty to pick up LJ. When the doorbell rang, I was in the bonus room playing pool while LJ was in the middle of the table knocking the balls in the holes when I missed the shot. I picked him up and ran downstairs to get the door. When I opened it, Collins smiled and came inside. He stood in the foyer and looked around with his hands inside the pockets of his long black trench coat.

"Wow, this is nice, man. You must hook me up with your Interior Decorator."

I smiled. "Naw, can't do that. She's my Ancient Chinese Secret."

"In other words, you don't want nobody's house resembling yours."

"Exactly."

He looked at LJ. "You have everything ready for him to go?"

"Yeah, just about. I was upstairs playing pool, so there's just a few other things I have to get."

"Pool, huh. You wanna shoot a game? I'm actually pretty good at it."

"I'm better."

Collins grabbed me by the shoulder. "We'll just have to see about that. Before we get down to business, though, would you mind showing me around? I'd like to at least get some ideas for my house."

I carried LJ and toured Collins through the lower level of my house. I bragged a bit about it, but I was sure Collins house wasn't short-stopping in Ladue. He stood in the doorway to my office and looked up at the Cathedral ceiling. I had an expensive chandelier hanging from the ceiling that gave the room a dim settle lighting.

"Now, this is an office. I would never leave my house if I had an office like this. My office has papers piled up everywhere."

"Yeah, it is one of my favorite places to be. Kind of relaxing, if anything."

We walked up the steps and went into my bedroom, since it was the closest to the staircase. Collins looked at the glass entryway and smiled.

"Now, how do you ever get down in your bedroom if people can see straight through here?"

"Easily. That glass is the last thing on my mind when I'm in here with a woman."

Collins laughed and I continued the tour. He stood in my bedroom gazing at the vaulted ceiling, the flat screen on the wall, the white fury chaise, and the fireplace in the far corner of the room. He shook his head, and sat down on my California king-sized bed covered with white and gold silk Gucci sheets. "Jaylin, how old did you say you were?"

"I didn't. But I'm thirty-three years young."

"You are blessed, my brotha. Truly, truly, blessed. I'm forty," he cleared his throat, "years-old and good fortune didn't come my way until three years ago. Just recently I was able to start my computer business in Detroit, as well as in St. Louis. I had to partner up with a few brothas just for that to happen. If you got it going on like this at thirty-three, and don't have to count on, or depend on anyone for anything, my hat goes off to you."

"Yeah, it feels kind of nice to stand alone." We walked out of my bedroom. "Now, Collins, your compliments will not stop me from giving you this ass whipping I'm about to give you playing pool."

He laughed and I continued the tour. I showed him the basement where I was in the process of having a theatre room added, a wine cellar, an oval shaped Jacuzzi built into the ground, and even an expanded work-out room so I didn't have to go to the gym.

Afterwards, we stepped into the bonus room, and when he took his coat off, we got down to business. LJ had fallen asleep, so I laid him down on the couch.

When it was all said and done, Collins lost four out of the five games we played. He leaned against the pool table and puffed on a cigar.

"You're pretty good, Jaylin."

I leaned over and shot the eight ball in to win the last game. It went in the hole. "Good at everything I do, Collins."

His cell phone rang. When he looked at it, he said it was Nokea and answered it. "Yeah, baby...I know. I'll be there in a few. Okay, I'm sure he won't mind."

He gave the phone to me. "Hello," I said.

"Do you mind if I come get my son now?"

"Collins here to pick him up. I know you ain't tripping?"

"I sent Collins over there almost two hours ago. I've been calling your house thinking the two of you got into it or something. Why haven't you answered your phone?"

"Because we've been playing pool. Come on over anyway, I want to tell you something in person."

Nokea hung up and we played one more game of pool. When she got there, we were sitting in the living room drinking some Cognac and talking. I opened the door and she immediately smelled the alcohol on my breath.

"I just know the two of you haven't been in here drinking with my baby around." She walked over to Collins and gave him a kiss.

"Naw, baby. He's been asleep for a while," he said, tipsy.

Nokea walked to the bottom of the stairs. "Is he in his room, or your room, Jaylin?"

"Neither. He's in the bonus room on the couch."

She looked at us and rolled her eyes. "That's dangerous. He could fall on the floor and bust his head. Careless, men, I tell you." She walked up the steps.

Collins and I looked at each other. "Good luck, man. She's a tough cookie," I said, shaking his hand.

"Isn't she? But, she's the boss." He smiled and winked. "I like to let her think that anyway."

We laughed and Nokea came down the steps with LJ. Collins met her at the end of the steps and took LJ's diaper bag off her shoulder. I took LJ out of her hands and kissed him. When Nokea reached out to take him back, I gave him to Collins.

"Take care of my son, Collins. I want him to come home safely."

Collins put LJ on his shoulder and grabbed my hand. "You bet ya, I will. And have a Merry Christmas, Jaylin." He walked out of the door with LJ, but Nokea stayed behind and gave me a hug.

"So, what did you want to tell me in person?" she asked.

"Call Pat, she's ready to talk."

"And how do you know this?"

"Because, I just do," I said, giving her Pat's new telephone number.

Nokea walked towards the car, then turned and looked at me, as I stood in the doorway.

"I love you," she motioned with her mouth.

I placed my hand on my heart and nodded my head.

After they pulled off, I went upstairs to my room, took a shower and lay in my bed. I picked the phone up and my voice mail said that I had thirty-five messages waiting. After I spent fifteen minutes listening to the calls, I jotted down the important ones and deleted the rest. Daisha, Shane, Stephon, Brashaney, Felicia, Ray Ray, Higgins and Schmidt called several times, Mackenzie and Scorpio called once, Nanny B called to check on me, and Pat called to thank me for bringing LJ over to see her. I wasn't sure if my visit was a success or not, but the rest was up to Nokea and her.

NOKEA

Collins' house in Detroit was awesome. He played it down like it wasn't as spectacular as the house in St. Louis, but this one was the best. And he had the audacity to brag on Jaylin's house. With decorating, yes, Jaylin had him beat, but since I was infatuated with the size of the house, rather than the look, Collins had it going on. I found myself comparing the two of them a lot. Sometimes I had to catch myself when talking to Collins, but when I apologized, he said that he understood. After so many years of being with Jaylin, it was hard not to compare the two of them.

Anxious to call Pat, I told Collins I had to make an important phone call and went into his Study. It looked like a library and had books lined up on a built-in bookshelf that covered an entire wall. I sat down in the chair behind his desk and dialed Pat's number. When Chad answered I almost hung up, but I was anxious to talk.

"Hi, Chad. Is Pat there?"

"Yeah, Nokea, hold on."

Pat took a minute to pick up, and when she did, she was laughing. "Hi, Nokea, hold on while I go shut the door." She put the phone down then came back. "Okay. Where are you? I tried calling you today and your machine said you were gone for the holidays."

"I'm in Detroit with Collins. Didn't Jaylin tell you when he spoke to you?"

"Yeah, he mentioned it, but we mainly talked about what happened between you and I. Listen, don't think I haven't thought about what you said. I just needed time to figure out what was really going on with Chad. Now that I know, I want to tell you how sorry I am for saying those things to you. I was just so angry with you about the Jaylin and Stephon situation that when you told me about Chad, I really thought you had lost your mind."

"Pat, you know me better than anybody. Even though I was going through hell at the time, I never would have wanted you to suffer with me. I was weak and Chad saw an opportunity."

"Yes, he did. I actually just got up enough nerve to talk to him about the ordeal last month. He admitted it and explained to me his reasoning. He claimed I had an attitude like it was all about me. He wanted children, and I didn't. He didn't want me to work, and I did. He wanted a new house, and I didn't. The list goes on and on. And the bottom line is when I didn't compromise, he felt like he needed something else. You weren't the only woman he approached. But the question is, do I agree with his reasoning? No, I don't. But we've been married for twelve years, Nokea, and to me, my marriage is worth saving."

"But why haven't you called me to say that? I've been miserable without our friendship. You were the only true friend I had and you have no idea what it did to me when I lost that."

"Again, I'm sorry. Please understand how hard it was for me to swallow. Thing is, I just didn't have the nerve to call you and tell you I was wrong. You know how stubborn I can be. Not only that, I was embarrassed and ashamed about the situation. My husband wasn't supposed to be that way. He wasn't supposed to do those kinds of things. I put him so high up on a pedestal, and didn't realize he was capable of doing what any other person might do. Note that I said person, and not just men, because women are capable of doing the same thing too, trust me. I'm speaking from experience."

"Well, I'm glad everything is going to work out between the two of you."

"I'm glad too, but we have a long road ahead of us. One thing I did learn from this was to never judge a woman in her situation again. I thought about all the times I came down hard on you because of Jaylin, only to find myself fighting through the same mess. I always talked about how I would never put up with this, or put up with that, but honey, you never know what you'll do until it becomes a reality for you."

"You're right. You're definitely right about that. Anyway, did you get a chance to see my handsome baby?"

"Girrrrl...he is adorable. Jaylin and I were fighting over him. I begged him to let LJ stay but he wouldn't let him. I cried as I held him in my arms and after he left, I made up my mind."

"You're going to try and have a baby, or adopt one now?"

"Nooo, ah, ah. I'm going to creep into your house and take yours. If not, I must get me a dog." We laughed. "By the way, next time you talk to Jaylin, thank him. He really cares about you Nokea.

All these years I thought he was full of shit, but I saw a side of him I never knew existed."

"I told you. He's not all that bad."

"No, he's not. But, he's still a ho, let's not forget that." We laughed again. "So, last question, then I'm going to let you get back to your new man. I want to meet him as soon as you get back. Anyway, Jaylin told me how much you've changed since you've met Collins, and I can hear the happiness in your voice. Question is…are you still in love with Jaylin?"

I looked down at the desk and rolled my finger around on it. I took a deep breath and answered Pat's question as best as I could. "Pat, my love for Jaylin will always be buried deep in my heart. Collins or any other man will never be able to replace what I shared with him. So, do I love him? Yes. Am I in love with him? Yes, I am. But it's a love that I have no desire to go back to."

"Well, I'm happy for you. But honestly, I think—and please don't take this the wrong way. You know how I always have to voice my opinion. But I think the two of you still love each other and want to be together. Now, again, that's just my opinion."

"You're wrong Pat, but I respect your opinion. Anyway, tell Chad I said hello and I'll see you when I get back. I'll bring Collins over to meet you and then you'll see for yourself how happy I am."

" I don't doubt your happiness, however, I do doubt your heart. Bye Girl. Have a Merry Christmas and kiss my baby for me. I love you."

"Love you too."

We hung up.

After talking to Pat, I called my parents to let them know we made it. As usual, Daddy was upset with me for not being at home for Christmas, but he really needed to let go and let me live my life. Mama told me to have a good time and said that she'd see us when we got back.

When I hung up, I sat in the Study for a while and thought about what Pat said. Honestly, I really wasn't sure how I felt. Only time would tell. I at least knew for right now, I was happy and that's all that mattered.

Collins was standing in the doorway holding LJ. LJ had a fudge cookie in his hand and had chocolate all over his face. He looked so cute and after seeing them together, I hoped more than anything this would all work out for the best.

Since Collins' family was coming in tomorrow, we had one night to spend together alone. Around eleven o'clock I laid LJ down for the night so we could spend some quiet time together. When I came downstairs, he was leaning over the fireplace, and poking at the fire trying to get it to flame up. I sat down drinking some hot chocolate he'd made us, and watched him with a thick heavy blanket covering me.

When the flames kicked up, Collins lifted me up from the chair, and sat me on his lap.

"Are you cold?" he asked.

"No, I'm fine. This blanket is just so warm I couldn't let it go."

He took the cup of hot chocolate out of my hand and kissed it. "How did Jaylin ever let you get away, Nokea?"

"Don't know. But I'm so glad that I found you."

"How glad?"

"Really glad."

"How glad is really glad?"

I stood up and dropped the blanket to the floor. He smiled and looked at my naked body. "So glad," I said. "And it would be an honor for you to make love to me right now."

"Well, I'm so glad you asked." He stood up and wrapped his arms around me. "And you must know, the honor is all mine."

240

Collins and I went to his bedroom and made love. He was so into me as much as I was into him. After we finished, he held me in his arms and we fell asleep.

About six o'clock in the morning, we were awakened by a knock on his bedroom door. When his mother and father came in and saw us in bed, naked, I was so embarrassed. That was not how I anticipated on meeting them. His mother announced that they'd be downstairs and closed the door.

I placed my hands over my face. "Now, that was embarrassing. I thought you said they wouldn't be here until noon."

Collins kissed my forehead, and continued lying in bed, smiling. "It's okay, baby. Trust me, it's okay."

"For me it's not. You can't tell me it's okay that your mother just saw me naked in bed with her son. It might be okay for your father, but moms, I don't think so."

"Nokea, calm down. It's not like they just walked in on some teenagers, or a one-night-stand. I've talked to my parents about you. They know how I feel. And I'm sure they know you and I make love. After all, they're the ones who taught me sex is a beautiful thing when it's shared with the right person."

Collins put me somewhat at ease, but I was still a bit uncomfortable by the whole thing. We got up, showered, and got dressed. Before heading downstairs, I went into the other room to check on LJ and Collins headed downstairs. LJ was still asleep, so I headed downstairs without him.

Collins mother was in the kitchen putting some groceries in the refrigerator. Collins and his father were sitting at the kitchen table talking. As I walked further in, Collins stood up, came over next to me, and introduced me. His father shook my hand and introduced himself as James, but his mother just smiled and waved. Completely ignoring me, she went back to putting the groceries up. Trying to break the ice, I asked if she needed help, and when she nodded her head saying no, I looked at Collins like, 'I told you she was upset.'

Collins, James, and me sat back down at the kitchen table. Knowing that his mother had an attitude, Collins was looking at her while biting into an apple. "Mama," he said, smacking on the apple. She looked up. "Are you mad about something?"

"No, honey, what makes you think I'm mad about something?" she asked, while holding her head down.

"Because you're not saying much." He bit into the apple again and chewed. "It's not like you to be so quiet."

She looked up and smiled. "Let the truth be told, Collins, nothing excites a mother about seeing her baby in bed with a naked woman. Especially one he's not married to." I gave Collins another look and didn't say a word.

"But Mama, your baby is forty," he cleared his throat, "years-old. Can I at least make love to a woman, in my own house, if I want to?"

By this time I was humiliated. Collins' mother wiped her hands on a towel and came over by the table. She put her hands on the back of my chair and looked back and forth at us. "Can a mother feel the way she wants to when she wants to? I don't care how old you are, you're still my baby." She leaned down and kissed him, then she kissed me on the cheek. "Nokea, you have a son, don't you?"

"Yes, ma'am, I do."

"Stella, call me Stella. But would you, or could you ever imagine yourself walking in on your son in bed with a naked woman and being excited about it?"

"No, I wouldn't. Even if she were his wife, I would be a slight bit bothered."

She looked over at Collins. "I love you, baby, but Mama's are always going to be Mama's." She kissed him again. He smiled and bit into the apple again.

I excused myself from the table when I heard LJ upstairs yaking. When I came back into the kitchen with him Stella had a fit.

"Chile, look at here, look at here." She took him out of my hands. "He is one handsome baby." She kissed him on the cheek and LJ reached for her long gray hair. When he placed his lips on her cheek and slobbed on it, as he tried to kiss her back, she was flabbergasted. They went back and forth playing the kissing game and when I reached for him, she snatched him away. "No way, honey," she said. "Go get your own. This here is my baby."

I laughed and walked back over to the table.

"Mama," Collins said. "I'm getting a little jealous, you know?"

"Well, too bad. Your Mama done found herself a new baby, since the old one won't do right."

Finally feeling at ease, I started helping Stella make breakfast for everyone. I did most of the cooking because she couldn't find it in her heart to part with LJ. When we were just about finished, Collins came into the kitchen, wrapped his arms around me, and kissed me. Stella playfully rolled her eyes, then took LJ into the other room.

After he smooched with me, he took my hand and walked me outside on the deck. It was cold, but he stood behind me and squeezed me tight.

"I'm falling in love, Nokea."

I turned around and placed my arms on his shoulders. "So am I. But, I'm scared Collins. This seems too good to be true. I keep thinking this is going to end up like Jay—

He kissed me. "I promise you it won't. All you have to do is open your heart and free him. Once you do that, this will all work itself out."

"But I have freed him."

"No, you haven't. I feel his presence in you right now. I feel it when I make love to you, and I see it in your eyes when you mention his name."

"That's because there's so much history between us. My time with you is going to hopefully wash those memories away. Now, if you're asking me to forget about him, I can't. But what I can do is move on with the man I love and that's you."

Collins nodded and before we went back into the house, he gave me a long and juicy wet kiss.

After his four sisters, along with their families, showed up the house was jammed packed. They couldn't wait to tell me all the crazy stories about how overprotective their older brother was and some of the things they told me I couldn't believe. He tried to deny it when his sister Charlotte said he beat up several of her boyfriends because he didn't like them and threw eggs at them when they came to the house. When Stella came out with the truth, he admitted to it and said that at least he apologized.

By Midnight, Christmas Eve, mostly everyone had gone to sleep. LJ was in the bedroom with Stella and James knocked out. I went into the Study to call Jaylin to let him know LJ was fine, but when he didn't answer I left a message on his voice mail and told him how well everything was going. Before I hung up, Collins stood in the doorway and heard me tell Jaylin that I love him.

I tried to explain. "That's just something we say to—"

Collins walked over to me and placed two fingers lightly on my lips. "Shh...don't. Don't explain. Let's just go to bed."

He turned the lights down in the Study, and I followed him into the bedroom. I sat on the bed and he headed for the bathroom to take a shower. I couldn't even imagine how he felt, but I truly meant no harm.

Trying to see what was taking him so long, I took my clothes off and went to the shower to join him. I stepped in, and his hands were pressed against the shower wall, as he was in deep thought. Hot water was dripping on him, but mostly on his face. When he felt me brush up against him, he turned and gave me a quick look, then turned back around and continued to face the wall. I wrapped my hands around his body and touched his chest.

"I'm sorry." I laid my head on his back.

"Don't be. Saying you're sorry all the time only means trouble in a relationship. Please, don't be sorry for something you truly mean. I know you love me, but I also know you love him too. Trust me, though, the better man will prevail, I know that I will."

We finished our shower and after he dried me off, we got in bed and lay down. Collins placed his head between my breasts and fell asleep. I stared at the ceiling for a while thinking about how God had blessed me with such a wonderful man, and shortly after, I dozed off.

SCORPIO

Mackenzie and I were having a pretty good time together. After Jaylin left she really didn't say much to me, and cried herself back to sleep. I was truly feeling her pain because I held her in my arms and cried right along with her. Thing is, we weren't sure if he was coming back this way or not.

By the next day, though, things started to get better for us. I took Mackenzie to work with me and everyone loved her. My boss let her take orders from a few tables and she got a kick out of all the attention. When he paid her twenty dollars for working, she was all smiles and said that she wanted to use the money to buy Jaylin a Christmas present. I promised her we would go to the mall and purchase something nice for him.

After work we bundled up and walked home together. And since it was snowing outside, she couldn't wait to play with the snow. We made snowballs and blasted each other with them. And when we got home, she rushed into the house to call Jaylin to tell him about her amazing day. Since he wasn't there, I told Mackenzie to leave a message.

The next day, I was disappointed when we hadn't heard from him. It wasn't like him not to call back, but I knew how upset he was when he left. Knowing him, he probably needed time to deal with the situation.

On Christmas Eve Mackenzie and I took a bus ride to the mall. We comb the shops looking for Jaylin something and when Mackenzie insisted nothing was good enough for him, I found him something myself. It didn't cost much, but it was a gold pen set, and I asked the woman who sold them if she would engrave his initials on the side for me. She said that she could for a small fee.

As we stood and waited on her to finish, I saw a man making ornaments with pictures on them. I rushed the lady with the pens, paid her, then we ran over to him so he could take our picture. After he did, he put our picture on a colorful Christmas ornament and scripted the words we love you right underneath our picture. It was so cute and I knew Jaylin would love it when he got it in the mail.

Mackenzie drove Santa Claus crazy telling him a list of things she wanted. And after I pulled her off his lap, we rushed to the post office to mail our package, so Jaylin would get it on time.

At the end of the day, we were so exhausted that we took a taxi home and ordered a pizza when we got there. I flopped down on the couch, and Mackenzie turned on the TV. When the phone rang she ran to the kitchen and answered it. I sat up and listened because I could tell by the excitement in her voice it was Jaylin.

"Yes, Daddy. I know. We bought you a present today," she smiled, as I walked into the kitchen. "I'm not going to tell you. You did? Okay, but when are you coming to get me?" She had a saddened look. "I know, but here's Mommy. I love you too."

Mackenzie gave me the phone.

"Hello," I said.

"Hey. I just wanted to tell you that I mailed Mackenzie a little something for Christmas. I also bought her a puppy, but I'm not going to pick him up until she comes back, or whenever she comes back."

"I'm sure she'll be excited to know that. And you know she'll come back to see you soon. So, don't even sound like that."

"Are you coming with her?"

"Jaylin, we already talked about this. I'd really like to stay here for a while. Mackenzie can go to school here. I already checked into it."

"So, I see your making some serious plans, huh?"

"If that's what you want to call them, then yes, they're serious. I still love you, but I am not coming back under the same conditions."

"Suit yourself, Scorpio. It's been over two months, and I'm not going to wait on you much longer."

"Don't. If you feel as if you need to move on, please do. Maybe you'll change for someone else. For me, it seems to be such a difficult thing for you to do."

"You can't change a man who don't want to change, baby. But you for damn sure can accept him for who he is. Adios Amigos, I'll talk to you soon."

"Jaylin! Don't hang up. Why is it that every time I talk to you, you have to hang up on me? Listen, I don't want you to move on with anybody else. You have all that you need right here. But I do want things to be a lot better between us. Just think about it, okay?"

"I've been thinking about it for months now. How much thinking do you want a brotha to do? How do you plan to work this out with me if you're in Denver and I'm in St. Louis? You're putting up a hell of an effort trying to work things out with me. I've been there twice, that's it for me. The only time I'm coming back is to get Mackenzie. After that, you're on your own and I mean it. So, keep playing around if you want to, you're going to miss me when I'm gone."

He hung up.

I hung up, and when Mackenzie wanted to call him back, I told her no. I told her he was leaving the house because I wasn't about to call back and kiss his ass.

When the doorbell rang I thought it was our pizza being delivered, but it was the United States Postal Service with Mackenzie's present. Jaylin said it was just a little something, but it was two huge boxes wrapped in green shiny paper and a big red bow was on top. I signed for the packages and closed the door.

Mackenzie couldn't wait to see what was in the boxes, so I let her open one up. She tore the paper off and when she opened the box she pulled out a white fur coat with a fur hat to match. Her eyes widened and when she put it on she looked like a million dollars. Inside that box was another small box with a card taped to it. I opened the card and one thousand dollars was inside. Then I read the card to her: *I'm sure you're going to need your coat living in Denver, and the money should take care of all the Barbie's you want until I get there to see you. As for the necklace, keep it close to your heart and think of me always, I love you, Daddy.* I laid the card down and we opened the small box. It was a silver heart shaped locket with a pink three-carat diamond centered in the middle. A picture of him and Mackenzie was inside and on the back was her initials, MJR, engraved along with Daddy LUV'S U.

I closed my eyes, and held back my tears so Mackenzie wouldn't see me cry. I didn't want her to think I was a basket case with all the crying I was doing, so I quickly got myself together.

Anxious to see what was in the second box, I let Mackenzie open it too. And just when I thought he had already done enough, she pulled out another white fur coat and hat, but this time, it was for me. Another necklace and card followed. The only thing my card said was for me to come home and it expressed how much he missed me. My necklace had a white diamond with only his picture inside and on the back were the initials SAR, meaning Scorpio Antoinette Rogers. I smiled and held it close to my heart. No doubt about it, it was time to go home and claim my man. I had put it off for as long as I could.

I rushed to call him and tell him my thoughts, but he didn't answer. Instead of hanging up, I thanked him for the gifts and told him how much I loved him.

On Christmas Day Mackenzie and I didn't get up until noon. We stayed up late watching the *Grinch Who Stole Christmas* and *Rudolf the Red Nose Raindeer*. I tried Jaylin at his house again, but still got no answer. Desperate to talk to him, I even called Stephon's house to see if he'd heard from him. When he didn't answer, I figured they were probably somewhere together, so I chilled, and waited to hear from him.

Mackenzie and I started on dinner late. Since it was just the two of us, there wasn't much to cook. More than anything, I wanted it to be a special day for her. She stood in the chair, and whipped up the chocolate cake mix. I checked on the baked chicken in the oven. Then, I put the boxed macaroni and cheese on the stove and waited for the string beans to cook.

When the phone rang Mackenzie and I both rushed to it, and truly disappointed, it was Jackson. He called to see how things were going with us and wished us a Merry Christmas. I only had a one-way line, so I rushed him off the phone just in case Jaylin tried to call.

By six o'clock, we set the table and blessed the little food we had. All Mackenzie ate were a few spoonfuls of the macaroni and cheese, and she picked over some of the chicken. When I asked why she wasn't eating she insisted she wasn't hungry. I pressed because I could tell something else was bothering her.

"Mackenzie, you can tell me, what's wrong?"

She kicked her feet underneath the table. "Nothing. I just don't like the chicken. It taste kind of funny."

"What's wrong with it? I thought you liked chicken."

"I do. But I like Nanny B's chicken. Even Daddy's chicken taste a lot better than yours."

"Well, thanks, honey. It really makes Mommy feel good when you don't like my chicken."

She frowned, looked at the chicken, then tooted up her nose. "Can I throw it away? It's spoiling my appetite."

"Yes, Mackenzie. Go throw it away. But don't ask for anything else to eat today, okay?" She got off the chair and dumped her whole plate in the trash, including her macaroni and cheese. "I thought you liked your macaroni and cheese?"

She shook her head. "That taste funny too. Can I have a piece of cake now?"

"No, you may not. If you didn't eat your food, then you can't have any dessert."

"That's not fair," she yelled. "I can't help it if you can't cook!" She turned and ran out of the kitchen. As she ran down the hallway, I heard her say she wanted her Daddy. Hurt by her words, I pushed the kitchen chair back, ran after her, then grabbed her arm.

"Listen, Mackenzie, I have no idea what is wrong with you, but watch your mouth. Do you understand?"

She shook her head and pouted, then she folded her arms and sat on the bed. Frustrated with her attitude, I turned her over and tore her behind up. I wasn't going to put up with her mess like Jaylin does. Just because she got away with clowning on him, she wasn't going to get away with clowning on me. The last thing I intended was for our Christmas to turn out like this. I had done everything I could do to make it a special day for her, but nothing I did was good enough.

I hit her a few more times on her behind, and afterwards she climbed in bed with her dolls. Being too hard on myself, I went into the bathroom and closed the door. I looked in the mirror, and felt badly because that was the first time I had spanked Mackenzie. Feeling that maybe it was because I was disappointed since Jaylin hadn't called, made me feel even worse.

I stayed in the bathroom for a while, splashed water on my face, and dried it off with a towel. I went back into the bedroom, and Mackenzie had fallen asleep cuddled up with her dolls and her fur coat. I kissed her on the forehead and grabbed a book on my dresser titled "How Can I Be Down?"

After reading several chapters, and munching on some popcorn, I glanced over at the clock and it was almost seven o'clock. I was wondering why Jaylin still hadn't called. I at least thought he would call to speak with Mackenzie, but the night was still a bit young. Slightly worrying, I started reading again, and was anxiously waiting for him to call.

JAYLIN

I didn't get an ounce of sleep last night thinking about LJ and Mackenzie. I wondered how their Christmas Eve was going, and wondered if they were missing me as much as I was missing them.

I lay in bed for countless hours looking up at the ceiling, and listening to my phone ringing off the hook. In no mood to talk to anyone, I picked up the caller ID to see who it was and put it right back down. But when Daisha called for the fourth time since six o'clock in the morning, I finally answered. She insisted that I shouldn't be alone on Christmas and wanted me to go to church with her. When I declined she begged me to go and said it would truly brighten my day if I did. After her being very persistent, I told her I'd be ready in an hour.

I got up, showered, and changed into my dark gray suit, then put a white dress shirt underneath. I chose a tie Nokea bought me to match the suit and slid into my shoes.

As I was brushing my hair, Daisha was already ringing the doorbell.

Classy, I thought, when I opened the door and checked her out in her dark gray silk suit, with a gray and white scarf gathered around her neckline. Her curly short hair was neatly cut and not one strand was out of place. We laughed and talked about how well we matched each other and didn't even plan it.

When we arrived at church, it was packed. She introduced me to everyone as a long time friend and smiled when some people talked about what a cute couple we made. During the short service, I glanced at Daisha a few times and she was all into it. When the choir sang, she squeezed my hand, and laid her head on my shoulder. I saw a few tears roll down her face and I reached over and wiped them.

Afterwards, she introduced me to a few more people and we jetted. On the drive home, she asked me if I enjoyed myself and I told her that I did. I kissed her and thanked her for the invite. Little did she know, though, I really did enjoy myself. Pastor Davis' message was quite interesting and the choirs' singing brought tears to my eyes. I couldn't help it because the thought of LJ and Mackenzie being without me kept coming to mind.

Before we headed back to my place, we stopped off at the cemetery where her brother was buried and laid flowers on his grave. Daisha said he was her twin brother and said that he was killed in a car accident almost five years ago. She said she always visits his grave because she never wants him to think he's been forgotten.

I felt bad because since mama had been gone, I never went to the cemetery to visit her. I guess I was so upset about her leaving me, that I never thought much about it. When I talked to Daisha about my feelings, she told me it wasn't like Mama left me by choice. I agreed, but I still had a hard time understanding why Mama wasn't a part of my life when I wanted her to be so badly. Now, though, I had Nanny B and for me, that was good enough. I could feel Mama's presence in her, and actually, when I thought about it even more, I had been feeling Mama's presence all along.

Instead of going to my house, Daisha wanted to stop by Stephon's place to give Mona her present. I didn't get Daisha anything and felt kind of bad. When I apologized she told me not to worry about it. She said it wasn't a big deal, since she hadn't gotten me anything either.

Stephon and Mona knew we were coming, so the door was already open for us.

No sooner had we walked in, Mona rushed to the door, and flashed an engagement ring on her finger. After I congratulated her, I politely asked her where the groom was and she pointed to the kitchen and said that he was in there with Shane. I pushed through the kitchen doors.

"Oh, no, you didn't!" I yelled.

"Oh, yes, he did!" Shane said, sitting at the table next to Stephon. "And did it straight up behind our backs."

"Y'all brothas know how I feel about Mona. So, don't pretend that y'all didn't see the shit happening," Stephon said.

"Honestly, I didn't." I peeked out of the kitchen door to make sure Mona couldn't hear me. Her and Daisha were talking, and opening up their gifts from each other. "Man, you just told me you were with Rachelle the other night," I whispered. "Come on dog, what's up with that?"

"I know," Shane said. "Brother just told me he went and knocked Felicia out for one last time. Man, you seriously should have thought about shit before making such a commitment."

"Shane! Jay! Get out my business. I know what I'm doing. Yes, I'm forever going to be a dog, but I also need a stable secure woman who understands that. Mona understands me. She knows what I want, and she knows what I need. Most of all, she ain't tripping off no other females. So, prepare yourselves, she's going to be my wife whether you fellas like it or not."

Shane and I looked at each other and shrugged our shoulders. "Stephon," Shane said. "I'm happy for you but—"

"Shane, please don't start with all that theoretical bullshit." Stephon moved his chair back, walked over by the kitchen counter, and leaned against it. "Life ain't about that all the time. Y'all brothas both know that the chances of anyone having a monogamous relationship these days are slim. If the woman ain't cheating the man for damn sure is. All I'm saying is enjoy what you have, for as long as you can have it."

I walked over by Stephon and held my hands out in front of him. "This time, I hope it's right. I support you because I love ya. However, I do not agree with any of that bullshit you just said. Marriage is supposed to be a sacred thing between two people and two people only. I can't seem to get to that point yet, but if you insist that maybe one day you will, congrats, and I wish you well." Stephon and I hugged each other.

"Get your ass over here and give me a hug, nigga," Stephon yelled at Shane. Shane stood up and gave his congrats too.

We all stood around in the kitchen talking. "You know what's funny?" Shane said. "Why every time a man announces he's getting married it feels like he's planning a funeral—looking at it from his boy's point of view. It's just so hard for us to be happy no matter how hard we try. I can recall all the fellas who stepped to me and said they're getting married, I was doubtful to simply say congratulations."

"I know man, it's scary," I said. "Things are just not what they used to be."

"But you can't let statistics scare you out of it," Stephon said. "See, Mona understands that you have your Good Dogs and your Bad Dogs. A Good Dog will take care of his woman, take care of the kids, and take care of the finances. He, however, will occasionally slip into something every once in a while, truly meaning no harm, and wouldn't give up his wife for nothing in the world. But a Bad Dog, he's dissing his woman, not taking care of the kids, barely hanging onto a job, and fucking everything in sight. He will trample from one woman to the next and get married about three, pho, five times, if need be. Problem is, too many women be liking these Bad-Dogs. Why? I haven't a clue."

"So," Shane said. "Do you really consider yourself a Good Dog?"

"Mona thinks I am, or if not, she thinks I can be. Honestly, though, I'm just a Good Dog who loves a woman with some Bad-ass pussy, that's all?"

We all laughed and gave each other five.

"Mr. Shane?" I said. "Whatever happened with you and Jeanette? Daisha told me you decided to kick it with Amber. What's up with that?"

"Well, if you would answer your damn phone, or call a brotha back sometimes, you would know. I just felt a better connection with Amber. And yes, I did get down with both of them that night, but I talked it out with Amber, asked her if we could still kick it and she's cool. It's nothing serious, we just kick it every once in a while. What about you? I see you're hanging pretty tight with Daisha. Does that mean Scorpio's history? If so, let a brotha know so he can make his move, please."

Stephon had the nerve to give Shane five. I looked at both of them and smiled. "Never, ever, ever, ever, will I let her go. You brothas need to hang it up. Daisha's cool, digging her like a motherfucker, so who knows. But Scorpio's right here." I placed my hand on my heart and winked. "And Nokea's right there too."

"Fuck you man," Stephon said. "I'm giving up on your ass. You don't know what the hell you want."

"Ah, I know what I want. Thing is, though, I don't have to choose. You're the one getting married, remember, not me."

"Well, Jay, let me put it to you this way," Shane said, getting ready with some more of his theoretical bullshit. "If the world was ending and God said you can choose one woman to live the rest of your life with in heaven, and Scorpio, Nokea, and Daisha were standing right in front of you, who would you take with you?"

Stephon moved in closer so he could hear. "You brothas all up in my bit-ness, ain't y'all? But, uh, to answer your question, I'd quickly take Scorpio's beauty, her sexy ass body and good as pussy, then I'd take Nokea's charming, loving, and so thoughtful ass caring ways, then Daisha's sexy, intelligent, smart, creative, spiritual mind and wrap them all up in one. After that, I'd get the hell out of there."

"You are so full of shit," Shane said. "But if it ever comes down to it and you have to decide which one of them you want to be with, what you just said about them might help you find your answer. What is the most important thing to you? Scorpio's good ass loving, Nokea's thoughtful caring ways, or Daisha's spirituality."

"It's called variety, Negro," I said. "I like variety, so I'll never choose. The truth is, if I did choose, eventually I would get whatever additional things I needed from just one of them—for my fulfillness. That's just the type of women all three of them are."

Our conversation was getting pretty deep, so Daisha and Mona came into the kitchen to shut us up. After sitting around kicking it with them until five o'clock Daisha said she was ready to go. Shane left and said he was going to spend some time with his ex-girlfriend's family, and Mona and Stephon were anxious to spend their first night together as an engaged couple.

On the drive to my house Daisha talked about how happy she was for Mona and prayed that Stephon would treat her right. I didn't say a word because I knew deep down he wouldn't be right. He just didn't have it in him and neither did I.

Daisha and I walked towards the door, and there was a small package in the doorway. When we entered the house the phone was ringing, so I laid the package on the bottom step.

I rushed to the phone and when I saw Scorpio's number on the caller ID, I just let it go into voice mail. I had listened to her message last night, as she thanked me for the gifts, but I wasn't in the mood to talk to her.

Ready to get my grub on, Daisha and I took the turkey, dressing, ham, scallop potatoes, greens, yams and cornbread that Nanny B cooked out of the refrigerator and warmed it up. After we fixed our plates, we went upstairs to my bedroom to get comfortable.

I lit the fireplace and turned on the TV. And before we sat down in bed to eat, Daisha reached for my hand and blessed our food. After she finished, we took our shoes off, rested our backs against the headboard, and started to grub.

"This is really delicious," Daisha said, with a mouthful. "Did you say your nanny cooked this for you?"

"Yes. She is an awesome cook. That's why I have to faithfully work out because if I don't my ass will be in trouble."

"You do have a nice body, Jaylin. How often do you work out anyway?"

"I used to work out every day. I've been kind of getting lazy, so now, I'm down to about three or four times a week."

"And how often do you get a work out from having sex?" She looked at me and bit down on her fork.

"Are you asking me if I've had sex since I was last with you?"

"Yes."

"No, I haven't. But I do like to *work* it out at least—"

"Be honest, Jaylin."

"Okay, honestly, I like to work it out about seven days a week. Five days would suffice, but seven days would be perfect." I reached over and put some potatoes in Daisha's mouth since she didn't have any on her plate. She chewed them. "So, what about you," I said, "how often do you like to *work out*?"

She swallowed the potatoes. "Those are delicious, and I should have put some on my plate. Anyway, I could probably work out seven days a week too, depending on who I'm with. However, as busy as my schedule permits me to be, I'd say I could probably get around to it...maybe, once or twice a week." She reached over and put some collard greens in my mouth. "Now, did I just blow my chances with you?"

I smiled and chewed the greens. "No, you didn't. The key words you said were depending on who you're with. And depending on who you're with, your busy schedule isn't going to stop you from making love to a brotha if he's good." I reached over and put another spoonful of potatoes in her mouth. "Wouldn't you agree?"

She chewed. "I guess, but he has to be awfully damn good."

I took her plate and put it on top of mine. Then I laid both plates on my nightstand. I scooted over and Daisha raised her skirt

257

and straddled me. She took her scarf from around her neck and wrapped it around mine. I started to undo her blouse. "Damn good, huh? What if he were extremely damn good?" I asked.

She leaned forward and whispered in my ear. "Then I'd sex his sexy-ass up seven days a week, or until he had enough of me."

The phone rang. Daisha raised up and when I looked at the caller ID it was Stephon. I picked it up.

"What fool, what?" I yelled.

"Damn! That's how I get treated?"

"I'm in the middle of something, man."

"I'm sure you are, but I was just calling to tell you that you left your Rolex over here. Now, if you want me to take this motherfucker to Lee's Pawn & Jewelry and pretend that I didn't see it, I will."

"I'll pick it up tomorrow. So goodbye." I hung up on him and the phone rang again. I quickly answered. "Now what, Nigga?"

"Hello, Jaylin." It was Scorpio.

Daisha quickly grabbed the phone. "Look, Stephon, you and Mona really—" she paused. I snatched the phone from her.

I placed it against my forehead for a second, took a deep breath, then placed it on my ear. "Yeah," I said.

She hesitated to talk, as I could feel her pain on the other end. "Uh...do you have company?"

"Yes."

She hung up.

I put the phone down and looked up at Daisha still sitting on top of me.

"That wasn't Stephon, was it?" she asked.

I shook my head. "No, but don't worry..."

"I'm sorry. Had I known I never would have grabbed the phone."

"I know, and as I said before, don't worry about it." I started to undo her blouse again. "Anyway, where were we?"

"You were just about ready to show me how extremely damn good you are."

"That's right, I was, wasn't I?"

I sexed Daisha up and showed her just that. She whispered to me several times during sex that it couldn't get any better than this and I agreed.

After she had fallen asleep, I took our plates downstairs to the kitchen and washed them. On my way back upstairs, I noticed the package that I had earlier laid on the steps. I picked it up, sat down on the couch, and opened it. When I did, enclosed was a pen set with my initials engraved on them, and the other box was an ornament with a picture of Scorpio and Mackenzie cheek to cheek, smiling. The words we love you were underneath. I placed the ornament on my lips and kissed it, then I put it back into the box.

Sitting in the dark and thinking, I leaned back on the couch and looked up at the blinking lights on the Christmas Tree. It was high-time that I let it all go. How I was ever going to be able to move on, I wasn't sure. But one thing I knew, and that was I couldn't stand to hurt Scorpio anymore than I had already done.

I closed my eyes and thought deeply about her. But when the music throughout the house played loudly, I listened to Aliayah sing, "I Care For You." I was smiling as Daisha sang and slowly came down the steps heading towards me. When she reached me, she straddled my lap and continued to sing, as she asked me to wipe the tears from my eyes and claimed the other woman was out of her mind to let a fine man like me get away. When she finished, I clapped my hands.

"You're trying to seduce me, aren't you?" I said, holding her hips.

"No, I just want you to forget about where you've been and think about where you're going?"

"Is that with you?"

"I hope so. But you tell me, is it?" Daisha leaned forward and kissed me.

"Wait a minute." I backed up and looked at her. "I thought church girls are supposed to be nice."

"We are nice, very nice I might say, but we also know how to get down when we have to."

"Ain't nothing wrong with that."

I kissed Daisha and lay her naked body back on the couch. We started having sex again, and as I tried hard not to think about Scorpio I couldn't shake her from my mind for shit.

After ten minutes into it, my rhythm got faster and faster. I was sweating and breathing hard trying to catch my breath. Daisha held me tightly around my neck, and we both looked down and watched me slide in and out of her. Excited about how wet my thang was, and at the peak of us coming together, she yelled my name and I yelled out...Scorpio's name. Damn! I thought. I dropped my sweaty forehead on Daisha's chest.

She lifted my head and looked at me. "What did you just call me? Did you just say what I think you said?"

"Daisha, I'm sorry. I just—"

"You just need to get up off me."

"Look, I understand how you feel, but I just got caught up in the moment."

"With her or with me? So, please, get up," she said, calmly.

There wasn't anything else I could say to Daisha to make this uncomfortable situation any better, so I raised up. She didn't waste any time going upstairs putting her clothes on and leaving. Since I stayed downstairs on the couch, all I heard was the front door slam behind her after she left.

Feeling so badly about what had happened, I rushed to the door to catch her, but when I did, her car had already gone down the street. I slammed the front door and sat on the steps. I think what hurt me the most is that I knew I had just blown it with a very special woman. I had never in my entire life called a woman by another woman's name. Especially, during sex.

I went into my office, called Daisha's voice mail and left her a lengthy message apologizing to her again. When I hung up I called Scorpio and tried to clear shit up with her. When she picked up on the first ring, I could tell she was wide-awake. There was no doubt that she was waiting on my call.

"Say, are you busy?" I asked.

"Yes," she said, in a shaky voice. I could tell she'd been crying.

"I just...I just called to apologize for earlier. A friend of mine—"

"Jaylin, please don't. There's no need to explain. I'm tired, baby, and I can't do this anymore," she cried. "Mackenzie's unhappy, and I'm unhappy and all because I can't make it without you. All I ever wanted was for you to love me, but your way of loving me has hurt me more than anything in my entire life has. After tonight this will all be over with. You will never have to worry about me again."

"Wait a minute. You're not thinking about killing yourself, are you?"

"I don't know what I'm thinking, but just know whatever I decide to do it's for the best."

"Scorpio, don't be talking like—" She hung up.

I called back and the number was busy. After calling back several times and still getting a busy signal, I started panicking. Fearing the worst, I ran upstairs and put some clothes on. I called the airport to see when the next flight was going to Denver from St. Louis, and when the lady told me not until four o'clock tomorrow afternoon I slammed the phone down. I immediately called Enterprise Car Leasing and had them bring me a car.

If Scorpio killed herself, I would never be able to live with myself. And Mackenzie, I thought, what about my baby Mackenzie? Thinking about her, I started rushing even more. I could be in Denver between ten or eleven hours. Either way, nothing was going to stop me from going.

I reached downtown Denver at twelve-fifteen in the afternoon. When I pulled in front of Jackson's house, I hopped out and left the car door open behind me. I unlocked the door and when I went inside, no one was there. I looked around and didn't see anything unusual. But when I went into the bathroom, there was a Tylenol bottle right by the sink. I looked inside and it was empty. I stood there for a minute, then I remembered Scorpio telling me about her working at a cafe not too far from here. I rushed back outside and got into the car.

Hating myself for putting her through so much, I slammed the door and sped down the street. After the car slid a few times on the ice, I finally slowed down. I drove down several streets and when I saw her walking down the street with her hands in her pockets, and turning her face away from the gusty cold wind, I pulled over to the opposite side of the street in front of her. She looked up and was shocked as hell to see me. I opened the car door and got out.

261

"Get in the car," I asked calmly, but with attitude. She rolled her eyes and kept on walking. I ran up behind her and grabbed her arm. "It's too damn cold out here to be bullshitting, Scorpio, so get in the fucking car!" I yelled.

She snatched her arm away. "Fuck you, bastard, and let my damn arm go!" She tried to pull it away, but I had a tight hold on it. Hard enough that I pulled her ass to the car, opened the door, and shoved her inside. When I closed the door and walked over to the driver's side, she opened the door and tried to get out. I ran back over to the passenger's side and stood in front of her, as the door was in between us.

"Get back in the car so we can go talk about this, please," I said.

"No," she shouted. "Why can't you just leave me alone? There's nothing else for us to talk about, okay?"

"No, it's not okay. Let's just go back to the house and talk. If you want me to leave after that, I promise you I will leave."

She hesitated, but sat back down in the car. I closed the door.

We silently drove back to Jackson's place and when we got there, she got out and rushed inside. I popped the trunk and pulled out two black suitcases. I went inside the house and walked into the bedroom where she was. I tossed the suitcases on the bed and opened one.

"Get your shit and let's go. Where's Mackenzie?" I asked. Scorpio didn't say a word. She stood up and headed towards the door. I quickly pushed her back on the bed. "Don't fuck around with me, woman! Where's Mackenzie?"

She sat up on her elbows. "She's next door playing with the neighbor's daughter, and we're not going anywhere with you Jaylin."

"Like hell. This goddamn game you're playing is over! It ends today, baby, and I mean that shit!"

I went over to the closet, opened it and started pulling her clothes out. As I slammed them into the suitcase, she took them back out. We went back and forth for a few minutes, then I got seriously tired of her resisting. I grabbed her wrist and twisted it back.

"Leave the damn clothes in the suitcase!" I yelled.

"No," she yelled back, then she took her fist and punched me on the face.

In a serious rage, I grabbed her by her hair and tripped her ass to the floor. When she fell hard to the ground, she started crying. I didn't give a fuck because my head was banging from her punch.

I leaned down, and grabbed her by the collar, then pulled her up on the bed. I was about to light her ass up with my fist, but instead, I shoved her backwards and went back to the closet and continued to fill the suitcase. I opened the dresser drawers and cleared them out. She scooted back on the bed, covered her face with her hands, and cried. I ignored her, opened the other suitcase, and filled it with some of Mackenzie's belongings and her shoes. I pushed everything down inside the suitcases and locked them. I put one of them on the floor and held the other one in my hand, then reached my other hand out for her to take it.

"Come on, let's go," I said. She wouldn't take my hand, so I dropped the suitcase on the floor. I plopped down next to her, moved her hair away from her face and put my hand on her cheek to wipe her tears. "What do you want from me, baby? I've begged you to come back with me. I've come here three times and you still tripping. Tell me, what more can a brotha do? "

She held my hands on her face and looked me in the eyes. "Change. All I want you to do is change the way you are. Not only for me, but also for yourself. You can't be happy with the way you are. With how you treat people and how you talk to them. There's no way you're happy with yourself. There are so many good things about you, but what's really important is how you treat me."

"What do you mean by how I treat you? I've done more for you than anybody. I've bent over backwards for you just to make you happy. But if my changing is going to get you out of this…this hellhole today, then I'll change." I stood up. "So, come on. Let's go." She still didn't move.

"You know you don't mean it. You're just saying that to get me to come back with you. I guarantee you the same ole stuff is going to happen over and over again—"

"No it won't." I took her by the hand and pulled her off the bed. I wrapped my arms around her and pecked her on the lips. "I promise you this bullshit between us ends today." She dropped her head and looked down at the floor. I lifted her head and kissed her again. "I'll change. It doesn't matter if it's for you, or for me. I'll do it

263

because I love you and I don't want to live another day without you. I lost one good woman, baby, and I'm not about to do it again. I'm sorry it had to take this for me to realize you're the woman I want to be with, but believe me when I say that I've had an emptiness in my life since you've been gone."

She rubbed my face. "Please don't say this to me if you don't mean it. I can't—"

I kissed her over and over again. And our lips smacked as they touched, and we floated our tongues in each other mouths.

Not wanting to let go we stood there for a moment in a tight embrace.

"Let's go get Mackenzie and tell her Daddy's taking her home," I said.

Scorpio rubbed her fingers across my lips, "No, not yet. I just need to hold you for a little while longer. I've missed you so much and I can't go another second without making love to you first."

She started unzipping my pants, but there was no way I could get down with her before taking a shower. Daisha and I had just done our thang several hours ago, and it didn't even dawn on me to hit up a shower before I left. As for taking a shower here, that was out of the question. Knowing that it was, I was pleading for us to hurry up so we could get down when we got back home.

I moved back and grabbed her hand, as she touched my thang. "Baby, wait. I got something special waiting for you at home. Let's wait until then, okay?"

"This won't take long, Jaylin. I've been without you for months, and this will be a quick one, I promise you."

Quickly, I moved back, and sat her down on the side of the bed. I lifted her waitress uniform, and kneeled down on the floor in front of her. She leaned back, and I rested her thighs on my shoulders, then removed her wet silk blue panties. In a trance, and gazing at what I had so long hoped for, I took my fingers and lightly rubbed her neatly-shaven soft hairs. With my dick at full attention, I dipped my tongue deeply inside of her. I licked against her walls, and tightened my lips over her hard clitoris. She held my head as tight as she could so I wouldn't move.

"Jaylin, I miss this sooo much, I swear I do," she said, moaning, and rubbing her fingers through the curls in my hair. "If you ever, ever make me do without you again I swear I—" her body jerked and I slid my tongue out.

"You'll what?" I smiled, and looked up at her.

"Damn you!" she yelled, and squeezed her legs tightly together. "Don't fuck with me, please, not right now!"

I opened her legs again and finished the job. In less than two minutes she came. She was dying to have sex, but I couldn't play her like that and give her Daisha's left over juices. Again, I promised to make it up to her later.

I didn't know who was the most excited, Mackenzie or I. She ran into my arms and held me so tight that I could hardly breathe. We sat down talking in the living room, and Scorpio ran around the house packing everything she needed. I told her she'd have to probably come back for some things because there was no way everything would fit into the car.

Mackenzie was jumping up and down on the sofa next to me. "Mackenzie, stop that before you fall," I said, holding her so she wouldn't.

"I'm sorry. But Daddy is Nanny B at home?"

"No, but she'll be there later. Why?"

"Because I'm hungry. Mommy made a yucky dinner for Christmas and I didn't want to eat it. She got mad at me and cried when I said it was nasty. Then she spanked me for not eating it."

"Well, Mackenzie, you probably hurt her feelings. You have to be careful what you say to people because words can be hurtful. As for the spanking, I'm sure she didn't mean it."

"Yes she did. But what kind of words, Daddy? Do you mean words like Bitch and Slut—words like that?"

"Where do you get all this stuff from, Mackenzie? And yes, I do mean words like that, but you shouldn't be saying them. If you've heard me say them, I was wrong and I don't ever want you to say them to anyone, okay?"

She shook her head, laid her head on me, and wrapped her arms around my neck. After a few minutes of holding me, she stood back up on the sofa and whispered in my ear.

"Daddy, I got a secret."

"Oh yeah, what kind of secret?"

"It's about Mommy."

"Really? And what might that be?"

Mackenzie whispered in my ear again. "She kissed another man the other day."

I turned and looked at Mackenzie. "Say she did. Who was it?"

"The extermer...I mean, the bug spray man."

"Really?" I looked to see if Scorpio was listening to us. "How many times did she kiss him?"

She tilted her head like she was thinking, then smiled. "Uh, I think three times."

"Did he ever spend the night?" I asked. Machenzie shrugged her shoulders. "Did you ever see him in bed with her?" Mackenzie shook her head saying no. "Did you ever see them—"

"No, no, no," Scorpio said, standing in the doorway to the living room. "You know you need to stop asking her all those questions. If you want to know, ask me and not her." Scorpio looked at Mackenzie. "Besides, she shouldn't be running her mouth anyway."

Mackenzie looked at Scorpio. "Sorry, Mommy, but Daddy told me to tell him if you were cheating."

I took a deep breath. "Come on, are you ready?" I said, looking at Scorpio. "This child is too damn smart for her age. I told her to keep an eye on you, that's it. Where all this cheating stuff comes from, I have no clue."

"I agree. And yes, I'm ready."

Scorpio grabbed a few more bags, and I took everything else out to the car. While she locked the door to the house, I gave Mackenzie a high-five and thanked her for telling me the truth. Even if Scorpio was in Denver getting down with the Exterminator, I couldn't be mad because I for damn sure was in St. Louis doing my thang.

As I drove, Scorpio reached over and rubbed the back of my head.

"I miss these ole nappy curls. Straight up missed running my fingers through them."

"If they were nappy, you wouldn't be able to run your fingers through them, so watch it now. My curls are naturally, beautiful, and soft curly-curls. If anything, you must be thinking about the Exterminator, right?"

She laughed. "I knew you were going to go there. You just couldn't leave it alone, could you?"

"You're damn right I couldn't. Especially when you pretended to be so alone, and so lonely. Those nights I called and you had the phone off the hook, you were getting your fuck on, weren't you?"

"Ooo, Jaylin. Now, you know better. I'm nothing like you. He was just someone to help pass my time away. The only thing we ever did was kiss a few times, and that's it."

"That's it?"

"Yeah, that's it. As fast as I came today, and you have the nerve to ask."

I looked back at Mackenzie. She was playing with one of her dolls. "You'd better watch what you say. You know who back there will be at school telling the teacher how quickly her Mommy came."

We laughed.

"But since we're on the subject. Who was that who took the phone from you?" she asked.

"Daisha."

"Daisha Voo."

"No, Daisha McMillian, a really nice woman I met when you were away playing games."

"So where's Daisha at now. I know you don't still plan on seeing her?"

"Nope."

"Why not? All your other women seem to always keep hanging around."

"Well, she's different. Besides, she's upset with me for calling her your name."

"That's understandable. It's a good thing you're still alive." Scorpio moved her hand from behind my head. "It wasn't during sex, was it?"

"Naw, it was during one of our conversations." I knew damn well that I was lying.

"Whew...I was getting ready to say. If it was during sex, and you didn't die, she's definitely a better sista than me."

I looked over at Scorpio and smiled.

By the time I pulled into the driveway I was exhausted from driving. We got everything out of the car and went inside to chill.

Mackenzie was asleep, so Scorpio carried her up to her room and laid her down. Then she came into my room, fell back on my bed, and stretched her arms out. I stood in the closet and took my clothes off.

"Home at last," she shouted, and looked up at the ceiling. "Thank God I'm finally home at last."

"What do you mean by home?" I asked. "The key to your condo is on the nightstand." I walked over to the nightstand, picked up the key, and gave it to her.

"You can throw that key away, or give it to someone else. Since you forced me out of Denver, I'm staying right here with you."

I tossed the key back on the nightstand. "You're lucky I'm renting the place out. If I wasn't, you'd be up in there right now."

"Is somebody already living there? And what about my car? Where's that at?"

"Shit, I sold that car to one of my neighbors. If you look out of the window, you'll see it right in their driveway. Their daughter turned sixteen less than a month ago and he bought it for her."

"Now, you know you ain't right. You act like I was gone for years or something."

"I didn't know if you were coming back. I was just trying to get some of my money back. Besides, I had something else to do with the money anyway."

"So, in the meantime, what am I supposed to drive?"

"I don't know. The junkyard might still have your get-out-and-push Cadillac you came over here in. I'm sure nobody else wanted it."

"For your information, Negro, that Cadillac got me from point A to point B. It sure as hell got me over here to fuck your brains out that night."

"Okay, then let's not talk about the Cadillac. If you need a car, you can drive mine. I'm kind of getting tired of the Cedes anyway. It's time for something new. Besides, I still have the Porsche."

"I see how you are. Give me the old car, huh? You can let me drive the Porsche, can't you."

"Naw, that's my baby. And are you out of your mind? What sista wouldn't like to drive around in a black 500 SL Roadster Convertible Mercedes Benz?"

"Not too many. So, make sure I get a key tomorrow."

After I changed the sheets on my bed, I went into the bathroom and started my water. When it was finished, I stepped in and reached for the phone to check my messages, since Scorpio was busy hanging her clothes up in the closet. LJ's Da-Da calls put a serious smile on my face, and Nokea said they'd call me as soon as they got in. Nanny B said she'd be back by Saturday and Felicia called again. Whatever the hell she wanted, I didn't know and personally didn't care. There was no message from Daisha, and not that I expected there to be, but I at least wanted to know if she accepted my apology.

I sunk my body deep down in the tub filled with hot steamy water and bubbles. Relaxing, I sat there thinking what a lucky man I was. All this chaos was finally over. My woman was back and all I had to do was change in order for her to stay. I knew it was going to be difficult, but all I could do was try.

When my bubbles started to dissolve, I turned the lights down, and added some more hot water and bubbles. Scorpio came in with a lit scented candle and laid it on top of the Jack and Jill sinks. She slid out of her clothes and came over to the tub. When she stepped in, I was mesmerized and watched her slide down backwards between my legs. I must have seen her naked body a million times before, but each time felt like the first. She pulled her hair to the side and leaned the back of her head against my chest.

"Must your thang be poking me in the back like that?" she asked. "You can't be that hard already." She put her hands in the water and touched me. "Oops sorry, I forgot how—"

"How big it is. And it is starting to rise, right now. You can't expect to put all that in my face and for it not to respond."

She smiled and turned back around on my chest. I rubbed up and down her arms, then took her hands and held them together with mine.

"I'm so glad to be back home with you," she whispered. "I've dreamed of this moment for many nights."

"Shh…listen," I said, as Natalie Cole was singing "INSEPARABLE" on the radio. I reached up for the intercom knob and turned it up. I kissed Scorpio on the back of her head, as we listened to the song together. When it was over, I reached up and turned the music down. Scorpio turned around to kiss me, but when she tried, I moved my head to the side.

"Quit playing with me," she said, trying to kiss me again. I moved my head to the other side. She grabbed my face and forced her tongue inside my mouth. She backed up when she felt something inside and took it out. "What's this in your mouth?" She curiously looked at it. It was an 8.0-carat Princess Cut Platinum diamond ring with baguettes on each side.

"You never did answer my question." I said, feeling the trembling in her body.

"Wha...what question?" she asked still gazing at the ring.

"The necklace. When I mailed it to you, on the back were the initials SAR. You still haven't responded."

She looked at me. "I haven't responded because you've never asked."

"Well, I'm asking now. Would you, Scorpio Antoinette Valentino, have me Jaylin Jerome bad-ass Rogers, for better or worse, rich or for richer, in sickness and in health, and nothing will keep us apart?"

She grinned, as I could see tears rolling down her face. She wiped them. "Only if you get on your knees and ask. You know, I'm just not feeling the effect of your proposal with you still soaking in this tub."

I laughed, got out of the tub, and kneeled down beside it. I took her hand, placed the ring on her finger and kissed it. "I love you, Pretty Lady, but I am not going to repeat myself again. So, are we going to do this or not?"

She grabbed me around my neck and pulled me back into the tub. Water splashed everywhere, as I wrapped her legs around me and looked her in the eyes. "Yes," she said. "I would love more than anything in the world to be your wife."

"Are you sure that's what you want more than anything in the world. I thought you might want this...this big ass dick I'm about to lay into you right now."

She smiled. "The wife and the dick thing are a tie. But right now, if I have to choose, please give me what you got and give it to me good."

I grinned because all she had to do was ask. We got our dripping wet bodies out of the tub, and I carried her into the bedroom. After I laid her on the bed, and knowing exactly how I like it, she rolled over on her hands and knees. I moved her back to the edge of the bed and stood up behind her. Before inserting myself, I held her pussy in my hand and massaged it. Juicing up her insides, I slowly rolled my fingers around deep inside her. As I touched her wet walls, she lowered her head and started to moan. Trying to rush me, she stopped me, turned around and swallowed all of me in her mouth. I stood there and closed my eyes, as I could feel her tightening up on my head when she sucked it between her lips. And before I could even think about coming, she pulled me down to the floor, straddled herself on me and slammed my thang inside of her. I sat up holding her breasts and sucking them, while she took deep fast strokes on top of me. And as she seemed to be having her way with me, I laid back, closed my eyes again and enjoyed the ride.

Scorpio and I exchanged juices for at least an hour as we got down on the floor. Knowing that she was somewhat wearing me down, she stopped my last come, brought her pussy up to my mouth and rolled it around on my lips. I opened my mouth wide and sucked her until she couldn't stand anymore. And when she tried to move away, I wrapped my arms tighter around her thighs and munched down.

"Jaylin, stop baby, please," she moaned softly, as the taste of sweet cherry lemonade was floating in my mouth.

I licked my lips, looked up at her, and shook my head. "Naw, baby, I can't stop. Not after fucking me the way you just did. This ain't over until I say it's over. Besides," I said, changing positions and putting one of her legs high up on my shoulder. "You asked me to give it to you good, didn't you?" I slid my dick inside Scorpio again.

"Yes, I did. But never in my wildest dream did I imagine you would give it to me this damn good. You must had really missed the hell out of me."

"I did, baby. I missed you and this good-ass pussy you be dishing out. If I had to go another day without it, I would have lost my mind."

Scorpio smiled and continued to let me have my way with her. She had even tightened up a bit, but the warmth inside of her that I

271

always felt was still there. After we finished our business on the inside, we grabbed some blankets, lit a few candles, and went outside on the balcony. She leaned over it and I fucked her like fucking was going out of style. I'm sure the neighbors got sick of hearing my name being yelled, but if anything they all should have been outside taking notes.

By morning, we had fallen asleep on the chaise cuddled up in the blankets. I woke up before Scorpio, and when I did, I put some clothes on, and went downstairs to my office.

Having everything already planned out, I typed up my resignation to Schmidt and thanked him for my thirteen years at his brokerage firm. I drew up the Amendments to my WILL making Nanny B my sole beneficiary, and LJ and Mackenzie my contingents. I wasn't sure what to do about Jasmine yet, but I recently put another detective on the case to find her, since the one I hired before had given up so easily. And as much as I loved Scorpio, a prenuptial had to be prepared. She wasn't going to be happy about it, but I was sure that she'd understand.

After I finished up my paperwork, I wrote a healthy check out to the orphanage I was in for two years, as I always did approaching the New Year, then called my attorney and made an appointment with him for Monday. He had other suggestions about my assets and said he'd talk to me about them further on Monday.

The rest of my day went down as one of the best days of my life. We picked up Mackenzie's poodle, and the smile on her face made me want to cry. She, of course, named the poodle Barbie, but as long as Mackenzie was happy, I really didn't care. The remainder of our day we spent catering to the dog, watching movies, and eating up everything in the house.

Everything was peaceful and was going smooth. When Nanny B came home on Saturday, we told her about the engagement. She was thrilled and cooked a wonderful dinner to celebrate. I had no plans on telling anyone who she really was because it was our secret. However, she did ask me to tell Mackenzie and LJ the truth when they were old enough to understand.

New Years came and we didn't do much at all. Scorpio and I took Stephon and Mona a bottle of wine, but we weren't ready to make our engagement known until a definite date was set. Stephon questioned me about the ring on Scorpio's finger, but I told him it was a well overdue Christmas present. I could tell Mona was jealous because every time she looked at Scorpio, she couldn't keep her eyes off the ring.

During our visit, though, I pulled Mona aside and asked her how Daisha was doing. She kind of ignored me, but then said that Daisha was doing fine. Occasionally still thinking about Daisha, I asked Mona to tell her hello, and after she said that she would, Scorpio and I left to enjoy our New Year and new life together.

Nokea and Collins finally made it back from Detroit with LJ. I asked Nokea to bring him over, but she explained how exhausted they were from the ride. Wanting to see him so badly, Scorpio and I drove over to Nokea's house to get him.

Nokea opened the door with LJ in her arms and invited us in. I reached for him and he damn near jumped out of her arms to get to me. I kissed him and sat him down on my lap, as we sat on the couch. Scorpio and Nokea stood by the kitchen's doorway and talked.

When Collins came into the room he spoke to me, and Nokea introduced him to Scorpio. I glanced at him and noticed how he lustfully checked her out like every man does when she crosses his path, but I wasn't the least bit bothered. I went right back to playing with LJ, and Collins came over and sat in the chair beside me.

"Did you all have a good time?" I asked.

"Yes, we had a wonderful time," he said. "How about you?"

"Best time of my life."

"Good. Glad to hear that, but you almost didn't get your son back. My mother fell in love with him and we had to literally fight with her to get him out of her arms."

"Yeah, he is quite charming, isn't he?"

"Yes, he is. But I didn't mention that once we got him away from her, we had to get him away from my sisters. Nokea barely got a chance to hold him the whole time we were there."

"I sure didn't. And I was mad too. But they really showed both of us a lot of love, Jaylin." She walked over and sat on Collins lap. Scorpio sat next to me and reached for LJ. I gave him to her and Nokea had a look like it still bothered her.

After we talked for a little while Nokea asked if we wanted anything to eat or drink, then asked me to come into the kitchen. As soon as I walked in, she drilled me.

"So, what's up with the ring on Scorpio's finger? Are the two of you engaged or something? I don't mean to pry, but I couldn't help but notice."

"Nokea, you know I've always been up-front with you, so yes, we are."

"When is the wedding?" She had an attitude.

"Don't know. We haven't set a date yet."

"Soon? A year or two from now…when?"

"Nokea, when we decide, I'll tell you, okay? Are you upset with me?"

"No, I'm happy for you."

"Well, why are you sounding so harsh?"

"I'm not."

I moved closer and stood in front of her. "Yes, you are."

"Okay, I am. I guess I'm a tiny bit jealous, but that's to be expected."

"You're right. But don't waste too much time on it. You have yourself a decent brotha. Don't blow it."

She reached up and touched my eyebrows to straighten them, "If it doesn't work out, you know I'm always here, don't you?"

"I'll keep that in mind." I embraced her, then kissed her on the cheek. "I love you SHOR-TAY."

She smiled. "Don't be calling me that. That name is only for Stephon to call me. And I love you too, Mr., soon to be married man."

Nokea told me her and Pat mended their friendship. And when I broke the news about Stephon's engagement, she damn near threw me out of the house, and implied we were both out of our minds.

After Scorpio and I left with LJ we stopped by London & Sons Wing House to get some chicken so Nanny B didn't have to cook again. I was worried about her doing so much at her age, but she was claiming to be young in body, mind, and in spirit. One of my main reasoning for retiring was so I could help her out with Mackenzie and LJ. And since Scorpio was already planning on returning to school, I would be there to help Nanny B when Scorpio wasn't around.

275

JAYLIN

After several months of being a changed man, things couldn't be better between Scorpio and I. Since we still hadn't decided on a date, we continued to keep everything on the down low. I was ready to do the marriage thing and get it over with, but she wanted everything to be right. She said that she wanted to make sure I was a changed man before she gave me a date and I was cool with that. Basically, I just went with the flow.

She was already back in school and I was at home being the nanny for the kids. Instead of Nokea's mother watching LJ while Nokea was at work, she brought him over every day and if she was too tired to pick him up, or wanted to spend time with Collins, she let him stay the night. I didn't care because if I had it my way he would be living with me on a regular basis like Mackenzie was.

As for Mackenzie, these days, she was quite a character. Scorpio and I knew we had our work cut out for us, and no matter how much we pretended that it wasn't happening, she was getting out of control. Every time I'd try to spank her Nanny B would save her behind. If not that, she'd cry and make me feel sorry for her. I couldn't find it in my heart to hit her, but Scorpio could. She feared Scorpio more than she did me. And every time she did something wrong, all I had to do was say Scorpio's name and she'd straighten up for a minute, then go right back to doing whatever she was doing.

Family day was on Saturdays so we went to Plaza Frontenac to look for Scorpio's niece a present for her graduation. We sat down and had a bite to eat first, then started walking around the mall to find a present. As Scorpio stroll LJ around in his stroller, and I held Mackenzie's hand looking through the store windows, I noticed Mona and Daisha going up the escalator. Scorpio had stopped to look at some shoes and I watched them behind some dark shades I was wearing, as they got off the escalator. Daisha looked different. And when Mona stepped out from in front of her, Daisha looked like she was pregnant. I hadn't talked to, or heard from her, but I remembered how funny Mona seemed on New Years.

Anxious to find out the down low, I told Scorpio I thought I saw an old friend of mine from college, and I was going to go catch up with him. She went into the shoe store and told me to meet her back there when I was finished.

I rushed up the escalator and looked around. When I saw them heading for the parking garage, I ran and tried to catch up with them. They got on the elevator and it closed before I could catch them. I watched the numbers to see if the elevator was going up or down and when it showed down, I started running down the stairs. By the time I got to the first floor, I could see them walking to the car. Mona opened the door to Stephon's BMW and when Daisha opened the passenger's door, I ran up to the car. Slightly out of breath, I walked over to Daisha and grabbed the door.

I looked down at her stomach. "Are you pregnant?" I asked. "Please don't lie to me because by the looks of things, it's obvious."

She looked over at Mona, then looked back at me. "Yes, I am."

"Is it my baby?"

"Jaylin, look, I'll call you later, alright?"

"No, Daisha, just tell me. I need to know, please."

She looked at Mona again. "No, it's not your baby."

I pulled Daisha away from inside the car door and closed it. "You're lying. I know you're lying because I can tell by how nervous you are. Please, Daisha, tell me the truth. The truth is so important to me."

She dropped her head and looked at the ground. "Yes, Jaylin. This is your baby." She looked back up at me with watery eyes. "Our first time together, I conceived a child. I didn't want to tell you because I didn't want to interfere with your life. I heard about how happy you were and I didn't want to mess anything up for you."

"I am happy, Daisha, but you couldn't possibly think I wouldn't want anything to do with my child."

"I just didn't want you trying to talk me into having an abortion. This is my first child and I want to have it. An abortion is not even an option for me."

"Who said anything about an abortion? We could have talked through this. I don't want you going through this alone."

Mona cleared her throat. "Look, Jaylin, we gotta get Stephon his car back so he can get to the shop. Why don't you just call her later?"

"Is that okay? Can I call you later?" I asked.

"Yeah, I guess." She opened the car door and got in.

I leaned down beside her and placed my hand on her stomach. "We can work this out, okay?"

"That's what got us in trouble to begin with. Remember, all that *working out*?" she smiled.

"Having a child is never trouble, Daisha. It's all about how you handle the situation. I'll call you later."

I stood up and watched as Mona and Daisha pulled off.

Why now? I thought. When everything in my life was going perfect. I rushed back inside the mall to find Scorpio. When I saw them standing in line getting some cookies, I slowly walked towards them thinking how another woman being pregnant could mess this entire thing up for me.

Scorpio saw me coming and started waving to make sure that I saw her. For the past several months, she had been on cloud nine. All the trouble we went through just to be together and now this. I really wasn't sure how I was going to tell her, but I knew I couldn't keep it a secret for long. If I did, that would be like denying my own child and I had no intentions on doing that.

Mackenzie ran up to me and took my hand. We walked back over by Scorpio and LJ and Scorpio opened a bag to show me the shoes she bought.

"Baby, did you see them?" she asked.

"Yeah, that's nice," I said, dazed, and barely looked at them.

"Are you okay? Did you catch up with your friend?"

"Yeah, I did. That's what took so long."

"Well, you don't look too good." She took her hand and felt my head. "You're not warm, but maybe we need to get you home into a nice comfortable bed and place a beautiful woman beside you."

"Uh-huh."

"Jaylin!" she yelled. "What is wrong with you?"

I snapped out of it and kissed her on the cheek. "Nothing, baby, I'm just tired. Listen, can we go? I need to lay down for a while."

After we got the kids some cookies, we headed home. I didn't say much in the car and I could tell Scorpio knew something was wrong. I went from being perky to being a complete slug.

At home, I asked Nanny B to take the kids because I needed some quiet time alone with Scorpio. I thought about what to say to her, and knew the faster I came out with it the better.

Scorpio was putting her bags up in the closet, and I sat on the bed staring at her. Noticing my mood, she stopped in her tracks. "Jaylin, why don't you just get some rest. You haven't been getting enough sleep, and I'm sure all this ripping and running you've been doing with me and the kids is wearing you down."

"Yeah, it might be, but, uh, come here for a minute." I scooted back on the bed and patted my hand on the spot in front of me. "Sit down right here for me."

She took a deep breath and sat down in front of me. "Baby, you're scaring me. I don't like it when you have that look. Are you sick or something? Please don't tell me..." her eyes quickly watered. Knowing that I promised myself I would never hurt her again I placed my fingers on her lips.

"Don't say anything. I have something I need to ask you, okay?" I said, softly. She shook her head. "How do you feel about having another baby around?"

She gave me a strange look and touched my hand. "You know about the baby? How did you find out about the baby?"

"What do you mean by how did I find out? I just found out today."

"But I...I haven't told anyone about the baby yet. I wanted to surprise you and tell you over a nice quiet dinner tomorrow. So, how did you find out I was pregnant when I just found out a few days ago?"

I sat there in disbelief and couldn't believe what she just said. "Are you telling me you're pregnant?" My mouth hung open, as I waited for an answer.

"Jaylin, you just out of the clear blue sky asked me how I felt about having another baby. I assumed that you knew. But since you've blown my surprise, yes, I'm a little over four months pregnant. Can't you tell how fat I'm getting? And not only that, sweetheart, I have a date for our wedding in mind."

279

I sat there stunned by her news. "So, you're pregnant?"

"Would you snap out of it, yes, you're going to be a daddy again."

"You're sure you're pregnant?"

"Yes! And I have the ultrasound picture to prove it." She went to the closet and pulled a card down from the top. She opened the card and took the picture out of it. "I was going to give this card to you tomorrow along with the picture." She handed the picture to me. I looked down at it.

"But, this is just a black and white sketchy picture."

"And this is the baby," she pointed to a tiny dot on the picture. "Right there."

"Right where?"

"There!" she pointed to it again.

"Are you sure?"

She snatched the picture. "Jaylin! If you're not happy about the baby, then don't be. I'm sorry, I thought you truly would be." She looked disappointed.

"Baby, I'm sorry." I pulled her close to me and lay her head on my chest. "I am happy about the baby. Stunned more than anything, but you...you just caught me completely off guard. I didn't think you wanted anymore children."

"Excuse me, but all this fucking we be doing and you never thought about me getting pregnant. Especially lately. We've been having sex every single day, two and three times, and you didn't see this coming? Besides," she said, twirling her fingers around in my hair. "I always thought about having a blood child with you. And since you're such a wonderful father, and we're going to get married, I've thought about it even more. When the doctor confirmed it, I was shocked, but I immediately thought about that day we were in the kitchen making love and you asked me where did I see us five years from now. Do you remember?"

"Yep. I remember it like it was yesterday. I asked you that question thinking it was over because I was in love with Nokea. In my mind, I was planning a future with her, but you still had hopes for us."

"You're right, I did. And I knew how much you loved her. But at that moment I said I saw us with some more children. I visualized what he or she would look like. And you know what else?" she said, looking at me smiling.

"What?"

"You'd better be careful because twins do run in my family."

I shook my head. "No, not twins. Twins would send me over the edge."

Scorpio laughed and asked me if it would be okay if she broke the news to Nanny B and Mackenzie. I told her it would be fine and she ran downstairs to share the news with them.

Not being able to swallow the news about having two babies on the way, I took my shirt off and lay flat on my back looking up at the ceiling. What in the hell was I thinking? Thirty-three, five children, and by four different women. I for damn sure was headed for a life full of chaos. There was no way in hell Scorpio would marry me knowing that I had another baby on the way. And Daisha, she was too much of a good woman to be played off by anyone, especially at a time like this when she needed me the most. What in the fuck am I going to do? This was one time I had no solution.

Running around the house excited about the news, everyone had finally shut down for the night. Scorpio and I made love for hours celebrating our new baby and the wedding date was scheduled one year from today. A whole lot of things could happen in a year's time, but one thing I was certain of and that was I was going to do everything in my power not to hurt Scorpio again.

Not being able to sleep, I soaked in the tub for a while then slipped into my khakis and put my soft baby blue Polo shirt and cap on. I quietly slid on my loafers, and needing some fresh air, I drove to AJ's liquor store on Union Boulevard and bought a bottle of Hpnotiq and a six pack of Bud Light.

I drove to Forest Park, parked my car near the Art Museum, then climbed all the way to the top to sit down. I took a few swigs of the Hpnotiq and popped open several cans of beer. Feeling the way I did, I dared anyone to come fuck with me right about now, including the police. I looked up at the stars, and tried to find Mama so we could talk.

After getting sick to my stomach from drinking, I poured a little alcohol on the ground for my relatives who weren't there. If anything, I figured since I was pop'em out like crazy, I'd have this family back to its entirety in no time.

I got fucked up and stumbled back to my car. Missing Nokea's comfort at a time like this, I was on my way to see her, but when I thought about if Collins was there, instead, I found myself driving to Daisha's house.

I was parked in her driveway for a while and tried to sober up. When I thought I did, I got out and rang the shit out of her doorbell. Barely being able to stand, I leaned against the screen door and waited for her to open. When she did, she just stood there and looked at me like I was out of my mind. She moved aside and I stepped into her house. My eyes watered, as I fell to my knees, wrapped my arms around her waist, and pressed my head against her stomach. Not saying a word, she rubbed her fingers through my hair, as I knew she understood my pain.

I looked up, "Just...hold me, please baby, just hold me."

She kneeled down, put her arms around me then looked me in the eyes. A tear rolled down her face. "I love you, Jaylin. From the first day I met you I knew that I was going to fall in love with you."

I released my arms from Daisha, and crawled my way into her living room. Not even deserving a woman like hers love, I rolled over on my back and lie there thinking about where in the hell I truly wanted to be.

The thought of Scorpio being pregnant by the Exterminator was fresh in my mind, but when I thought about maybe it was my way of trying to walk away from our commitment I dropped the thought. Then Nokea, damn was I deep down missing her. I just threw her to a brotha like Collins who was for damn sure waiting for the catch. It was times like this she could make me smile, and make me feel as if I didn't have a worry in the world.

Still soaking in my pain, my head started spinning around the room. Soon after, a blurred vision of Daisha's naked body stood before me. I felt her hands touching my body, but I didn't have the strength or the courage to stop her. Feeling a draft as she unzipped my pants, I tried to force my eyes to stay open. She straddled herself on top of me, leaned forward, and whispered something in my ear. All it sounded like was mumbo jumbo to me, but whatever she said I definitely knew where this night was headed. I grinned, as she placed my hands on her thick breasts, and when I felt her juicy insides sliding up and down on my thang, I closed my eyes again.

The sunlight beaming through the window is what awakened me. My head was banging and I rolled over on the floor trying to figure out where in the hell I was. When I looked down my dick was slanging and I was naked. I tried to get up but the pounding in my head wouldn't let me.

After lying there for a few more minutes, I took a few deep breaths and managed to maneuver myself over to the couch. Having a vague memory about last night, I sat there rolling my temples around with my fingers. I glanced at my watch and it showed nine-fifteen in the morning. Knowing that Scorpio was going to kill me, I stood up to find my clothes, only to fall right back down.

Trying hard to get myself together, I looked around the room for Daisha and noticed an envelope on the table with my name written across it. I picked it up, leaned back on the couch, and started to read. *Good morning, handsome. Your son and I had a few errands to run this morning, but I'll be back soon. Last night was magnificent, and I'm so glad you finally found your way back to me. I prayed many of nights for your return, and now after you confirming your love for me last night, I truly understand your purpose for being a part of my life. Breakfast is on the kitchen table and I'll understand if you're not here when I get back. Take all the time you need to break the news about your change in plans to Scorpio and call me if you need a shoulder to lean on. Love Ya, Daisha.*

I tore up the letter and hadn't a clue what the fuck Daisha was talking about. My son? Love and change in plans? I thought. What in the hell did we talk about last night? By the looks of things it was obvious we had sex, but damn, other than that I couldn't remember shit.

As I sat on the couch, and thought about what I could have said to Daisha, I stood up and picked my pants up off the floor. I pulled my cell phone out and called the house to talk to Scorpio. I wasn't sure what I was going to say, and when she answered I had a lost for words.

"Hello," she said again.

"Baby, it's me."

"Jaylin, where are you? I rolled over in the middle of the night and you were gone," she said, hurtfully.

"I'm, uh, on my way home now."

"Okay, but, where have you been?"

"I went for a drive to clear my head."

"All night? You know, I thought these days were over between us. There's no way in hell you've been just riding around in your car all damn night, Jaylin."

"You're right, I haven't. But I'll tell you what happened when I get home."

Scorpio hung up.

Feeling down on myself because I was on my way home to tell the biggest lie of my life to keep my woman, I walked into Daisha's kitchen and sat down at the table. There wasn't no need for me to rush because it was obvious the damage had already been done.

On the table, Daisha had four buttermilk pancakes stacked up on a plate with some cheese eggs, hash browns, and grits on the side. In the center of the table were some yellow daisies in a vase with a note saying: pulled from the garden especially for you. I smiled, as I cut into the pancakes, then I thought about my requirements from the beginning that I'd always wanted my woman to have. I'd often said that she must be African American, bodacious, have a degree, be able to cook, have a good job, drive a nice car, no kids, and be willing to cater to my needs. Daisha was all that and then some. The total package and there I was with Scorpio, the woman I love, who had only met a few. It wasn't that I was disappointed because it reminded me that sometimes what I ask for I sure in the hell won't get.

After I finished eating, I put my plate in the sink and washed my hands. I put my clothes back on and got ready to head home to make things right with my woman.

As I was standing in the hallway looking in the mirror, and brushing my hair getting ready to leave, I heard a car door slam. Feeling terrible about telling Daisha I made a big mistake last night, I stood there and waited for her to come in. When she didn't, I laid the hairbrush down on the table and walked over to the front door. And when I opened it, I damn near lost my balance. Scorpio was standing on one side of the door, and Daisha on the other side. My heart dropped, as I grinned and tried to play it off like everything was cool.

284

Scorpio looked at me with a devilish look in her eyes and punched me hard in my right eye. Feeling it swell, I touched it, dropped my head, then realized at that moment a *"CHANGE DON"T ALWAYS COME IN THE MORNING."*

ORDER FORM AND COMMENTS

Please use this form to order additional copies of novels written
by
Brenda M. Hampton
Any comments or questions, send to P.O. Box or send to email
address at: brendahampton_1@netzero.net

Books	Price	Quantity
1. *How Can I Be Down?*	$15.00	
2. *Two's Enough Three's A Crowd*	$20.00	
3. *My Way Or No Way*	$25.00	

Subtotal $_____
Shipping $_____
Total $_____

Shipping: $1.50 per book

Make money orders or checks payable to:

Brenda M. Hampton
P.O. Box 3007
Bridgeton, MO 63044

Autographed copy: ☐ Yes ☐ No

Your Name:_____
Address:_____
City:_____ State:_____ Zip:_____
Phone: _____ Fax: _____
E-mail: _____
Comments:_____
_____
_____
_____

ABOUT THE AUTHOR

Brenda M. Hampton is the author of *My Way Or No Way*, *Two's Enough Three's A Crowd*, and *How Can I Be Down?* She is currently working on her up coming novels: *My Best Friend's Man*, *Tomorrow Never Dies*, and has several other projects in production. Hampton is the president of a locally owned insurance business and the founder of a non-profit organization designed to encourage and empower women. She has twin daughters in college and lives in St. Louis with her son.

Printed in the United States
66149LVS00005B/249